READING MENNONITE WRITING

READING MENNONITE WRITING

A Study in Minor Transnationalism

Robert Zacharias

THE PENNSYLVANIA STATE UNIVERSITY PRESS
UNIVERSITY PARK, PENNSYLVANIA

The editor and publisher would like to thank the Faculty of Liberal Arts & Professional Studies, York University, Toronto, Canada, for the financial support it provided to this work.

Library of Congress Cataloging-in-Publication Data

Names: Zacharias, Robert, 1977– author.
Title: Reading Mennonite writing : a study in minor transnationalism / Robert Zacharias.
Description: University Park, Pennsylvania : The Pennsylvania State University Press, [2022] | Includes bibliographical references and index.
Summary: "Examines Mennonite fiction, poetry, film, and criticism from Canada, the United States, and Mexico"—Provided by publisher.
Identifiers: LCCN 2021061267 | ISBN 9780271092744 (hardback) | ISBN 9780271092751 (paper)
Subjects: LCSH: Canadian literature—Mennonite authors—History and criticism. | American literature—Mennonite authors—History and criticism. | Literature and transnationalism.
Classification: LCC PR9188.2.M45 Z329 2022 | DDC 810.9/212897—dc23/eng/20220224
LC record available at https://lccn.loc.gov/2021061267

Printed in the United States of America
Published by The Pennsylvania State University Press, University Park, PA 16802–1003

The Pennsylvania State University Press is a member of the Association of University Presses.

It is the policy of The Pennsylvania State University Press to use acid-free paper. Publications on uncoated stock satisfy the minimum requirements of American National Standard for Information Sciences—Permanence of Paper for Printed Library Material, ANSI Z39.48–1992.

Aber freilich, alle Begriffe sind nur beziehendlich, sie haben im Werden der Menschheit nur eine bestimmte Dauer. Danach werden sie unwahr . . .

[But admittedly, all concepts have context, they have only a limited time of usefulness. After that they become untrue . . .]

—Dietrich Neufeld, *Ein Tagebuch aus dem Reiche des Totentanzes* (Emden: Selbstverlag des Verfassers, 1921)

for mom

CONTENTS

ACKNOWLEDGMENTS

I have been circling around the issues explored in this book for some time, and several sections of it have been previously published in different form. My introduction here builds on, and at several points includes brief direct passages from, my arguments in "'A Garden of Spears': Reconsidering the Mennonite/s Writing Project" (*Mennonite Quarterly Review* 90.1 [2016]: 29–50) and my introduction to *After Identity: Mennonite Writing in North America* (Pennsylvania State University Press, 2015). A shorter version of chapter 3 was previously published as "The Mennonite Thing: Identity for a Post-Identity Age," in the *After Identity* collection, and my discussion of *Irma Voth* in chapter 4 includes a revised paragraph from my earlier review of the novel for *Journal of Mennonite Studies* (30 [2012]: 379–81). I am grateful for having permission to reprint this material here.

Each of these chapters relied on the generosity of other scholars in one way or another. In drawing heavily on the existing Mennonite/s Writing bibliographies, chapter 1 relies heavily on the work of Ervin Beck, who created and maintained the bibliographies for several decades, and Daniel Shank Cruz, who continues to maintain the bibliographies today. My thanks to the librarians at Conrad Grebel University College, Ruth Steinman and Mandy Macfie, who helped me scour their databases for publications from 1986; to Kyle Gerber, whose work is expanding those efforts further; and Ann Hostetler and Sharon Mack at Goshen College, for their timely help with the Pinchpenny booklets. My thanks, too, to Daniel Shank Cruz for passing along a pdf of Togane's collection, which is difficult to find, and to Sofia Samatar, who shared it first with Cruz and later put me in contact with Togane. The archival research at the heart of chapter 2 required me to work through Al Reimer's papers at the Mennonite Archive and Heritage Center (MAHC) in Winnipeg, and to virtually peruse Neufeld's papers held at the Mennonite Library and Archives (MLA) at Bethel College in Kansas; my thanks to both Conrad Stoesz at MAHC and John D. Thiesen at MLA for their support of those efforts. My thanks, too, to Sam Steiner, who, in giving me his copy of the 1930 edition of Neufeld's diary, unwittingly set me off on the journey recounted in that chapter. I am also deeply thankful to Ed Zacharias and Derek Gingrich for their help with translation from the German throughout, but especially in my work with Neufeld's diary, and to Jon Isaak at the Canadian Conference of Mennonite Brethren Churches archive for helping me with the Anna Baerg diary. Thanks again to Kit Dobson for his close reading of an early version of chapter 3. Chapter 4 has the longest gestation of any of the work included here, sections of which were presented at the 2015 North Eastern MLA in Pennsylvania and the 2016 Encuentro Conference in Santiago, and which received much-appreciated feedback from Smaro Kamboureli and Ato Quayson, as well as two anonymous reviewers via *PMLA*. Chapter 5 has been strengthened by the lively discussions about Plett's *Little Fish* I had with the students in my *Contemporary Canadian Writers* classes at York (2019, 2020). I am also thankful for the generous permission I received to quote directly from numerous poems.

Accepting a manuscript for publication and preparing it for press is a collective effort, as well, and I am thankful to Emily Howe for her valuable research assistance throughout, and to Kathryn Yahner at PSUP, for her timely work on the project. I am also thankful to PSUP's two anonymous readers, whose deeply informed and generous engagements as peer reviewers of the original manuscript strengthened the project and saved me embarrassment, as did the careful copyediting of Dana Henricks. All the remaining errors and embarrassments, of course, are my own.

Thanks, finally, to my friends and family, who have made the project possible in various ways, including Corey and Lynlee, who allowed me to use their house for a much-needed writing week. And, of course, thanks to my family: to Arvelle, for patience and support as I tool around with my books, and to our children, Adiah, Samuel, and Talia, deep readers who are fast becoming fine writers. To my father, Les, surely the only person who has read all my scribblings, and certainly the only one to have them on display by his reading chair. I dedicate this book to my mother, Marrian, who was diagnosed with pancreatic cancer and passed as I finished its final polish for publication. I doubt she would have read it, but I know she would have loved it.

INTRODUCTION

Mennonite Literature as a Case Study in Minor Transnationalism

In a brief 2013 essay entitled "Sunday Morning Confession," the noted American poet and critic Julia Spicher Kasdorf paused to reflect on the sixth Mennonite/s Writing conference, which had taken place just a few months earlier on the lush campus of Eastern Mennonite University in Virginia. The essay begins with a concise articulation of what Kasdorf suggests had become the conventional history of the small but vibrant body of Mennonite writing in North America, beginning with a trailblazing author-hero from central Alberta whose first novel shocked the conservative Mennonite world in 1962, preparing the way for a surge of Mennonite writers in Canada and the United States a generation later. As an introduction to the concerns of this study, Kasdorf's retelling of this account is worth quoting at some length:

> From the first of these Mennonite/s Writing conferences, Mennonite writers have gathered and told one another the story of Rudy Wiebe's troubles after *Peace Shall Destroy Many*. It's a story that says the publication of a work of literature by a big, worldly press (McClelland and Stewart) was so transgressive that Wiebe became an exile. That's more or less true, but the story has become a freighted myth of origins for Mennonite writers, which goes

> something like this: for his sin, Wiebe was cast out of the Garden. [. . .] We have said that ever since the publication of *Martyrs Mirror* in 1660, there was no *serious* Mennonite literature until *Peace Shall Destroy Many*. [. . .] The writer steals the fire of authority previously held by the big men in the church, and from that small flame literature blazes. (It's Adam and Eve and Prometheus and James Joyce all at once!) (7)

In Kasdorf's account, the conventional literary history of Mennonite literature in North America is less a straightforward description of the field's past than it is a potent mix of literary, biblical, and classical allusions, perpetuated by a set of cultural gatekeepers invested in the patriarchal trappings of literary celebrity. It leaps from the *Martyrs Mirror*, that vast seventeenth-century martyrology recounting the trials of the early European Anabaptists, to Wiebe's 1962 *Peace Shall Destroy Many*, a protomodernist account of Mennonite settlers on the Canadian prairies, by the logic of something called literary "seriousness," effacing several centuries of writing in the process.

Although Kasdorf is clearly slipping into parody, she is not exaggerating the field's iterative return to Wiebe's novel—Paul Tiessen calls *Peace* the "urtext within Mennonite literary culture" ("Double" 70), for example, and Jeff Gundy calls it the "inevitable starting point for discussions of contemporary Mennonite writing" ("Doubt" 337)—nor is she the first to ponder its implications. In a brief but remarkable 1997 essay, Mavis Reimer asks why "academic readers so quickly enshrined Wiebe as origin of modern Mennonite writing" ("Literary" 119) and points to the institutionalization of Mennonite studies "within the secular university" as a possible answer (120). "Reading Wiebe as a Mennonite writer is reading backward" (119), she insists; it was not Wiebe but later critics who were keen to establish the world of Mennonite writing that they described as the consequence of his work. Crucially, Reimer follows up this insight with a question I will attempt to answer at some length in this study. "Recognizing that our reading of Wiebe as origin itself produces Wiebe as origin," she writes, "might also lead us to ask what writers or traditions of writing we ignore and devalue in creating this historical narrative" ("Literary" 120). Some fifteen years later, Kasdorf reiterates Reimer's question and her call to action. After reflecting on her own role in the establishment of this critical narrative—what are the "ghoulish or egotistic appetites the transgressive myth satisfies for individuals like me who keep repeating it," she asks by way of confession (8)—Kasdorf closes with a set of questions clearly meant as a challenge to the field at large. "I wonder what possibilities might open up for Mennonite writers if we told other myths of origin when we gathered," she writes, encouraging scholars to "ask not only what new stories (and poems and essays) we can write [. . .] but also what new histories of this literature can we tell" (10).

Reading Mennonite Writing is, in one sense, an extended effort to test, engage, and expand on such calls to rethink the standard critical narratives of Mennonite literary studies in North America. As Reimer's early insights suggest, Mennonite literary studies has a long history of self-consciously interrogating its own founding narratives, which I have traced elsewhere as a form a metacriticism.[1] Although I have begun this study with Kasdorf for her clarity and wit, a surge of recent work in this area suggests this metacritical tradition may be reaching a head, with scholars reconsidering not only the field's past but also, increasingly, the plausibility of its future. This study takes its larger impetus, then, from a host of related work in the field, which, while varying widely in its proposals and its assessment on the health of the field itself, has collectively articulated a pressing need for Mennonite literary studies to interrogate its founding narratives, methodological assumptions, and, perhaps, its viability as a scholarly field. With Kasdorf and Reimer, I am interested in reexamining the field's so-called mythic origin, but I also want to consider the impact of another one of the field's originary narratives—this being the one that historicizes its emergence as a minority literature in the 1980s and '90s—in order to problematize the larger call for new histories that has been at the heart of the field's metacritical concern of the past two decades. Here I will have my own set of confessions to make, having worked hard to write that account of the past myself.[2] What if a key step toward opening "new possibilities" for Mennonite literature is not simply moving past the field's so-called "mythic origin" by more fully historicizing its emergence as a minority literature, but to consider how literary history itself, far from a neutral methodology for engaging the past, has been quietly working to limit the field's present?

In looking at literature by and about Mennonites from across North America, this book can also be read as a case study in the broader field of transnational literature. Paul Jay's much-quoted dictum that "nothing has reshaped literary and cultural studies more than its embrace of transnationalism" (1) remains true, but this study takes up Mennonite literature in North America—primarily, though not exclusively, in Canada and the United States—as a case study in the belief that the generalizations necessary for the theorization of transnational literatures are most useful and best tested in the narrower contexts of individual fields of concern. There is no question that the shape and tenor of Mennonite writing has been deeply informed by the immediate regional and national contexts within which it has emerged, and historicizing these specificities remains a productive and unfinished critical project. At the same time, one of the primary arguments of this study is that we must be careful not to allow a historicization of the field's emergence within particular contexts and communities to fully determine its broader parameters or possibilities. As Magdalene Redekop suggests in her recent *Making Believe*, local and national differences have often been ignored in the field in favor of the artificially "smooth finish of transnational Mennonitism" (168). One productive way to respond to such a condition, as Redekop does in *Making Believe*, is to delve more deeply into the regional and national specificities. Another way to respond, as I am doing in this study, is to rough up that "smooth finish" a bit, exploring the limits but also the possibilities of the transnational assumptions and aspirations that have long been expressed by the field itself. It is notable, after all, that scholars of Mennonite writing in North America have attempted to work across national, racial, ethnic, and denominational lines for so long. My argument here will be that taking those efforts seriously could offer not only a body of literature broader than has often been imagined but also a rich archive of critique and a unique articulation of cultural difference that, read carefully, can challenge the methodological nationalism, as well as the racialized and secularized assumptions, that have informed the identity- and nation-based study of minoritized literatures across North America over this same period. If recent work in the field has made clear that the aspirational rhetoric of inclusive transnationalism in Mennonite literary studies often obscures how thoroughly its practice has been directed by the ill-fitting critical discourses into which it emerged, it has also signaled something of the promise and possibilities of self-consciously reading across a broader set of texts, genres, locations, and contexts.

Accordingly, this introduction turns to Françoise Lionnet and Shu-mei Shih's influential articulation of "minor transnationalism," which interrogates "major discussions of transnationalism" ("Thinking" 6) and their implicit assumptions of a "universal minority position" (11). Lionnet and Shih encourage scholars to consider the specific shape, history, and trajectory of individual fields as they transverse not only geopolitical but also critical and conceptual borders. At the same time, they encourage scholars to emphasize and explore the specificity of minor fields, looking to explore the lateral networks of relation between and within minor fields rather than defaulting to define them in relation to dominant modes and discourses. Contemporary Mennonite literary studies in North America, I want to suggest—its subject a surprisingly diverse mix of faith and cultural communities, faith-based institutions, and a tangle of kinship and migration lines that stretch across and beyond the continent—are particularly well positioned to serve as a study of such a framework. In identifying ways in which critical discourses have "rendered invisible subject positions that did not readily fall into such accepted categories as those of official minorities" (4), Lionnet and Shih offer a means through which to consider a broader past and possibilities *specifically* of Mennonite literary writing and, perhaps, help us to enable the surprisingly radical possibilities of this small field. What, if anything, is unique about Mennonite literary studies, and how might we more fully appreciate and grapple with the elements that distinguish it from other literary traditions?

Like many other fields of identity-based literary scholarship that emerged as "minority literatures" during the 1970s and '80s, Mennonite literary studies is currently grappling with how best to build upon the work that enabled its formation in a contemporary context with often starkly different critical and political assumptions about identity and literature. Is it possible for the field to build on its earlier critical conversations without being forever tethered to its founding assumptions? Can we meaningfully reconsider the field's past without simply retracing the lines of thought that have led to our frustrated present? As the conversation moves into its fifth decade, it seems clear that the past of Mennonite literature in North America is up for grabs. And by "past," of course, I mean the future.

ON MENNONITE HISTORY AND/AS LITERARY CONTEXT

One of the challenges of working in a minor field of study is that, nearly by definition, scholars cannot assume much by way of general readers' prior knowledge of the subject at hand. This is the case for scholars working in Mennonite literature, certainly, who are routinely encouraged to preface their analyses of poetry and fiction with contextualizing remarks about Mennonites in general. The task of providing sufficient context for such work, however, turns out to be surprisingly tricky. As part of my argument in this study has to do with the way in which Mennonite literary critics handle the past—and because it seems only fair to follow Kasdorf's account with a confession of my own—I want to ask readers' indulgence to offer this context via a brief reflection on the historical overview with which I began the edited collection *After Identity: Mennonite Writing in North America*. I recount that passage in full here:

> The Mennonites of North America are descendants, by faith or birth, of the sixteenth-century Christian dissenters collectively referred to as Anabaptists. Stressing adult baptism, nonconformity, and nonviolence, the diverse Anabaptist movements that sprang up in Europe during the early sixteenth century were subjected to widespread persecution. The first large migration of Mennonites to North America occurred as part of William Penn's "holy experiment" in Pennsylvania around the turn of the eighteenth century. Many of the descendants of these Mennonites, often called Swiss Mennonites or Pennsylvania Dutch, later established the first Mennonite presence in Canada when they emigrated from the United States following the American

> Revolutionary War. The second major cultural or ethnic group of North American Mennonites, often referred to as Russian Mennonites, arrived from their once-prosperous colonies in present-day Ukraine in three mass migrations (1870s, 1920s, and 1940s). The larger Mennonite faith, however, has spread around the world through missionary efforts, and today there is a global Mennonite religious community of more than 1.5 million baptized adults, with the largest population in Africa. There are roughly five hundred thousand baptized members of Mennonite churches in North America, scattered broadly across some 150 different groups and denominations. Although the majority of North American Mennonites are assimilated into mainstream culture, others—especially those from Old Order or related Amish and Hutterite traditions—continue to live separated from "the world," maintaining distinct ethnoreligious traditions with conservative dress, unique dialects, and a reluctance to embrace modern technologies.

In *After Identity*, I followed this historical paragraph with an endnote comparing such passages to what Kasdorf memorably describes as the "autoethnographic announcements" common in ethnic literatures, those obligatory but charged moments when a literary text breaks its façade, and the author pauses to offer a set of historical and sociological details for an audience that is presumed to be outside the community. Mennonite literary criticism is imagined to be a form of nonfiction, of course, but it, too, is subject to its own version of this demand, and here, too, these brief historicizing gestures, destined by their brevity to be partial and misleading, erupt as moments of "*apparent* nonfiction" (Kasdorf, "Autoethnographic" 25) and risk being mistaken as determining the field's "real" referent and parameters.

I have quoted this piece of "apparent nonfiction" at some length here to provide general readers of this study with some basic historical context, of course, but also to illustrate something of the conundrum that historical contextualization poses for literary scholarship. Such passages are not simply context for the critical argument to follow but are—always and unavoidably—an important part *of* that argument. When faced with constraints of space and time, what do we select as the key contextual concerns for the field? What do we leave out? Revisiting the passage above in light of the claims of this project, several assumptions embedded within it seem clear: it presents the field of Mennonite writing as a minority literary expression of specifically Russian and Swiss (read: *white*) ethnic Mennonites, positioning the racial and cultural diversity of Mennonites as a global rather than a North American phenomenon, and subsuming the smaller but longstanding Asian, African, and Latinx Mennonite communities in Canada and the United States within the generic phrase of "different groups." It overlooks Mexico as part of the North American Mennonite context altogether and emphasizes migration even as it depoliticizes it. What is more, by introducing the notion of assimilation with the subordinating conjunction *although*, it seems to bend toward the exoticizing draw of the most stereotypical elements of Mennonite dress and culture. And, crucially for me here, it also affirms a narrative, linear form of history as the collection's primary method of engaging the past.

As this larger study will make clear, I do not mean to question the need for historical context for literary analysis, and I certainly do not mean to dissuade analysis of work that focus on even the most conventional of Swiss or Russian Mennonite narratives. My concern, rather, is to think more carefully about the shape and forms of history we collectively invoke, and in which we invest. Necessary as it may seem, offering these types of abbreviated narrative histories as the primary context for literary analysis may be affirming forms of community we might otherwise want to question, and retracing the types of methodological assumptions that continue to delimit the field's possibilities. I will explore the complexities of Mennonite literary history at some length in the pages below. First, however, I would like to turn to the field's complicated present.

MENNONITE LITERATURE IS DEAD; LONG LIVE MENNONITE LITERATURE!

To judge from the range and prominence of creative work by and about Mennonites as we begin the 2020s, it would seem clear that Mennonite literature in North America is in robust health. The last decade has seen a host of new writing by a range of the best-established figures in the field, including Rudy Wiebe, David Bergen, Jeff Gundy, Julia Spicher Kasdorf, Patrick Friesen, and Di Brandt. Following the 2018 publication of *Women Talking*, her bestselling novel set on a Bolivian Mennonite colony, Miriam Toews was the subject of glowing profiles in the *New Yorker* and the *New York Times*; the book itself has been optioned by Brad Pitt's film company, Plan B. Rhoda Janzen's quirky memoir, *Mennonite in a Little Black Dress*, reached the top spot on the *New York Times* bestseller list. At the same time, a new generation of Mennonite writers has been busy winning major awards and suggest a rich future for the field, including Casey Plett, whose celebrated *Little Fish* won the $60,000 CND Amazon Canada First Novel award and landed her a Hodder Fellowship at Princeton, and Sofia Samatar, whose evocative speculative fiction has been anthologized in numerous *Best American Science Fiction* collections and earned her the 2014 World Fantasy Award. Little wonder that a 2016 survey essay by Jeff Gundy marveled at what he called the "lovely excess of writing and writers" in the field, noting that there are "so many vibrant and varied voices echoing through the halls and corridors of Mennonite/s writing these days that it's impossible to do justice to them all" ("Mennonite/s"). More recent bibliographic review essays by Daniel Shank Cruz echo Gundy's assessment. "In 2017 the field is in full flower," he writes in one essay, noting "more Mennonite creative writers [are] active than ever before" ("Bibliography" 98). "Any reasonable observer of the field of Mennonite literature," he insists in another, "must agree that it is currently flourishing" ("Introduction").

As it turns out, reasonable observers do not agree. I began this study by invoking Kasdorf's call for new histories of the field, yet hers is but the clearest of a host of suggestions over the past decade that the broader field has reached something of a limit. When Kasdorf and I extended invitations to a group of leading or promising scholars in the field to convene at Penn State for a week to address concerns related to her 2013 "confession," all nine agreed to participate immediately. The resulting collection, *After Identity: Mennonite Writing in North America*, clearly reflects, as I put it in the introduction, a "shared frustration with the direction of the field" (11) and has been read as evidence the field is near a crisis.[3] Indeed, several of the most established scholars in that collection wondered openly at the enduring narrowness of Mennonite literary criticism's purview (Brandt, "In Praise" esp. 128ff.), or worried that its critical wheels are "spinning" so much that the field is "not making progress" (M. Redekop, "Is Menno?" 196). Even some of those celebrating the vibrancy of the field's literary production have expressed doubts about the direction of the critical conversation. In *Making Believe*, for example, Redekop celebrates the "embarrassment of riches" that is Mennonite literary production in Canada (165) but confesses a sense that her topic "could vanish into thin air at any moment" (xv). In the same review essay in which he applauds the range of contemporary Mennonite writing, Gundy casts a doubtful eye on the critical frameworks through which that work is being examined. "Maybe it's time for a new narrative," he writes, adding: "It's *always* already time for a new narrative, isn't it?" ("Mennonite/s") It's an argument I echo implicitly by searching for a new critical framework in my introduction to this study and have made more directly elsewhere, celebrating the growth of new writing by and about Mennonites while arguing that "the very foundations of the Mennonite/s Writing project are swaying" ("'Garden'" 29).

At times, this critical concern about the field's future has tipped beyond simple expressions of concern. Even Hildi Froese Tiessen, whose prominence and endurance in the field has led Cruz to christen her the "godmother of Mennonite literary criticism" (*Queering* 1), has wondered aloud if perhaps "critics would do well to abandon the notion" that Mennonite writing "can be considered collectively" ("Habit" 24), and suggests that the Mennonite literary text may need to be "liberated" from the critical conversation that has surrounded it ("After" 210). In the same paragraph where she notes, "Mennonite literature seems to be in no danger of vanishing" ("After" 220), Froese Tiessen suggests that "the conditions that sustained its origins and the early critical readings of it no longer compel many who have an interest in the field." Writing two and a half decades after she organized the first "Mennonite/s Writing" conference, she goes on to invoke Franco Moretti's suggestions that "literatures tend to remain in place 'for twenty-five years or so,' and that almost 'all genres active at any given time seem to arise and disappear together according to some hidden rhythm'" ("After" 220).

Froese Tiessen's arguments are complex and she routinely tempers such expressions of concern with notes of optimism, but others are more pessimistic. The editor's introduction to a recent special issue of the *Mennonite Quarterly Review* dedicated to Mennonite literature, for example, suggests the essays included therein "unavoidably raise questions as to whether the concept of 'Mennonite/s Writing'—and the conferences associated with it—is sustainable" (Roth 10) and asks if these essays might constitute "the valedictory commentary on 'a shape of life grown old'" (10). And, in an essay memorably entitled "The Voice Is Coming (Faintly) from the Grave and It Says Mennonites Are Dead, and So Is Mennonite Writing . . . ," the Canadian writer and critic Maurice Mierau flatly suggests the field has already died. When a term like "Mennonite writer" is applied to new writers, he insists, it is but "a marketing gimmick of decreasing effectiveness" (28).

From "flourishing" to "dead": How are we to judge these starkly different assessments of the Mennonite literature today? One way is to take the celebratory rhetoric surrounding the range and success of individual Mennonite writers as evidence of the health of literary writing itself and take the anxieties about its imminent demise as referring specifically to the state of the critical conversation that surrounds it. This study takes its initiative from what I have suggested is a shared sense of frustration with the critical conversation, after all, and who would deny that the best poetry, fiction, and drama of any literary field runs well ahead of its critical response? At the same time, it is something of a surprise to find many of the field's best-established critics openly worrying that the critical conversation—which is to say, *their own work*—is suddenly unequal to the task of engaging the literature it supports and surrounds, especially given that so many of them are counted among the field's most notable creative writers themselves. What is more, perhaps the central point of overlap between the scholarly work of Jeff Gundy, Di Brandt, Julia Spicher Kasdorf, and Ann Hostetler—all poets themselves, all major critical figures in the field—is that it so productively disregards the conceit of a sharp distinction between creative and critical work. Nor is this disregard restricted to the poets: *11 Encounters with Mennonite Fiction*, among the most recent edited collections of scholarly work in the field, begins with its editor explaining she "urged the writers to 'lean in the direction of a personal essay'" (Froese Tiessen, "Encounters" 1). Recent book-length studies by Magdalene Redekop and Cruz foreground the personal in similar ways, albeit for different reasons, with Cruz noting with agreement that Gundy argues Mennonite criticism "often disregard[s] the borders between the academic and the personal, opting instead for a hybrid of genres" (*Queering* 17).[4] Perhaps even more to the point, however, is the fact that it is a critical act to gather texts together under the title of "Mennonite literature" or "Mennonite/s Writing," the very act required in order to speak of individual texts in the collective terms of a body of literature whose health can be assessed.

Another way to look at the uncertainty and range of critical assessments of the field today is to suggest that it reflects a broader uncertainty about the framework and method by which Mennonite writing has worked to understand its past. Part of my argument here is that "Mennonite/s Writing," with the forward slash—first conceptualized by Froese Tiessen for the 1990 inaugural "Mennonite/s Writing" conference and adopted as a guiding term for the subsequent critical conversation and conference series—is deeply rooted in the field's emergence as a minority literature, and that much of the critical conversation is straining under that legacy. This is a decidedly less romantic account of the field's history, and if it, too, is now well established it is worth recounting in brief for our purposes here. In Canada, the federal government's efforts to foster a national identity via the arts dovetailed with its early multiculturalism policies during the 1970s and '80s, creating funding and publishing opportunities that helped a range of minority literatures—from Black Canadian literature to Italian Canadian literature and so on—establish themselves as areas of scholarly interest as the "cultural contributions of the other ethnic groups."[5] It was in this period and framework that the unlikely surge of writing by the so-called "Russian Mennonites" in Winnipeg was first fostered and celebrated as a "Mennonite miracle."[6] As a result, in the context of Canadian literature, "Mennonite" came to be understood nearly exclusively as "Russian Mennonite," and in ethnic rather than religious terms. In the United

States, by contrast, there stood a Puritan tradition of faith-based writing as a ready frame of reference,[7] and, as Ann Hostetler notes, a racialized discourse of ethnicity that emerged from political resistance movements and which arguably corresponded less easily with prevailing assumptions about Mennonites.[8] When well-received poetry by Swiss Mennonite writers in the United States began emerging slightly later than in Canada—including work by Jeff Gundy, Jean Janzen, and Kasdorf herself (who published work in several issues of the *New Yorker* in 1992)—it was encouraged by a critical conversation that was often self-consciously looking to build on the critical conversation that had begun north of the border, while remaining more open to engaging the religious elements of the work.[9]

The Canadian and American contexts have offered differing emphases for the field, then, and important work remains to be done understanding regional and national expressions of the field. However, the enduring emphasis on understanding Mennonite literature as a North American phenomenon has meant the national critical conversations were rarely fully separate.[10] Indeed, scholars routinely engaged the literature through an implicitly transnational frame, looking to reflect what John D. Roth and Ervin Beck have called the "truly international nature—and cross-fertilizing influence—of Mennonite writing" (viii). Although early critical efforts like John Ruth's *Mennonite Identity and Literary Art* (1978) and Al Reimer's *Mennonite Literary Voices: Past and Present* (1993) are clearly written from Swiss American Mennonite and Russian Canadian Mennonite positions, they routinely reach across the Swiss–Russian and US–Canadian borders, often without comment, to consider the prospect of a larger body of writing. Recent collections, anthologies, and scholarly monographs have confirmed the transnational framework for the field—including the field's most prominent literary anthology, Ann Hostetler's *A Cappella: Mennonite Voices in Poetry* (2003), which includes poets from Canada and the United States on the logic that the Mennonites' "religious, ethnic, and linguistic criteria cross national boundaries" (182). I will have more to say about the transnational nature of the field shortly but will pause here on Cruz's observation that "Mennonite literature has always treated being Mennonite as an ethnic identity in both Canada and the United States, and thus has always treated Mennonite literature as an ethnic literature" (*Queering* 7). While the critical emphasis on Russian and Swiss Mennonite ethnic identity in early discussions of Mennonite writing reflected both the prominence of work by writers of these backgrounds at this formative moment and the demographics of North American Mennonite communities in this period,[11] it also worked, in the United States as in Canada, to downplay religious difference and circumscribe the field as a minority literature expressing forms of white ethnic expression. In the terminology of Charles Taylor's work on identity that was so prominent at that time, we can say that through the logic of the politics of recognition, Mennonite literature—as "Mennonite/s Writing"—emerged as a transnational minority literature that gave both voice and audience to the newly articulated field.[12]

Scholars of Mennonite literature will recognize the project of historicization above and are likely to agree that much work remains to be done to fully explore the rise of Mennonite writing in its various regional, national, or transnational iterations. Part of the challenge faced by these efforts, I want to suggest, is that the methods and models of conventional literary history encourage us to route our historicizing efforts through the linear, developmental logic of the field's emergence as a minority literature. Once a dominant method of literary studies, literary history rose to prominence as part of the romantic nationalisms of the nineteenth century, selecting and plotting freshly canonized texts into narratives of progress to support claims of national maturation. By the first half of the twentieth century, such histories were widely recognized as forms of hagiography and roundly challenged, as David Perkins recounts, by scholars critiquing their emphasis on context over content and form; their reduction of individual books to manifestations of collective identity; and their reliance on teleological narratives of development that reduced the past into an authorization of a politicized present (1–2). Importantly for my argument here, however, Perkins and others have suggested that the developmental model of literary history retained its position in the latter half of the twentieth century primarily via its use in "sociological literary histories" (9), including those written by underrepresented communities "turn[ing] to the past in search of identity, tradition, and self-understanding" (10). In a parallel argument, Linda Hutcheon suggests it was the "potent combination of the nostalgic impact of origins (the founding moment) and the linear utopian projection (into the future)" (7) that made national literary history a powerful model. For scholars working from marginalized groups, she continues, the "strategic power of identifying with an obviously successful national narrative of progress outweighs at least temporarily the dangers of co-optation by a model that, after all, was often responsible for excluding the very groups these literary historians seek to represent" (6). In Gayatri Chakravorty Spivak's related argument, historiography was "embraced as strategy" by subaltern studies rather than as a final destination, wielded for its authorizing power rather than its critical nuance (285). The question, as Spivak writes, is whether such "strategic blindness will entangle the genealogist in the chain" (285). Or, as Stephen Greenblatt has cautioned about the "strategic appropriation of the national model of literary history—with its teleological, developmental narrative of progress—in order to confer authority upon an emergent group" (54–55): "Such groups may believe that they are appropriating traditional forms, but it may well be the forms that are appropriating them" (59). As we will see in the next section of the introduction, this is almost precisely the caution leveled to the field of Mennonite literary studies by Julie Rak, keynote to the 2017 Mennonite/s Writing Conference in Winnipeg, albeit in a slightly different register ("Interview").

How do such arguments relate to the search for new histories of Mennonite literary studies? They help us appreciate the challenge posed by the methodological pull of the relationship between literary history itself and the field as a minority literature, which always risks directing our gaze through the developmental logic that fostered and authorized its belated emergence as an "ethnic literature." There is little question that the iterative celebration of Wiebe's *Peace Shall Destroy Many* as a "mythic origin" for the field's development reflects what Hutcheon calls the "potent combination of the nostalgic impact of origins (the founding moment) and the linear utopian projection (into the future)" (7). There are, of course, no shortage of notable earlier works written in English by or about Mennonites in North America, including several published by major publishing houses dating back to the early 1900s, but when critics went looking for precedent for the remarkable community of "serious" Russian

Mennonites literary authors that had emerged in Winnipeg, they were uninterested in novels like Mabel Dunham's *Trail of the Conestoga*, the 1924 bestselling romance about Swiss Mennonites rambling up to Ontario from Pennsylvania—to say nothing of earlier works of science fiction or extended critical satires, or embarrassingly parochial biographies or didactically religious children's literature or self-published personal memoirs. Instead, using the developmental logic of conventional literary history, they looked for earlier works that were recognizable as clear antecedents to the work flourishing at the time and just happened to find it in the scandalous debut of the field's most celebrated writer. Wiebe's novel, in turn, would offer a "beginning" for the field in Edward Said's sense of the term, in that it designated "the possibility of, as well as the rule of formation for, subsequent texts," establishing a "discontinuity" with what precedes it and "an authorization for what follows" (34). The key point for me here is the tight relationship between the so-called "mythic origin" historical narrative and its ostensible corrective historicization. Identified as the field's urtext decades after its publication as part of the field's establishment, the selection and endurance of Wiebe's 1962 *Peace Shall Destroy Many* as Mennonite literature's "mythic origin" needs to be understood as a direct product of the field's emergence as a form of (ethnic) minority literature, rather than an alternative history. The designation of a mythological literary beginning is not in conflict with a linear, developmental understanding of literary history that relies on direct lines of influence, for both establish not only the "possibility" of a field of study but also, to a powerful extent, the "rule of formation" for subsequent work in the field. Is it really such a stretch, after all, to move from a "mythic origin" to stories of a "Mennonite miracle"?

Nowhere have these two lines of thought come together more clearly than in two recent essays by Mierau. In the first, which I referenced earlier, he flatly suggests that both Mennonites and Mennonite writing are "dead" ("The Voice" 27). Although few have been so blunt, the arc of his argument will be familiar. Authentic Mennonite literature was, he argues, the product of a clash between the isolated, German-speaking Mennonite villages of the Canadian prairies and contemporary culture. With the loss of the linguistic and cultural markers that attended the assimilation of these Mennonite communities into a secular, English mainstream, he reasons, Mennonite literature itself is finished—because there can no longer be such a thing as a "Mennonite writer." Mierau is a provocateur and the essay is highly stylized, but he returned to this argument in his introduction to *Rhubarb*'s 2017 fiction anthology, *9 Mennonite Stories*. Quoting his previous essay at some length, Mierau insists that "producing more Mennonite writers will be difficult, and maybe impossible" (1), given the "disappearance of [. . .] distinctive Mennonite theological and cultural markers" (6). The stories selected by David Bergen for the larger anthology affirms the narrow view of Mierau's introduction: all nine of the authors highlighted in the collection are of Russian Mennonite descent; all are Canadian and eight of them are from Southern Manitoba; half of the stories were first published decades ago.[13] If there are good reasons for this narrow focus, Mierau never presents them, choosing instead to present the narrow collection of stories as if it were reflective of the larger field. If the categorical error here seems obvious to the point of being trite, it is also necessary to articulate clearly: in these essays, Mierau is conflating one particularly prominent strain of writing by Russian Mennonites in Manitoba with the field of Mennonite literature itself, metonymically presenting the decline of the specific set of historical and cultural contexts that cultivated the former with the decline of the latter.[14]

Mierau's high rhetoric is most useful as something like a limit case, but part of my argument here is that his conflation of a specific set of its key texts and formative contexts as the implicit parameters for the broader field, or even its stated "default," is indicative of how the specifics of the field's inauguration as a minority literature in Canada can work to limit the broader possibilities of Mennonite writing in North America.[15] It funnels our critical gaze not only to a specific time and place, with its canonical authors and texts—so that Redekop can quote Froese Tiessen to suggest there is a critical "consensus" that "'we cannot speak of contemporary Mennonite writing in Canada without placing at its center Manitoba, where it began'" (qtd. in *Making Believe* 168)[16]—but also to the assumptions, genres, conventions, and methods of that same period. Consider the fate of Dunham's *Trail of the Conestoga* in such an arrangement: a bestselling book by a Mennonite and about Swiss Mennonites, it quite literally put Mennonites on the Canadian literary map.[17] But Dunham's work was dismissed by early scholars as being just "marginally attributable to the Mennonite people" (J. Thiessen 70), and, along with Paul Hiebert's *Sarah Binks* (1947), as being "isolated literary phenomena" that can be "regarded only peripherally as 'Mennonite'" (A. Reimer, *Mennonite* 20). As Reimer's description of Dunham as "isolated" suggests, *Trail of the Conestoga*—about Swiss Mennonites in Pennsylvania and Ontario, written in Ontario in 1924—was firmly ahead and outside of the development of Mennonite literature as a body of literature. Before a critical mass of Manitoba-based Russian Mennonite writers made it possible to think of their work as a body of writing in the 1980s, as Froese Tiessen reports, there was simply "nothing that could be identified as a Mennonite 'literature'" ("Habit" 12). Writings by Mennonite authors such as Hiebert and Dunham, she observes, were "unlikely to be thought of by anyone except, possibly, Rudy Wiebe, in the same breath" ("Habit" 12). As an account of the field's consolidation and subsequent development, these are simple statements of fact. But given the ways in which a developmental literary history encourages a teleological account of the field's past and possibilities, it is worth asking whether we have consistently drawn a clear enough distinction between the historical development of Mennonite literature as a conceit and as a field of study—between the authors, texts, and contexts that made it possible to think about Mennonite writing as a body of writing in the first place—and the broader history of literary writing by and about Mennonites in North America, along with its presumably much larger set of figures, texts, and contexts. Now that the critical discourse of Mennonite literary studies is well established, is there any reason why we would continue to allow those early parameters to shape our understanding of the broader history of Mennonite writing in North America so sharply? Why is it that as I write, *The Trail of the Conestoga* is *still* missing from the "Mennonite/s Writing" bibliographies, the field's most extensive bibliographic projects?[18] What other texts, authors, genres, and geographies have been similarly unrecognizable from the perspective of the field's founding terms and concerns?

Let me close this section of this introduction with several clarifications. The first is that I certainly do not intend to suggest the field can be understood as being sharply divided between scholars looking to restrict the field to a specific version of its past and those pushing to move it forward into a broader future. To the contrary, what I mean to suggest is that this tension exists *within* many of our accounts of the field, even where careful scholars are wrestling directly with the question of literary history as part of our collective effort to rethink the field's possibilities. Given that this account grounds the field in the early work of Russian Mennonites in Canada, it may not be surprising that we seem to find this tension most often in the work of Canadian critics of Russian Mennonite descent, including myself. In *Rewriting the Break Event*, for example, I worked hard to historicize the emergence of Mennonite Canadian writing as an "ethnic literature" in Canada and traced the revisions and rewritings of a single historical account in the field. I stand by the project but acknowledge it remained largely within the boundaries it was looking to critique—one of the factors motivating my return to similar questions in this study.[19] Recuperative projects have already begun to complicate the field's narrow past—Cruz's efforts to establish a genealogy of queer Mennonite writing is especially notable in this regard, as is Kasdorf's edited edition of Joseph W. Yoder's 1940 bestseller *Rosanna of the Amish*—but an additive model will always strain against the centrifugal pull of the field's established literary history as a minority literature. This is why, in chapter 1, I adapt Franco Moretti's notion of distant reading as an alternate form of literary history, and why, in the next section, I suggest the possibility of intentionally moving outside the minority literature frame.

So, is Mennonite literature in North America flourishing or dying? Understood as a body of works in Canada and the United States bound to the most traditional elements of euro-Mennonite identity, animated by a literary history that tethers it to the villages of Southern Manitoba via its development in the charged conflict zones of Swiss and Russian ethnocultural Mennonite identity—that is, as a form of ethnic minority writing—Mennonite literature may well be at risk of disappearing along with the villages themselves. Understood in a broader sense, however, as a critical framework for gathering and engaging the larger, longer, and ever-increasing production of literary works by or about Mennonites across North America, it seems clear that Mennonite literature is continuing to thrive. In the next section, I will look at some of the many ways in which Mennonite literary critics are working to expand the field and will suggest these efforts might be fostered by thinking about the field as a case of what Lionnet and Shu-mei Shih call a minor transnationalism. In moving away from the widest paths of literary critical discourse, it is possible—perhaps even probable—that the critical interest in Mennonite writing as a minor transnational literature will prove less substantial than it has been as an ethnic minority literature. Academic popularity is hardly the strongest of arguments, however, and as I argue in my next section, it is also possible that the field will have more to offer as a minor literature working self-consciously outside the parameters of "mainstream" criticism than it has had as a minority literature attempting to work largely within it. In the end, then, it is possible that both assessments of the field may be true: as a form of minority literature, Mennonite literature may be nearing an end, even as its future as a literary tradition outside that frame is bright indeed. Mennonite literature is dead; long live Mennonite literature!

TOWARD A MINOR TRANSNATIONALISM

Reflecting on her experience as the keynote speaker at the eighth Mennonite/s Writing conference in Winnipeg in October of 2017, Julie Rak offered a word of caution. Of Mennonite literature specifically in Canada, she suggested it might be best understood as a "minor field of study oriented towards (and mostly not within) English-Canadian literature as a whole" ("Mennonite/s" 19). By "minor field," of course, Rak meant not to indicate that Mennonite literature was insignificant but rather that it is relatively small, and—importantly—that it does not fully adhere to the assumptions and models of the dominant critical discourse in the country. For Rak, the fact that the field's size and specifics set it outside the mainstream of literary studies was not a limitation but rather an opportunity. Indeed, efforts to move the field toward a "recognition by the larger paradigm," she cautioned, could be understood as an example of what Lauren Berlant refers to as "cruel optimism," in that "what might be desired that could be an obstacle to its flourishing" (Rak, "Interview" 19; see also Berlant, *Cruel Optimism*). Striving for recognition by the larger paradigm, Rak argues, requires minor fields to emulate the logic and methods of that paradigm; in the process, they risk adopting the limitations of the dominant modes of critique and losing what makes them of value as a specific field. Although Rak's comments were made specifically in relation to the Canadian context, they resonate with my sense that the value of the larger field lies in the specificities that are obscured when we attempt to route it through the language and logic of conventional literary studies. Given that Mennonite literary study's "audience, its premises and even its sense of history are very different" from conventional literary studies, Rak concludes, perhaps its most productive direction would be to intentionally "work differently as a subfield" ("Mennonite/s" 21).

Calling for the field to self-consciously estrange the minority writing frame and strategically embrace its specificities as a minor tradition is meant to help us recognize and foster the ways in which it has sought to "work differently." As I expect is already clear, I am in full agreement with what I take to be the spirit of Kasdorf's call for "new histories" of the literature, as well as with Gundy's assertion that it is "*always* already time" for renewing the critical narrative—along with his earlier exhortations for critical humility, in which he described individual critics as "walkers in the fog" inescapably reliant on each other to gain a fuller picture of the field.[20] Despite the expressed anxieties of the field's stagnation, it appears there are a host of renewal projects already underway, including: an affirmation, via the rising field of theopoetics, of the field's religious foundations (*Crosscurrents* 60.1 [2010]; *Conrad Grebel Review* [*CGR*] 31.2 [Spring 2013])[21]; and fresh explorations of overlooked genres, such as the related field of Amish romance novels (Weaver-Zercher 2013), personal narratives (*Journal of Mennonite Studies* [*JMS*] 36 [2018]), documentary creative writing (*Journal of Mennonite Writing* [*JMW*] 10.4 [2018]), and speculative fiction (*JMW* 11.1 [2019]). There are efforts underway to expand the field toward the US-Mexican border (*JMW* 10.1 [2018]); to explore the field's connections with related work in visual arts (Redekop, *Making Believe*); and, perhaps most notably, there are recuperative projects exploring racialized and, especially, queer Mennonite writing (Samatar; Cruz;

Guenther Braun; Plett). In a small field sustained by the committed work of a few dozen scholars, this breadth of work—alongside the recent publications of substantial manuscripts and edited collections[22]—suggests to me less a field in "crisis" than one in the midst of a critical renewal. It is worth asking, however, whether our existing frames will be able to sustain this promising expansion of the field into new concerns, genres, and communities. Might there be a way to reconceive the field's critical frame so that it fosters these expansive efforts, rather than resists them?

Françoise Lionnet and Shu-mei Shih's influential 2005 collection of essays, *Minor Transnationalism*, offers one possibility. Even as they celebrate the possibilities enabled by the transnational turn that has occurred over the past several decades in literary criticism, Lionnet and Shih caution that the generalizations required for these broadening scales of study risk distorting the shape of the fields they help bring into view. The "major discourses of transnationalism and globalization," they argue, "assume that ethnic particularity and minoritized perspective are contained within and easily assimilated into the dominant forms of transnationalism" (6–7). Engagements with minor discourses tend to read them through their "vertical" relationship to the major, they argue, obscuring the "lateral networks" of relation and the specificities of individual traditions (1). "For tactical and strategic purposes," they write, "minority identities have been constructed in strong and bounded terms that have unfortunately rendered invisible subject positions that did not readily fall into such accepted categories as those of official minorities" (4). Rejecting the conceit of a "universal minority position" (11), they call for a rejection of the "compulsory mediation by the mainstream for all forms of cultural production" (2), as well as a "'historicizing'" of "the field of minority discourse production" in order to "show how transdisciplinary academic practices can construct transnational objects of knowledge, thereby transforming our established interpretive frameworks and disciplinary conventions, while also producing alternative genealogies and narratives of the past" (15).

In making space for a reconsideration of the specificities that are often lost within dominant discourses of minoritization and transnationalism, Lionnet and Shih's "minor transnationalism" offers a critical discourse that can help us register the "cruel optimism" that has tied Mennonite literature's ostensibly unique and transnational form of cultural difference to productive but ill-fitting critical paradigms. Indeed, as Vijay Mishra (2006) writes in his brief but careful engagement with Lionnet and Shih's work, the "minor" as a category is "often elided [. . .] in many generalist works on transnationalism," positioned as intrinsically secondary and constituted in relation to the dominant modes and flows. Accordingly, he argues, the minor "requires analysis (as transnationals)" on its own terms. Understanding the "transcultural dimensions of literary production require[s] a rather different interpretative model," he continues, one that "break[s] away from the binaries of culture and knowledge (the latter, as the European argument goes, something that great works of the West produce, the former no more than an anthropological archive from the periphery), high and low." As the larger collection makes clear, Lionnet and Shih are not arguing for a false depoliticization of minority writing but rather arguing against its *restriction* to an oppositional politics that obscures its wider possibilities while implicitly re-entrenching its supplementary status within an expanded transnational scale that replicates the marginalizing logic of the national frame.

How might reconceptualizing Mennonite literature as a form of minor transnationalism encourage us to think differently about the field? Estranging the linear, developmental model of history that has tethered the field to the framework of its emergence should encourage not only archival explorations of underappreciated periods, genres, or movements from the field's enlarged past but also alternative ways of engaging well-known works and new methods of historical scholarship. Similarly, understanding Mennonite writing as a form of minor transnationalism also encourages us to interrogate the assumptions of high *literariness*—read: "seriousness"—that the field inherited from the dominant modes of critique. This can lay an affirming critical foundation to explore a range of work long dismissed as unworthy of critical interrogation, some of which can be seen as central to Mennonite writing, including personal narratives, such as diaries and memoirs; children's and young adult literature; speculative fiction; and, of course, religious writing. Exploring the stakes and possibilities of such work is the project of the chapters to follow.

If part of the argument of my account of Mennonite literature's emergence as a transnational phenomenon was that the transnational rhetoric of the field has obscured the ways in which it remains invested in an understanding of Mennonite cultural difference as a form of ethnicity, it is also true that the field's forty-plus-year archive of transnational work places a productive pressure on the ways in which the transnational itself is conventionally theorized in North America. The oft-repeated critical lament about the relative absence of Canada within hemispheric studies, for example, is the result of a number of overlapping pressures that are relevant to my project here—including an emphasis by American scholars on the country's southern border (Sadowski-Smith and Fox 15), and a palpable anxiety among Canadianists that the transnational "often functions as an alibi for multinational processes in which dominant American perspectives define all others as 'local' understandings" (Berland 100).[23] The transnational flows of Mennonite literary studies, however, run almost directly counter to the directions we have come to expect in North America: it is the United States' northern border that has been most relevant to the field; it is the Canadian context that is understood to have initiated the critical conversation; and it is Canadian authors who have garnered the most sustained attention.[24] Mennonite writing in North America is valuable, in such a context, not only because it inserts Canadian texts and contexts into a US-dominated critical discussion but also because it serves as a reminder that such wide-ranging critical frameworks are most useful and best tested at the level of individual fields. In Mennonite writing, it is the Mexican–American border that has long been ignored, despite the hemispheric-wide migration patterns of Russian Mennonites having established long-running colonies in Mexico and South America, and its early emergence in Canada initially left American critics thinking "wistfully about the lively Canadian Mennonite literary scene, with its high-profile and controversial writers" (Gundy, "U.S." 5), and hoping that one day Mennonite "Canadian and U.S. creative writers and literary critics will, at last, meet as equals" (Roth and Beck viii). Herb Wylie is correct to argue that critics interested in hemispheric literary studies must thus take into account the "fundamentally asymmetrical" balance of power between the United States and Canada (49), but twentieth-century Mennonite literary studies is a notable case in which the nature of this asymmetry was complicated, if not outright inverted.

The most immediate and substantive consequence of reframing Mennonite literature as a case study in minor transnationalism, however, is its marking a shift of the field from its emergence as a form of *minority* writing and reconceptualizing it as a *minor* field.[25] In the most basic sense, I am using *minor* in this study to mean *smaller* and *outside the mainstream*, while by *minority* I mean, in keeping with its common usage in North American literary studies, *racialized* minority. While there are, of course, no shortage of cases in which a subsection of a national literature is both minor and minoritized in these ways, I would suggest that it is a categorical error to equate the two, and that Mennonite writing is a case in point. Here I worry that even Lionnet and Shih slip too easily between the terms, for it seems clear to me that the construct of the "minority" is itself part of what can be productively transversed and interrogated by the "minor."[26] Because the term "Mennonite" is first a religious designation (around which several distinct cultural and ethnic identities have coalesced but with which they cannot be fully equated), it makes more sense to refer to Mennonite writing as a *minor* literature. Where Mennonite writing happens to be written by a subject racialized in the North American context—say, in the poetry by the Japanese Mennonite writer Yorifumi Yaguchi—there is no contradiction at all: it is both a work of *minor* and *minority* literature. Indeed, the fact that the lateral, cross-cultural networks that Lionnet and Shih suggest are underappreciated *across* minor fields are also in operation *within* Mennonite writing is central to the field's potential contribution to the larger study of literature. Cruz's argument that "Mennonite literature's inclusion of multiple Mennonite ethnicities along with its transnational nature are rarities in literary studies" (*Queering* 9) registers the potentiality of "lateral networks" within the field that have yet to be fully explored.

Embracing a minor frame can also help to estrange a presumption of whiteness that the field inherited from its formation as an ethnic minority literature. While this frame was arguably an accurate reflection of the specific texts and contexts that marked the field's emergence, it is not only clearly inappropriate today as a *prescription* for the field, but it was notably out of step with the larger conversations about race that were occupying the broader Mennonite church in that formative period. "Between the 1950s and the 1970s conversations on race in the church highlighted the anxiety that Mennonites felt about being a 'white' church," writes Felipe Hinojosa, "forcing them to take into account the needs of Latinos and African Americans, to diversify their church structures, and for the first time to consider new definitions of Mennonite identity in the United States" (*Latino* 215). Those debates can be tracked in several notable works exploring nonwhite Mennonite traditions in North America published in the period—including Le Roy Bechler's *The Black Mennonite Church in North America* (1986) and Rafael Falcón's *The Hispanic Mennonite Church in North America* (1986), both published by Herald Press, as well as Hubert L. Brown's *Black and Mennonite: A Search for Identity* (1976), published a decade earlier—but they are all but completely absent from the formative works of Mennonite literary criticism from this period. As Jeff Gundy has noted, the first substantial effort to theorize Mennonite literature in North America, Ruth's *Mennonite Identity and Literary Art* (1978), was written at a time when "civil rights and feminism were transforming American culture and (more slowly) the Mennonite church" and "the gay rights movement was slowly gaining momentum as well," but it "shows little interest in any of these issues" ("Explorations"). This may be true, but it is also true that Ruth was far from alone in such oversights. The Mennonite writing of the latter twentieth century was rightly celebrated for its gendered and theological critiques of Mennonite patriarchy and religious fundamentalism, and its emergence among the white "Russian" and Swiss Mennonite communities is hardly a surprise, given that this community—then as now—constituted the large majority of North American Mennonites. In hindsight, however, we can see how the emergence of Mennonite writing specifically as a form of ethnic minority literature functioned to extend the normative whiteness of institutional Mennonite identity at the very time when it was elsewhere under critical interrogation. Understood alongside studies like Hinojosa's *Latino Mennonites: Civil Rights, Faith and Evangelical Culture*, it is clear that the mobilization of Mennonite cultural difference as a form of "white" ethnicity in literary studies took place in the larger context of a "twentieth-century racial crisis in the

Mennonite church" that was "turn[ing] ethnic Mennonites into white Mennonites" (216).

Shifting the critical frame from *minority* to *minor*, then, is not meant to evade the enduring questions of race, gender, and identity in the field but rather meant to help foster a renewed and more nuanced engagement with them. It may be true, as Michael Millner has reported, that the academic discourse surrounding identity is marked by "a sense of exhaustion around the whole project" (541); it is an exhaustion that has been expressed in Mennonite literary criticism, to be sure, as well as by Mennonite historians expressing surprise that the field's literary critics and writers "continue to reflect on identity issues" (M. Epp 12).[27] It should be clear, however, that the intersecting problems articulated by the poststructural and postcolonial critiques of the 1990s and early 2000s have not been adequately addressed and resolved, and that brushing aside enduring concerns about gender, class, race, and ethnicity would only work to affirm the flawed models we continue to inhabit. "There is no dispensing with identities," as Anthony Appiah argues in his 2018 study, *The Lies That Bind*; "but we need to understand them better if we can hope to reconfigure them, and free ourselves from mistakes about them" (xvi). Indeed, as Millner goes on to suggest, scholars are exhausted in large part by the need to return to them via the same structures and institutions that have been recognized as complicit with the essentializing logic they have set out to critique—a complicity inherited in part, as I've argued above, by a strategic reliance on recognizably flawed methodologies, but also by the institutionalization of minority difference by government policy and academic practice. In Roderick A. Ferguson's provocative account, the rapid institutionalization of minority difference within the American academy was as much about rearticulating that difference in manageable terms as it was about empowerment and meaningful change. The post-1960s institutionalization of resistance movements into academic fields "would discipline through a seemingly alternative regard for difference" (6), he writes, with the result being "an abstract—rather than a redistributive—valorization of minority difference and culture" (8). Ferguson's assessment of the regulatory/disciplinary role of minority difference in the US academy resonates with comparative accounts of the "sedative politics" of Canadian multiculturalism, whereby the radical elements of Quebecois sovereignty and racialized minority movements were depoliticized, redirected, and disciplined into academic and cultural performances of difference.[28] For scholars and academics whose thinking has been enabled by these same disciplines and institutions, part of the challenge is engaging the enduring terms and concerns that surround identity without replicating or reinvesting in its restricting logic—to work, in the resonant terms of Ferguson's epigraph, "in the institution but not of it."

Reframing the field as a minor literature may help refresh the field's engagement with identity in two directions. The first is to help us better appreciate the early and enduring function of tropes of ethnicity, authenticity, and whiteness within the field as a minority field. It is when the field is understood as the natural expression of a coherent and homogenous community, after all, that it is subject most forcefully to the demand that the writing be an earnest, mimetic re-presentation.[29] Rey Chow's articulation of coercive mimicry, or the processes by which "those who are marginal to mainstream Western culture are expected [. . .] to resemble and replicate the very banal preconceptions that have been appended to them" is instructive here (107). This is the challenge, surely, of Taylor's logic of multiculturalism as a politics of recognition, in which cultural production must replicate audience expectations in order to circulate within the discourse—it demands, in Chow's terms, that subjects "objectify themselves in accordance with the already seen and thus to authenticate their familiar imaginings of them as ethnics" (107). Chow's terms offer a concise way to understand Kasdorf's experience of being received as an "ethnic" Mennonite writer in the late 1990s: "As a Mennonite author, I have become both spectator and sight," she writes, "conscious of conventional expectations about my background and the ways that my work fulfills or fails to meet those expectations" (*Body* 53). Here, too, the unvarnished, straightforward prose of so much early Mennonite writing—"From the beginning," writes Reimer, "the Mennonite literary imagination seems to have been drawn to a gritty realism serving didactic purposes" (*Mennonite* 11)—seems to have dovetailed conveniently with critical demands for writing that is readable as autoethnography. In several chapters of this study, I engage this history in order to better understand its function in the field: in chapter 2, I consider how the perceived "authenticity" of life writing was strategically marshaled by early Mennonite authors and scholars alike, for example, and in my discussion of the Mennonite Thing in chapter 3, I trace how the contemporary field continues to wrestle with the cultural force that remains attached to the most recognizable, essentializing imagery that surrounds Mennonite identity across the continent.

Having estranged the specific set of identity-based concerns that have settled onto it as normative via the minority literature frame, the second critical direction fostered by a minor literature frame is to deepen our appreciation of identity categories underappreciated in the field to date. "I hear Mennonite writers and critics in North America talk about being tired of identity discussions, of desiring to get past and away from Mennonite identity," writes Sofia Samatar, "and I think of how different those discussions would be, how newly troubling and electric, if we considered ways of being Mennonite outside Dutch-Swiss-German ethnicity and the North American context" ("Scope"). Samatar's welcome suggestion is anticipated in an earlier issue of the *Journal of Mennonite Writing*, where editor Ann Hostetler notes that "the Mennonite literature curriculum needs to more actively seek out and include Mennonite writers of color," and that with Mennonite colleges having "been producing writers and cultural critics for several generations now—it is time to recognize the infusion into Mennonite literature of non-Eurocentric viewpoints" ("Learning"). Those scholars working most closely and productively with identity in Mennonite writing today are pushing against the heteronormative, Eurocentric presumptions of the field's origins as a minority literature. Perhaps the most sustained of these recuperative efforts have been in the productive field of queer Mennonite writing, but Mennonite writing also offers both early and recent critiques of the presumed whiteness of Mennonite institutions.[30] I explore both these conversations further in chapter 1 and, especially, chapter 5 of this study, but perhaps the most stinging critique of this history is to be found in the voices absent from the field altogether.

Of course, the dominant identity marker of Mennonite cultural difference is religious, and it is my contention that the minority literature framework, along with multiculturalist discourses, have often worked to render Mennonite religious difference in ethnic terms. As Michael W. Kaufmann has noted, contemporary literary studies have long been "generally accepted" to be "a decidedly secular enterprise" (607), but recent work contemplating what Jürgen Habermas influentially refers to as the "post-secular"—describing the "society that posits the continued existence of religious communities within a continually secularizing society" (329)—suggests a framework in which efforts to engage Mennonite religious difference might receive hearing. As it has been theorized to date, the post-secular tends in my view to engage religious thought with a grudging respect that sees it as unavoidable, much as when Stanley Fish (2005) identifies religion as the subject most likely to succeed the "triumvirate of race, gender, and class as the center of intellectual energy in the academy"—only to add it is "one thing to take religion as an object of study and another to take religion seriously." A similar division could be made in Mennonite criticism, where religion has not always been "taken seriously" as a "candidate for the truth," even when it has been recognized as an "object of study." It would certainly be too much to suggest Mennonite literary studies has outright ignored religion, but it is my hope that intentionally estranging the field's parameters as a minority literature may help us further explore the religious and theological aspects relevant to the field—recognizing how they intersect with, but should not be superseded by, questions of race, ethnicity, gender, and class. Rak, whose first book examined Doukhobor autobiographical discourse, points to "the radical possibilities of religious faith when it runs headlong into secular ideas about private property, education and so on," as well as the question of whether it is "possible to critique religious excesses and also think about radical potential" ("Mennonite/s" 22) as examples of the type of questions that, while currently outside the mainstream of literary studies, could be explored by a freshly engaged Mennonite criticism. Such topics, she suggests, should help it move beyond the "tendency to provide narrow genres and their industrial success as the indicator of success" for literary authors (19). Tanis McDonald has made a related point in somewhat different terms. Reviewing a recent work of Mennonite poetry, McDonald notes: "The place of faith in the contemporary world is perhaps the least cool subject on the planet, and in its uncoolness, one of the most urgent, desperately in need of discussion beyond demagoguery or cant, where its real human struggle and connections and overlaps between faiths and peace and compassion can find resonance" (398). Taking Mennonite religious discourse seriously will mean reminding ourselves of the long tradition of straightforwardly evangelistic writing by or about Mennonites that stretches back through and alongside the self-consciously literary tradition that was comparatively late arriving, as I do in chapter 1 of this study. It will also mean attending closely to the theological specificities of Mennonite thought necessary to appreciate and understand projects that might not immediately seem to foreground faith at all, as I do in chapters 4 and 5.

Finally, I want to suggest that understanding Mennonite writing as a minor transnational literature, at least as I am describing it here, would mean rethinking, perhaps even suspending, the foundational assumption of the field as it has been imagined since the early 1990s: that the purpose of Mennonite literary studies is to engage *literature that has been written by Mennonites*. As a broader field, Mennonite literature has long exceeded the church membership lists that might approximate the citizenship records that are the implicit foundation of national literary traditions and cannot be logically defined by the discourses of race or ethnicity that provide structure and political urgency to minority literatures. In lieu of such parameters, critics have—as I noted elsewhere—"consistently responded to problems of definition by outlining the parameters of the field as broadly as possible," even as it "remains fairly narrow in its strict devotion to authorial biography" (Zacharias, "Introduction" 2). These definitions include Hostetler's "diverse spectrum of sensibility informed by Mennonite experience" (*A Cappella*, xviii), or *Rhubarb* magazine's "diversely defined Mennonites[:] genetic, practicing, lapsed, declined, and resistant,"[31] or, paradigmatically, Al Reimer's "wide-angle lens": "the work of writers who spent at least their formative years in a Mennonite milieu—family and/or community and/or church—regardless of whether they now consider themselves 'Mennonite' in a religious sense, or in a purely ethnic sense, or in both senses, or in neither sense" (*Mennonite Literary Voices* 2). Much of the field's frustrations with identity, I have suggested, comes from our attempts to explicitly define the field in the broad terms but remaining tethered to the biography of the author—that is, in method and scope, within the logic of minority writing. The result is a slippage, or tension, within even the most careful works, so that even where scholars are explicitly straining to move away from identity-based readings of texts by Mennonites they continue to look for "traces" (Froese Tiessen, "Homelands" 22), "accents" (Redekop, *Making Believe* 208), or a "tone" (Nathan 181) that would provide evidence of that link, whether or not the works in question directly engage Mennonite characters or settings. Redekop's *Making Believe* is admirably clear on this point: "Nothing I have written here should be taken as support for the notion that readers should actively look for what is Mennonite about a particular text," she insists, only to add: "The fact remains, however, that for the purposes of writing this book I have necessarily had to separate out books written by authors with Mennonite names and that while doing so I have repeatedly registered Mennonite accents in the writing" (208). I recognize this tension—*The fact remains*— in my own work, as well. In my oversight of literary reviews at the *Journal of Mennonite Studies*, for example, it often results in an embarrassingly parochial form of biographical sleuthing in order to justify the inclusion of an author's work within the field. *Is that a Mennonite last name I see in this publisher's new catalog? Maybe she married in? What would he think about having his work reviewed as "Mennonite"?* Such decidedly uncritical questions are only rarely acknowledged, and yet they exert a powerful gatekeeping function in all fields that understand themselves as expressions of, or closely related to, specific communities.[32] How could we expect to move beyond the most conventional accounts of the field as an "ethnic" literature if our critical frame relies heavily on ethnic markers and kinship ties for inclusion?

As will become clear over the course of this study, I am most interested in writing *about* Mennonites rather than *by* Mennonites, which are often but not always the same thing. It is worth noting that when we look back at critical writing about Mennonite literature before the field emerged as—or should we say *transformed into*?—an area of minority literary studies, we can find cases of scholars happy to explore writing *about* rather than *by* Mennonites. Harry Loewen's influential edited collection,

Mennonite Images: Historical, Cultural, and Literary Essays Dealing with Mennonite Issues (1980), for example, notes that "Mennonites are receiving increased attention in certain creative works written by non-Mennonites" (2–3), and nearly half the essays in the collection's "Literary Images" section explore such work, including Victor G. Doerksen's examination of the eighteenth-century German author Heinrich Jung-Stilling; J. W. Dyck's essay exploring "The Image of the Mennonites in Josef Ponten's *Volk auf dem Wege*," and Loewen's reading of "Anabaptists in Gottfried Keller's Novellas." With several notable exceptions, such analyses have disappeared from the critical conversation, in keeping with the convention of minority literary studies to tie the field to the identity of the author rather than the content of the work—itself part of the Romantic ideal that a body of writing ought to reflect something essential about the community from which it emerges.

My hope is that Lionnet and Shih's notion of minor transnationalism, understood as I am adapting it in this introduction, may offer a methodology that can foster the expansive vision that the field has long anticipated and which I believe it is now struggling to enact. David Damrosch's influential work, which suggests "world literature" is best understood not as a single set of texts but as a way of engaging texts that circulate and are read beyond their immediate contexts, is a useful comparison point for what I am proposing. "World literature is not an infinite, ungraspable canon of works," he writes, "but rather a mode of circulation and of reading" (5). Just as reading a book as a work of "world literature" in Damrosch's terms is not to pretend it was written by "the world," to read a book as a work of "Mennonite literature" in the context I am articulating here is not to presume it must be read as the autoethnographic expression of a Mennonite author. Instead, it is to consider how the literary text, widely defined, intersects with Mennonite concerns, whether as a matter of character, setting, theology, or theme, or authorial position, and perhaps even a matter of genre or form, or some combination of these elements.[33] It is to interrogate the conceit of the "literary itself," not in order to ignore questions of complexity and quality but to recognize its shifting and socially conditioned nature, and, crucially, its gatekeeping function. Picking up on a distinction made in a different context by Terry Eagleton, we can say that to reframe Mennonite writing as a minor literature is to adopt a *functional* rather than *ontological* definition of the field (9), recognizing that Mennonite literature is a mode of reading rather than of writing—that it is not a *thing* that can be meaningfully defined but rather something we *choose to do with a text.*

READING MENNONITE WRITING: A STUDY IN MINOR TRANSNATIONALISM

In the chapters that follow, I undertake a number of experiments in understanding Mennonite writing as a minor transnationalism. Chapter 1, "1986: Toward a Minor Literary History," is a methodological experiment in nonnarrative literary history, drawing on work by Franco Moretti and the digital humanities to attempt an adapted distant reading of all the literary texts published in English by and about North American Mennonites in a single year. Suspending the teleological selectivity of conventional literary history, this lengthy chapter looks to reanimate the genres, texts, and concerns that have been lost in what Moretti (2000) calls the "slaughterhouse" of the field's literary history, revealing a rich set of writing that forces a reconceptualization of the early field. While chapter 1 explores a host of texts in a single year, chapter 2, "*A Russian Dance of Death:* Mennonite Diaries and the Use of Truthfulness," traces a single Mennonite diary across decades, countries, and languages. Arguing that the role of life writing in the establishment of the field has been vastly underappreciated, this chapter offers a comparative reading of the numerous editions of the Dietrich Neufeld diary—written in French and translated for self-publication in Germany in 1921, translated into English for publication in California in 1930 and retranslated as the inaugural project of the Canadian Mennonite Literary Society in 1977—to explore how the "autobiographical pact" (Lejeune 1989) functions within the context of minor transnationalism.

The third chapter, "The Mennonite Thing," draws on Slavoj Žižek's work on the inversion of ideology and the fetishistic structure of the

"Ethnic Thing" to explore the ironic function of identity in much of contemporary Mennonite literary studies. The Mennonite Thing, as I formulate it here, is the conceit of a static and "authentic" Mennonite identity expressed through (but not reducible to) stereotypical markers of Mennonite culture, language, and faith. In this chapter, I examine a prominent strand of writing in the field—from poetry by Jeff Gundy and Julia Spicher Kasdorf to the online satirical website *The Daily Bonnet*—that routes its engagement with the most conventional aspects of Mennonite identity through a variety of distancing gestures, strategically mobilizing notions of Mennonite cultural authenticity in ways that are not directly readable as autoethnography. My fourth chapter, subtitled "On Faith and Fantasy in Mexico," tests the geographic assumptions that have long circumscribed the field by pairing Canadian Mennonite Miriam Toews's novel *Irma Voth* (2011) with Mexican director Carlos Reygadas's celebrated film, *Silent Light* (2007). Reygadas's film is a set on a conservative Russian Mennonite colony in northern Mexico, using local colony members as actors and starring Toews, the Canadian author, in its leading role. I read *Irma Voth* as a careful and strategic retort to Reygadas's film: where Reygadas exaggerates the Mennonites' isolation to render it a form of fantasy, Toews returns the community to its broader social and historical context, affirming the flawed agency of individual colony members and critiquing the community's efforts at self-isolation as a catastrophic failure of the imagination.

The fifth chapter, "Endure," concludes the study's close analysis by reading Casey Plett's trans coming-of-age novel, *Little Fish* (2018) alongside Sofia Samatar's science fiction novella, "Fallow," to explore their shared interest in complicating conventional notions of a Mennonite past. In *Little Fish*, an opening debate about trans and cis experiences of time shifts into a trans woman's efforts to explore the possibility that her beloved Mennonite grandfather may also have been trans, while in the Afrofuturistic "Fallow" (2017), a young Mennonite activist undertakes a "rescue project" to inscribe her racialized family's history within the heavily protected archive on their intergalactic colony. Returning to the question of history with which I began this study, then, the chapter closes with the suggestion that *Little Fish* and "Fallow" insist that a reconsideration of the Mennonite past is a necessary step toward the enabling of the possibility of a broader, more inclusive future. It is an argument echoed in the book's brief summative conclusion, where I reiterate the major claims of each chapter and look to draw them together as a larger case study in minor transnationalism.

CHAPTER 1

1986

Toward a Minor Literary History

Let's begin with a list of Mennonite literary titles: *After the Revolution*; *The Bottle and the Bushman*; *Collaborators*; *Dear God, I'm Only a Boy*; *Surrendering to the Real Things*; *Dustship Glory*; *i sing for my dead in german*; *Rooms Overhead*; *A Stone Watermelon*; *Three Mennonite Poets*; and *Three Winter Poems*. Readers will be forgiven if none of these titles sound familiar—most of them will be unfamiliar to even those of us who have followed Mennonite literature in North America closely over the years—for their unfamiliarity is part of the point for my argument in this chapter. As I write, these are the eleven titles listed in the Canadian and American Mennonite/s Writing bibliographies for the year 1986, the provenance to which I will return shortly. Their shared publication date places these books squarely within the "Mennonite miracle" stage of the field's development: that long decade beginning in the late 1970s, when a rush of writing by and about Mennonites started to be published in Winnipeg (Manitoba), and ending with the 1990 conference, "Mennonite/s Writing in Canada," which responded to this writing and effectively established Mennonite literary studies as a field of academic inquiry. Quantitatively speaking, 1986 appears to have been a slightly above average year in this era of Mennonite writing, though to judge from the lack of critical engagement with works published that year, it has been mostly forgotten. With perhaps one or two exceptions, none of the year's publications have become critical touchstones for the field, and few are cited regularly in discussions of the field's development.[1] Instead, they have been left in what Franco Moretti (2000) has recently called the "slaughterhouse of literature," that vast majority of published books which, outside of sustained popular or critical interest, has been forgotten to history.

This lengthy chapter is a methodological experiment, undertaken in an effort to estrange the standard literary history that has created and sustained the parameters of Mennonite literary studies in North America. As national and ethnic literary studies have long relied on linear and highly selective narratives that string canonical texts along a developmental, teleological history in order to authorize a particular version of their present, this chapter looks to undertake literary history differently, returning to a (not-quite-random) year early in the field's development to attempt a cross-sectional reading of every Mennonite literary book published in a single year. My method here draws heavily on Moretti's influential articulation of the problem of scale that haunts conventional literary histories, but I want to suggest that the relatively small scale of minor fields of study changes the equation slightly and may open them to alternative forms of historicization. It may well be impossible, as Moretti insists, to read every literary text published in a major field, but what about a minor field like Mennonite literature? What would happen to our understanding of literary history if we attempted something similar: read everything published in an ostensibly forgotten year of a minor field's past?[2] And how might that expanded past help us better understand the present?

LITERARY HISTORY: ON SCALE AND ENCYCLOPEDIC HISTORY

In the introduction to this study, I noted that scholars have long been aware of the shortcomings of developmental models of literary history. As early as 1970, Geoffrey Hartman was able to sum up these critiques with admirable precision: "We are all disenchanted with those picaresque adventures in pseudo-causality that go under the name of literary history," he writes, "those handbooks with footnotes that claim to sing of the whole, but load every rift with glue" (355). If it is true, as others have suggested, that scholars of minority literatures responded in the 1980s and 1990s to the whitewashed canons of national literatures by working to recuperate ignored texts via narrative literary histories of their own, it is also true that many of these projects were undertaken in full awareness of the danger that such recuperative work might ultimately affirm the exclusionary methods that made them necessary. As I noted in the introduction, the challenge of wielding the power of developmental literary history, as Greenblatt put it, was whether minority literary studies were "appropriating traditional forms" of narrative history, or whether those "forms [were] appropriating them" (59). I am not the first to suggest contemporary Mennonite literary studies are subject to this type of challenge. Magdalene Redekop, for example, has prudently warned against investing in the "illusion that literature makes progress," noting it springs from the "nineteenth-century model of literary history that underlies the accepted account of the origins of the Manitoba Mennonite phenomenon" ("Is Menno?" 198). Similarly, Froese Tiessen has cautioned that Mennonite literary scholarship has "tended to rely on paradigms of ethnicity produced in the inaugural moment of the field" and thus "'run[s] the risk,' in the words of Susan Koshy, 'of unwittingly annexing the newer literary productions within older paradigms'" ("Habit" 22). If it was recognized that the "ethnic" minority literature framework so effective in establishing the field as an area of study in the 1980s and '90s has also worked to limit its possibilities, the continued reliance on a developmental model of literary history to historicize the field's emergence now risks becoming a methodological tether holding it to the minority framework it is straining to move beyond.

The limitations of conventional literary history are well known, then, but Franco Moretti's provocative recent work on "distant reading" has freshly articulated a set of related problems and has opened new avenues for consideration. Moretti's primary insight, in this context, is to tie the problematics of literary history to scale via the practice of close reading. Pointing to the irony of scholars claiming expertise in a massive field such as nineteenth-century British literature while having read less than 1 percent of the titles published in the period, Moretti suggests the canonizing logic of contemporary literary criticism is a product of our investment in reading texts as carefully and closely as possible: "The trouble with close reading (in all of its incarnations, from the new criticism to deconstruction) is that it necessarily depends on an extremely small canon. This may have become an unconscious and invisible premise by now but is an iron one nonetheless: you invest so much in individual texts *only* if you think that very few of them really matter. Otherwise, it doesn't make sense. And if you want to look beyond the canon [. . .] close reading will not do it" ("Conjectures" 57). Moretti argues elsewhere that this problem is not one that can be solved by reading *more*, even if one could somehow read it all. It is "not a matter of time, but of method," he insists: "a field this large cannot be understood by stitching together separate bits of knowledge about individual cases, because it *isn't* a sum of individual cases: it's a collective system, that should be grasped as such, as a whole" (*Graphs* 4). A supplemental model of recuperation might add a couple of heretofore ignored books to a major field's canon, but in Moretti's account it can do little to alter the fundamentally partial picture of conventional literary histories. At worst, it might subsume those "new" texts into an established critical discourse that is not only unaltered but strengthened for having appeared to address its gaps or occlusions. Close reading won't help us read *beyond* the canon, in other words, because it is the methodological bottleneck that created the canon. What is needed instead, Moretti insists, is "a new sense of the literary field as a whole" ("Slaughterhouse" 208), one in which a "quantitative approach" sets aside individual texts to grasp the field as a whole.

Mennonite literary studies in North America, small as it is, is subject to many of the challenges of canon formation and the delimiting tropes of literary history that Moretti convincingly identifies as problematic. Not only has the scholarly field settled into a set of canonical texts and authors as the basis for a narrative, developmental literary history, there is little question that, as Jeff Gundy has recently noted, the literature itself has "spread beyond the capacity of any one person to grasp fully" ("Mennonite/s"). These two phenomena, of course, are tightly related: as the volume of books increases, a selective focus that produces a canon would seem to be increasingly a matter of practical necessity. At times, this process is intentional and strategic: Al Reimer means to register his faith in the field's long future when he closes his 1993 *Mennonite Literary Voices* by noting "a canon of Mennonite literature is rapidly taking shape" (71); Ervin Beck lists seven of the field's key works as the "canon of transgressive Mennonite literature" (53) in order to indicate the significance they have held in the field to date.[3] Much more often, however, the canonizing logic of close readings and narrative literary history function implicitly, via patterns of citation and engagement in both an active and passive sense: *active* in the sense that recounting the past via key literary texts strengthens the version of the past those texts affirm, and *passive* in the sense that focusing on specific texts means necessarily ignoring others. What is more, this problem may appear to scale down: if the number of books in the full corpus of Mennonite literature is only a fraction of the number in a field like British literature, so too is the number of critics involved. The result is clear enough from a quick perusal of the bibliography: of the 178 literary authors included in the "Mennonite/s Writing" combined bibliography, just 20 are listed with more than 2 critical essays written on their work to date. Of the 350 separate essays dedicated to those 20 authors, more than half are focused on a single author—whose name I will assume you can guess.[4]

As an example of this process at work, let us return, one more time, to the standard account of the field's emergence, this time as offered in a 2005 essay by Ann Hostetler. Hostetler's account is worth including at some length not only because she is a major figure in the field but also because of how confidently she presents it as the field's accepted account. "The genesis of Mennonite literature written in English, in both the United States and Canada, has been chronicled in a number of places," she writes, "so I will rehearse it only briefly here." She continues:

> Broadly speaking: Mennonite literature was first recognized in Canada and has played a more prominent role in the literary scene there. This is not surprising when one considers that Mennonites in Canada comprise a larger percent of the population than they do in the United States. Rudy Wiebe's first novel in 1962, *Peace Shall Destroy Many*, is generally considered the beginning of Mennonite literature in English. Now recognized as one of Canada's leading novelists, Wiebe has since won the Governor General's

> award twice: in 1973 for *The Temptations of Big Bear* and in 1994 for *A Discovery of Strangers*. In the 1970s Patrick Friesen pioneered Mennonite poetry publication with several widely recognized collections and his strong publishing record continues to date. In the 1980s Mennonite women writers entered the literary scene, among them Di Brandt and Sarah Klassen, whose first volumes both won publication awards and who have continued to publish consistently since. [. . .]
>
> In the United States, Mennonite literature has developed more slowly than in Canada and its primary achievements have been in poetry. The publication in 1992 of Julia Kasdorf's first collection of poetry, *Sleeping Preacher*, winner of the Agnes Lynch Starrett prize from the University of Pittsburgh Press, and the publication of four of her poems in *The New Yorker* serve as a landmark for the recognition of Mennonite literature by a wider reading public in the United States. Since the publication of *Sleeping Preacher*, most of the literary activity in Mennonite literature in the United States has continued to be in the genre of poetry. ("Bringing" 138–39)

Hostetler's account is notable not because it uniquely accords with my understanding of the field's conventional version of its own past but rather precisely the opposite: it is thoroughly typical in its tone and tenor, as well as in the texts and moments it highlights. Aware she is on well-trod territory, Hostetler moves quickly. Positioning the Canadian scene as antecedent to that of the United States, she begins with Wiebe's *Peace Shall Destroy Many*, then leaps several decades to offer a few names from the 1970s and 1980s before moving on to the 2000s, and returning to the United States, where she mentions only Kasdorf's work by title. The literary texts strung along the larger essay's narrative of development will be immediately recognizable to anyone with a passing knowledge of the field—from Wiebe she will move on to Patrick Friesen, Di Brandt, and Sarah Klassen, then on to Sandra Birdsell, Armin Wiebe, and Miriam Toews; from Julia Kasdorf she will move on to Jeff Gundy, Keith Ratzlaff, Betsy Sholl, and so on—and she will justify their inclusion by listing their external awards or inclusion in highbrow publications. Hostetler is on well-trod territory, indeed: *In the beginning there was Rudy, and then, decades later, came the miracle of the others: first the poets and novelists in Canada, then the poets in the United States.* Viewed through Moretti's critical lens, crucially, the canon-forming selectivity of such accounts is best understood not as a shortcoming specific to a given critical tradition, and certainly not of an individual scholar. Instead, it should be read as a logical consequence of how literary scholars conventionally engage the past as they balance a general overview with noting those figures and works that have generated a critical discussion of closer engagements. The challenge for those who would like to complicate such histories, then, is not to simply add one or two more texts to the narrative but to look for a methodology capable of moving beyond its limits.

Moretti's imperfect solution, distant reading, is worth considering closely. Moretti encourages scholars to release even the desire to briefly engage individual texts and move instead toward a qualitative form of reading from afar. For Moretti, this type of "distant reading" is enabled by computational tools that can scan tens of thousands of digitized texts and be "read" or analyzed for patterns and outliers. With Moretti, I recognize the challenge of meaningfully engaging the past without replicating the shortcomings born of selection and canon formation, and I see the value of quantitative assessment of a given field as a means of enabling a larger scale of reading practices. At the same time, it seems crucial to recognize Mennonite literature in North America operates on a very different scale than Moretti's case studies, and, as such, may be open to a different set of possibilities. Indeed, I worry that much of the distance Moretti prescribes is predetermined by the very canonical logic that his project sets out to critique: the primary case studies that Moretti turns to making his case are nineteenth-century British literature and detective novels, two massive and well-established fields with the scale to make his model necessary and the institutional gravitas to earn it critical approval. He is completely overwhelmed when he speculates about the vast number of unread nineteenth-century British novels—"twenty thousand, thirty, more," he writes, "no one really knows" (*Graphs* 4)—and it is this overwhelming number of texts that makes his methodology of distant reading appear inescapable. But if it is clearly impossible to read every British novel from the nineteenth century, is the same thing true about a minor field like Mennonite literature—where books are counted by the hundreds, rather than the tens of thousands? What happens, I wonder, if we consider the problematics Moretti outlines in relation to literary history and canon formation, but within minor fields of study, where the smaller scale works to amplify recuperative gestures and may remain open to modes of reading that are neither strictly close nor distant?

As it turns out, the scale that Mennonite literary studies has been operating at can be measured with relative accuracy. For the better part of thirty years, Ervin Beck of Goshen College in Indiana built and maintained bibliographies of the literature and criticism by Mennonites in Canada and the United States, a project now continued by Beck's former student, Daniel Shank Cruz.[5] Cruz has suggested he sees his bibliographic efforts as constituting a form of literary history that can serve as a corrective to mistaken assumptions about the shape of the field ("Bibliography" 95, 99), and in this sense, my work in this chapter is following his lead. I recently spent a deeply dry several weeks inserting the two combined national "Mennonite/s Writing" literary bibliographies into an Excel database searchable by date, gender, and genre, as well as publisher, city, and country, in an effort to enable a different mode of literary history. As of the end of 2019, the combined bibliographies—hereafter simply referred to in the singular—list 627 English-language literary works in the field, beginning with Gordon Friesen's 1936 novel, *Flamethrowers*, and running through Dora Dueck's 2019 novel, *All That Belongs*.

Although the texts of the works themselves are not searchable, even the basic bibliographic data, combined in an Excel database, enables an informative pass at what Moretti calls distant reading. It allows us to describe the bibliographic field in a range of quantifiable terms that can be tracked for change over time.[6] I will return to the many caveats shortly, but here will suggest simply that the bibliographies offer a rough portrait of the field as it has been practiced, and the results are instructive: of the 627 total works listed, the field is split almost evenly between Canadian and American titles (325 titles, or 52%, are Canadian; 301 titles, or 48%, are American), with a slight majority of titles published by women (339 titles, or 54%, by women; 288 titles, or 46%, written by men). Roughly half the complete list of titles is fiction (309), a slight majority of which are written by men (57%) or by Canadians (56%). Poetry collections make up nearly 40 percent of the entire list at 239 of 627 titles (38%) and are roughly balanced between male (124) and female (115) authors; 128 of the 239 poetry collections, or a slight majority (54%), were published by Americans. This type of relative balance—in gender, genre, and nation—is notable in a larger literary context that might be presumed to be dominated by men, fiction, and the United States.

We can also read the bibliography for the quantifiable portrait it suggests about how the shape and balance of the field as a transnational literature has changed over time. Recall the portrait of the field's emergence presented by Hostetler in the passage I suggested was typical of the field in the introduction to this study: Canada is antecedent to the United States, with Wiebe's *Peace Shall Destroy Many* as origin point; a few key names from the 1970s; a "miracle" in the later 1980s; and a burst of American poetry in the 1990s. A quantitative analysis of the field's most comprehensive and authoritative bibliography offers a rather different account. Most obviously and immediately, it lists more than a dozen books published in the field prior to the 1962 release of *Peace Shall Destroy Many*. Far from being a field in decline, the database suggests a field that has never been more prolific: the list includes 16 books for the 1960s and 41 for the 1970s, and 181 titles during the so-called "Mennonite miracle" stage of the field: 65 titles in the 1980s and 116 titles in the 1990s. According to the bibliographies, nearly two-thirds of North American Mennonite literature has been published since 2000 (176 titles in the 2000s; 201 titles in the 2010s). The year with the most books of Mennonite literature published during the twentieth century was 1992, with 15 titles published, a number that is matched or surpassed by 18 of the 20 years listed in the twenty-first century. Breaking these numbers down by country suggests that the field's substantive publication history began not in Canada but in the United States (75% of the titles listed as published before 1970 were by Americans); was balanced between Canadian and American titles during the 1970s; then swung toward Canada for the 1980s and '90s (during which time approximately 60% of the titles were published by Canadians). Since

2000, however, the field has settled into nearly an even balance between the two countries: of the 376 titles listed as published over the past two decades, 190 books, or 51 percent, have been published in Canada; 186 titles, or 49 percent, have been published in the United States. Finally, the bibliographies suggest that the field began in fiction, settled into a remarkable balance between poetry and fiction throughout the 1970s–1990s, and has returned to an emphasis on fiction over the past two decades: prior to 1970, 85 percent of the list is fiction (23/27), with just 11 percent poetry (3/27); between 1970 and 1999, 45 percent of the list is fiction (100/222), and 45 percent is poetry (101/222); while since 2000 the list is 48 percent fiction (182/378) and 36 percent (135/378) poetry.[7] Just over half (54%) of the total list is written by men, but that slight majority is inverted over the past two decades, during which time 108 of the 201 titles have been written by women. And while slightly more than half the total number of poetry collections were written by men, nearly 60 percent of the poetry collections published during the crucial decade of the 1990s were by women.

The precision of such numbers should be received with some healthy skepticism, of course, but they can be understood to provide a relatively accurate quantitative assessment of the field of Mennonite literature in North America *as its critics have imagined it*. It suggests something of the scale at which the field has been operating, as well as the shape of that operation, including the shifting balance of gender, genre, and geographic focus over time. At 627 titles, the field may well be too large for any single scholar to master fully, but not so large, perhaps, so as to demand the type of telescopic distance Moretti envisions for the literary history of major fields that count their texts in the tens of thousands. Crucially, the bibliographies also include the critical essays published in the field to date, sorted by the literary author whose work is under examination. Accordingly, there is a sense the contents of the bibliographies do not simply reveal the predilections of the individual compilers but roughly reflect the field as it has been operating to date. And since, as we will see, it is far from an exhaustive account of all literature written by Mennonites in North America, it also has plenty to tell us about the gaps and assumptions that have been operative in the field to date.

Bibliographic efforts are also valuable because they force scholars to articulate the defining parameters of the field in a way that close readings of individual texts do not. Let us begin again, then, with explanatory paragraphs that precede the bibliographies. They read, in part:

> The bibliography includes work by Mennonite writers, that is, writers who are either ethnic or theological Mennonites (or both), whether they claim the identity "Mennonite" for themselves or not, and whether or not their work contains explicitly Mennonite characters or subject matter. [. . .]
>
> With a few exceptions, the bibliography does not include self-published books, book reviews, children's books, or individual poems or stories published in periodicals or miscellaneous collections.[8]

In defining Mennonite literature as literature *by* rather than *about* Mennonites, the Mennonite/s Writing bibliographies reflect not only the conventions of the field but also, I am arguing, the field's formation as a minority literature, wherein it is presumed to be the expression of a distinct communal identity. Notably, it defines this communal identity in the expansive manner typical of the field to date—we are assured "Mennonite" can be understood in "either ethnic or theological" terms—and a quick perusal will make clear that the term "ethnic" refers almost exclusively to Russian and Swiss Mennonite cultural identity. Notably, the explanatory paragraph also makes unambiguous a key element of this field's gatekeeping logic that is usually left tactfully unsaid, in that it explicitly reserves the authority to attribute the identity marker of "Mennonite authors" to the critics: the bibliography includes the work of Mennonite authors, it reads, "whether they claim the identity 'Mennonite' for themselves or not." In all this, of course, it is simply making explicit the assumptions and conventions that are widely agreed to govern the field's practice.

Thus far we have proceeded by analyzing the combined Mennonite/s Writing bibliographies to consider the portrait they offer of the field to date. What I would like to undertake for the remainder of this chapter, however, is an experiment aimed at dramatically expanding the bibliography to explore its gaps and exclusions. Rather than close reading the entirety of the field—surely an impossible task even for its relatively small list, and one that would, by definition, still focus only on those works already included in the field—the method I have in mind is a combination of Moretti's distant reading and the "encyclopedic" history as described by Perkins in his study *Is Literary History Possible?* I have already touched on Moretti's emphasis on quantifiable analyses, so let me turn briefly to Perkins's work. Encyclopedic histories, he suggests, look to solve the problem of selectivity by "attempt[ing] to embody our sense of the overwhelming multiplicity and heterogeneity of the past" (55). Perkins acknowledges that the accounts offered by encyclopedic literary histories—which he suggests "are sometimes called surveys, and might also be called compilations or aggregates" (53)—are ultimately limited by their fragmentation, yet he insists that this fragmentation is, in a sense, central to its effect. "The great advantage of encyclopedic form is its conspicuous difference from our notions of reality," he writes, "When we read narrative history, we may be tempted to suppose that the form of the discourse represents a—or even the—form in which events occurred in the past. But no one thinks the form of a past happening was encyclopedic, and the more encyclopedic the form [. . .] the less can we mistake it for the form of the past. [. . .] Like any form, it distorts the past as it presents it, but that the past is distorted is, in encyclopedic form, blatant" (54–55). Despite the promise that Perkins sees in the encyclopedic form, he ultimately moves away from it after considering the limitations of the experimental *Columbia Literary History of the United States* (1987) and *A New History of French Literature* (1989). Both works, he suggests, are promising but ultimately self-defeating efforts, failures in part because they are "piecemeal," "inconsistent," and are "admitted to be inadequate" (60). For Perkins, then, the tension between the cohesion of narrative literary history and the comprehensive nature of encyclopedic history is too much to overcome. "Every theorist of literary history—every practical attempt in the genre—ultimately shatters on this dilemma," he insists. "We must perceive a past age as relatively unified if we are to write literary history; we must perceive it as highly diverse if what we write is to represent it plausibly" (27). My contention will be that

Moretti's idea of distant reading provides a means by which to overcome Perkins's conclusion that the "piecemeal" nature of encyclopedic history fatally undermines its value, and that a modified version of Perkins's encyclopedic approach offers a method that can bring us closer to the individual text than allowed by Moretti's work.

A methodological shift toward an encyclopedic or distant approach does not constitute a move from a "minority" toward a "minor" literary history on its own. After all, there is no shortage of massive bibliographic projects compiled with the expressed aim of demonstrating the legitimacy of a minority tradition. George Elliott Clarke's massive bibliographic project *Odysseys Home*, for example, insists that a "bibliography is required to transform the phrase 'African Canadian literature' from rhetoric into fact" (327), while King-Kok Cheung and Stan Yogi's landmark project, *Asian American Literature: An Annotated Bibliography* (1988), aims to demonstrate, in its sheer size, the substantive nature of the field.[9] In shifting the methodological scale for literary history here, my initial goal is to estrange the existing frame rather than replace it. More works come into view as we step away from the canonical figures and forms, to be sure, but the dream of bibliographic completeness is a mirage, for one can always expand the frame further—to include more languages, more countries, more genres, more mediums, more venues. Nonetheless, I am hopeful such a project can help us become aware of the filtering effect that a minority literature framework has had on the field, including not only the way it has directed our critical gaze toward texts that align with autoethnographic accounts that display Mennonite cultural difference as ethnicity, but also the canonical assumptions regarding what constitutes literary value, artistic seriousness, and aesthetic accomplishment. As Eli MacLaren writes in discussing book history more generally, this type of encyclopedic history—which he describes as "enumerative bibliography"—has an "an epistemological significance in that it allows us to know what we know: it is the organized response not only to the daily increasing welter of published information but also to the oblivion into which this all too quickly slips" (800).

The scale of Mennonite literary studies, I want to suggest, enables a middle ground between the canon-forming logic of narrative literary history and the qualitative accounts of encyclopedic accounts of the past. The experiment I want to undertake is to return to a key period in the field's past and attempt a relatively exhaustive cross-sectional account of a single year, expanding the established bibliography to read every literary book published by or about Mennonites in North America in a single year, then reading the resulting cross-sectional account against the grain of the field's established literary history. I propose the term "cross-sectional" to describe this method rather than "bibliographic," "encyclopedic," or even "single-year survey" in an attempt to register something of the social sciences model, in which cross-sectional studies are routinely distinguished from longitudinal studies on the basis of their engagement with time. Where longitudinal studies attempt, rather like narrative literary history, to follow the development of a concern along a given number of years, cross-sectional studies attempt a wider portrait of that concern at a given moment in time. My hope is that this approach has the benefit of countering the methodological limits imposed by close readings, which routinely restrict our engagement with a period to a select few works, without working at such a far remove as to require us to completely give up textual analysis and thus what David Damrosch—who, as a scholar of world literature, knows something about problems of scale—has called "the pleasures of the text" (26). Understood not as a *replacement* but as a *complication* of the field's established history, usefully blatant in its distortion of more conventional accounts, it offers a form of reading that, if not truly "distant" in the sense articulated by Moretti, takes place at a productive remove that reveals a more comprehensive account of the past.

What happens to our understanding of the field's past, I want to ask, if we go back several decades to focus on a single year into the field's past—say, 1986?—and review all of the books that were being published by and about Mennonites in North America at that time? In the narrative histories of the field's past, after all, 1986 is part of the formative period of a fast-emerging field soon to be framed as a dynamic new minority literature, squarely in the midst of a Mennonite cultural explosion so surprising as to be described as a "miracle." Were there really only eleven literary books published by or about Mennonites in 1986? What would we discover if we were to peruse the library shelves, search engines, and periodical indexes for literature by and about Mennonites published that year? How much could we expand that list, and what might the details of those additions tell us about how the field's past has been imagined to date? What happens if we go back, in other words, and pick up the Mennonite writing from the year's slaughterhouse floor and read it all?

1986: ADVENTURES IN CROSS-SECTIONAL READING

I began this chapter listing eleven works of Mennonite literature published in 1986, and it is worth reminding ourselves of those titles here, in alphabetical order: *After the Revolution*; *The Bottle and the Bushman*; *Collaborators*; *Dear God, I'm Only a Boy*; *Surrendering to the Real Things*; *Dustship Glory*; *i sing for my dead in german*; *Rooms Overhead*; *A Stone Watermelon*; *Three Mennonite Poets*; and *Three Winter Poems*. At eleven publications, 1986 was, by the bibliography's count, the most productive year of the decade, which averaged a publication of just over 7 books a year. The established bibliography's list for the year is distributed roughly evenly between both Canadian and the American authors (5/6) and between men and women (5/6); they are mostly poetry (7) and are published almost exclusively by secular presses (10 /11). Three works—or roughly a quarter of the books listed—were published by Winnipeg's Turnstone Press, well known for its role in helping to establish Mennonite writing as a field. How might we test this version of the field's past?

After compiling the existing bibliographies within an Excel spreadsheet, I set out to see if I could find examples of literary books published by Mennonites in 1986 that were missing from the existing Mennonite/s Writing bibliographies. I expect it will be no surprise—especially to the bibliography's caretakers—that I quickly established the combined bibliography to be something less than a comprehensive account. Even when restricting my search within the institutional parameters of texts already identified as "Mennonite" by library and subject heading, or by bibliographies within Mennonite publications, the list expanded briskly. A simple database search with Ruth Steinman and Mandy Macfie, librarians at the Milton Good Library at Conrad Grebel University College in Waterloo,

Ontario, nearly doubled the number of books on my list; a long afternoon working my way through the library's shelves added several more. A search through the *Mennonite Life*'s annual "Radical Reformation and Mennonite Bibliography" for 1986 offered more yet.[10] When I opened my parameters to include life writing, children's and young adult (YA) literature, the list nearly doubled again. In all, my final expanded bibliography—surely still incomplete—includes forty-six books of Mennonite literature formally published in 1986.

To be sure, a single year is far too small a sample size to suggest anything approaching definitive about the field of Mennonite literature overall, and there is a sense in which the parameters of my expanded bibliography remain partial: it almost entirely excludes those works of short fiction and poetry that were published in literary journals, for example, as well as all self-published material.[11] At the same time, my hope is that the partial nature of this expanded bibliography is usefully "blatant" in the sense that it reminds us of the similarly partial and ad hoc nature of existing bibliographies, its distribution of texts presenting a useful contrast to the existing portrait offered by the established Mennonite/s Writing bibliography. A comparison of the genre, gender, geography, and publisher of the two bibliographies can be found in table 1.[12] The most immediately notable difference in this context is that the texts that are not included in the original bibliography of the field are overwhelmingly in one of several genres: life writing, or children / YA literature. Notable, perhaps, but not surprising, as literary criticism as a whole was slow to engage children's and YA literature as serious enough to warrant critical attention, and life writing has only recently begun to be widely considered within the framework of literary studies. Indeed, nearly 50 percent of my expanded Mennonite literature bibliography is aimed at children or young adults, and another 15 percent of it can be categorized as memoir or auto/biography. The overrepresentation of men's literature in the established bibliographies versus the expanded bibliography is unsurprising, as well: 68 percent of the expanded bibliography is written by women, compared to less than half the established bibliography (45%). While this imbalance is perhaps especially frustrating given the notable prominence of female literary and critical figures in the early field, reading across the chart demonstrates the close relationship between genre and gender—that is, between which types of writing are taken seriously by critics, and who just happens to write it: the gender gap between bibliographies match closely onto the children's and YA novels, nearly all of which (twenty of twenty-one) were written by women. As Kathy Meyer Reimer notes in her valuable survey of Herald Press's long history of publishing children's literature, it is somewhat "ironic that, although we have not historically heard many women's stories, Mennonite publishing for children is dominated by women." The established bibliography's overwhelming emphasis on works published by secular publishers surely reflects similar gatekeeping processes and assumptions about literary quality that rely on discourses of prestige, and which have tended to offer a straightforward equation of "secular" with "serious." No less than twenty-eight additional books come into critical view for the year's publications if we suspend this assumption for the duration of the chapter.

A brief distant reading of the field of Mennonite literature in 1986 suggests that at the height of the "Mennonite miracle" stage of the field's early emergence, the majority of the literary publishing by and about Mennonites in North America was being done by American women, was aimed

	Mennonite/s writing bibliography	**Expanded bibliography (includes the established bibliography)**
Total number of books	11	46
Canada	5 (45%)	14 (30%)
United States	6 (55%)	32 (70%)
Women	5 (45%)	31.5 (68%)
Men	6 (55%)	13.5 (29%)
Fiction	3 (27%)	29.5 (64%)
Poetry	7 (64%)	8.5 (18%)
Life writing	1 (9%)	7 (15%)
Children	0	14 (30%)
Young adult	0	7 (15%)
Secular press	10 (91%)	17 (37%)
Church or Mennonite affiliated press	1 (9%)	29 (63%)

at children or young adults, and was published by church or Mennonite-affiliated venues. A consideration of the works included in the expanded bibliography that are missing from the established bibliography reveals what type of works the field has been underappreciating from the year: of these thirty-five books, 74 percent are written by Americans; 76 percent are written by women; 80 percent are published by church or Mennonite-affiliated presses. Even with the various caveats required when relying on small sample sizes and imperfect data, a surface reading of the results suggests a result that few of those who are familiar with the field would find surprising: to date, Mennonite literary criticism in North America has tended to lean toward a disproportionate focus on writing by Canadians, poetry, and works written by men. Correspondingly, it has underappreciated writing by Americans, women, fiction aimed at younger readers, and life writing. It has almost completely ignored work published by church or Mennonite-affiliated venues.

This type of basic distant reading provides an alternative perspective on the shape of the field at this crucial stage in its development, but it tells us frustratingly little about what those books are about, about how strong the field was, or about trends in form or focus. Moretti suggests that it is the sheer size of literary fields that makes distant reading a methodological necessity, but a cross-sectional approach within the smaller context of a minor literature provides an opportunity to undertake a closer look across the material published for a single year. If a scale of forty-six books remains daunting, it is not insurmountable, and the rewards may prove substantial.

Let us begin with the six works of life writing published in this year. The only work of life writing included in the established bibliography for 1986 is Menno Duerksen's episodic memoir, *Dear God, I'm Only a Boy*, published by Memphis's Castle Books. Born into a conservative Russian Mennonite family in Oklahoma in 1919, Duerksen left his dustbowl community and his Mennonite roots to work abroad for the United Press in Germany and the Middle East in the aftermath of the Second World War before ultimately returning to work for a newspaper in Memphis. Each of the thirty-four chronologically ordered chapters of *Dear God* offers a charged vignette from a fascinating life. The book is ably written: Duerksen is a natural storyteller, and the work's structure and pacing echo the news story structure of his day job. Each chapter begins with a sharp hook followed by setting cues and a detailed narrative before closing with some reflection, and—nearly always—a tidy conclusion as the episode returns to the opening hook. The tone of the book is characterized by a bend toward hyperbole and melodrama: the opening chapter begins by promising a story about the "wildest sex fiend" he ever met (we soon learn it is a horse); a bothersome rabbit from his childhood is referred to as "buck the terrorist," and so on. Duerksen leans toward hyperbole in his presentation of his Mennonite family and faith, as well, alternating between the absurd and the abusive: revival tents full of "surrealistic hodgepodge" (29) terrify the young Menno to repeatedly fake his salvation in hope of escaping hellfire, for example, and his father is described as a "groveling, crawling, praying, beseeching pilgrim" (381). In general, however, it is a structure and tone that works well in the most personal sections of the book, where it helps him to imbue his parochial struggles with a sense of lighthearted significance, as well as to establish the weight of loss when his father and his first wife pass.

Duerksen's reliance on tight story arcs and hyperbolic language is considerably less well suited to the middle section of the memoir, where he recounts his dramatic experiences as a newspaper reporter in postwar Germany and Palestine. It undermines, for example, the gravity of his descriptions of decapitated Jewish corpses, as well as his reports from the courtrooms of the Nürnberg trials and the trial of the infamous Ilse Koch. At times, his bend toward cliché leads him to rely on problematically racialized tropes: he compares a Palestinian battle to a "perfect Hollywood set" for a movie about cowboys and "Indians" (267), for example, and describes the British soldiers as protecting a house of Jewish families from a "horde of bloodthirsty Arabs" (275). Memoirs reflect the assumptions and discourses of their time, surely, but such passages lack the sensitivity that might have enabled his account of his many travels to move beyond what now read as ethnocentrist—especially when contrasted against his (admittedly self-aware) indulgence in nostalgia for his Germanic roots.[13] *Dear God* remains of interest, however, in part because of these very limitations, which provide insight into the assumptions operative in this period, as well as because of its modest accomplishment as a work of life writing. Duerksen himself spoke self-deprecatingly about the project, but his consistent use of literary forms and tropes, along with its tight narrative structure, suggest literary aspirations. Moreover, there is reason to believe there was some demand for the book: it was subsequently republished (gently revised with an eye for modesty, it seems) and was excerpted in a 1987 issue of *Mennonite Life*.[14]

Ruth Unrau's *Encircled: Stories of Mennonite Women*, published that same year by Faith and Life Press, stands in a productive tension with Duerksen's memoir. Where *Dear God* is a thirty-four-chapter episodic account of one man's dramatic life—very much in the *author-as-hero* mode of masculine memoirs—*Encircled* is an edited collection of thirty-three brief portraits of Mennonite women from across the past century. Twenty-four of the biographical sketches are written by Unrau, the collection's editor, nine are undertaken by eight different women, and one was written by someone Unrau refers to as the collection's "token man" (7). Originally invited by the "Commission on Education of the General Conference Mennonite Church" to collect the stories of thirty women who have made a significant contribution to the community and the church" (1), Unrau's collection, as the epigraph suggests, presents its subjects as a "crowd of witnesses" regarding the faithfulness of God, with favorite scripture verses sprinkled throughout. These portraits of Mennonite women largely privilege the historical details of their subjects' lives rather than the author's commentary upon them, but if the introduction suggests these will be lives recounted mostly in their own words, direct quotations from their subjects are surprisingly rare—even when the women in question had published substantial memoirs or autobiographies of their own, as is the case with both Elva Leisy (146) and Polingaysi Qoyawayma (172).[15] Overall, however, *Encircled* is well researched and well written, admirably consistent in its tone, messaging, and frame.

From the perspective of this study, *Encircled* is notable not only as an example of the type of life writing routinely overlooked by contemporary scholars but also as a faith-based, cross-cultural account of Mennonite identity that spans the globe in its varied settings. The stories following the transatlantic trajectories of Russian and Swiss Mennonite migration history are productively complicated in the collection with the lives of Polingaysi Qoyawayma (Elizabeth Q. White), a Hopi woman from Arizona whose father's work with the nearby H. R. Voth family resulted in the nickname of "Little White Man's Rooster" (165); Caroline Banwar Theodore, a Bengali doctor who was "underpaid and overworked" at the mission hospital, but who was given an entire village—or at least the tax revenues derived from it—for the "dramatic success" of an impromptu surgery in Champa, India; and Julia Yellow Horse Shoulderblade, a Cheyenne convert who is shown to have struggled but ultimately succeeded in blending her Indian and Mennonite heritages. At times, these admirable efforts to acknowledge Hopi, Indian, and Cheyenne differences in the collection are undercut by the evangelizing framework of the collection, which leads to rather celebratory accounts of assimilation, including unquestioned discussion of Hopi children being "forbidden to speak the Hopi language" and "learn[ing] also the sinfulness of their ancient beliefs" (166). At other times, however, the range of narratives manage to speak back to each other in compelling ways: an early chapter criticizes the Cheyenne Native American Church's "mixing of Christian and traditional practice" (including the use of peyote in communion [47]) and suggests that "to save the Indians' souls they knew they must destroy the pagan practices" (46), but a later chapter celebrates Shoulderblade for "bridge[ing] two cultures" (317) and applauds her singing of Cheyenne spiritual songs in defiance of missionary norms (321).

I have spent some time on *Dear God, I'm Only a Boy* and *Encircled: Stories of Mennonite Women* as they suggest something of the range of polished Mennonite life writing in 1986, but they are far from alone. Penny Armstrong and Sheryl Feldman's *A Midwife's Story* (New York: Arbor House), for example, is a bestseller recounting the experiences of an Amish midwife released by a major publisher, hinting, perhaps, at the explosion of popular interest in Amish romance narratives to come a decade later. Another notable trend in this genre is the formally published missionary narratives, including James R. Klassen's *Jimshoes in Vietnam: Orienting Westerner* (Scottdale, PA: Herald Press); the collectively edited *On Wings of Faith: A Tribute in Memory of Irwin G. Schantz* (Red Lake, ON: Northern Light Gospel Mission); as well as Helmut Huebert's *Kornelius Martens,*

Our Skillful Advocate: A Brief Biography and Collection of the Poetry and Other Writings (Winnipeg: Springfield Publishers), the latter notable, in this context, for its (admittedly hagiographic) positioning of Martens as a literary figure. The dominant mode of this latter set of memoirs is to view its subjects within a thoroughly religious framework, positioning both challenges and successes as evidence of God's faithfulness. With the exception of some of the poetry included in the Huebert text, this latter set neither aspires toward nor achieves the quality of writing that would reward literary analysis.

One final work of published life writing worth pausing over at some length here is Hannah B. Lapp's startling memoir, *To Belize with Love*, released by Brunswick Publishing Company of Lawrenceville, Virginia. *To Belize* is centered on the large Lapp family, several of whom leave their home in northwestern United States to serve as missionaries in a small village in Belize. The surprising trajectory of the Lapp memoir is established early. Lapp's parents, readers are informed, "had been born and raised in the Amish church, and for many years they knew nothing better. It was their religion and belief and they pursued it devoutly—until they ceased to be satisfied with a religion that doesn't live up to its claims, nor to the requirements of Scripture" (3). *To Belize with Love* is full of these types of offhanded but devastating critiques of both Amish and Mennonites, as the family rejected both traditions in order to find (or, better, to found) a faith of their own. Hannah is one of the family's many children—eleven "besides the one that left our belief" and so is no longer counted (3). The Lapps were preceded into rural Belize by a Mennonite missionary whom Lapp describes as giving "unsound" teaching that led to a "false peace" in the village. "There could come no blessing from such a weak and cowardly thing," she writes, adding of the locals that following the Mennonites "was the mistake that led to their own downfall" (10). They meet others who had similarly "given the Mennonites a try," and she acknowledges that their "holy-appearing way of life has an appeal" but insists it is outside of "the real Truth." "The main obstacle was the traditions [that the Mennonites] tried to impose on these truth-seeking people," she writes, indicating that they chose instead "what is right, a life submitted to the will and ways of God" (13). Lapp is a true believer in the church established by the family and writes of their flagging missionary efforts with colonializing zeal. "The superstitions" of the locals are "deeply rooted beliefs in witchcraft and spirits [that are] hard to leave behind," she writes, "but those that come to know Christ eventually can see that there is no use for those things of the godless life" (22). *To Belize with Love* recounts the younger Lapp's five-month stay at the family mission and includes scripture-quoting family letters and extensive black and white photographs. The memoir concludes with an epic thirteen-page poem, "The City of Our God," which replicates the awkward but earnest didacticism of the memoir itself.

The vast majority of the year's life writing, uncounted in either the established biography or my own, was self-published. Many of these works, including Abram J. Friesen's *God's Hand upon My Life: Autobiography* and George Wall's *Living in the Realm of the Miraculous*, are explicitly religious in nature, recounting stories of benighted lives and individual spiritual development. The *Mennonite Life* bibliography is littered with genealogies and family histories—there are at least twenty-one of such texts by my count. Some, such as Nancy B. Jones's *Annie of Mole Hill: A Biography of Annie Shank Weaver*, Virgil Litke's *A Journey with My Grandfather: Jacob W. Buller*, and Caethe Klassen's *My Father Franz C. Thiessen*, are generously painted biographies of locally notable figures; others, such as Katie Friesen's *Into the Unknown* and John V. Friesen's *Never Never Give Up: An Autobiography*, are autobiographies that emphasize their authors' perseverance through dramatic events. Overall, the self-published works lean heavily on the missionary tone and focus of the Unrau collection but are considerably less polished. Although their use of history to justify their present is rarely as explicitly acknowledged as it is in the conclusion of Friesen's work—having accepted his past "as it was," he writes, means that "I can make the past serve me" (205)—it is perhaps the dominant logic that extends over these works as a whole. The *Mennonite Life* bibliography for this year lists another half-dozen or so similar titles.

It is unsurprising, perhaps, that the Mennonite memoirs and biographies of 1986 have garnered little scholarly attention. As I discuss at some length in my next chapter on Mennonite diaries, life writing has only recently become a subject of sustained scholarly attention more generally, and the individual examples discussed above are uneven in quality, largely hagiographic in tone, and predictable in their accounts of challenges faced and faith affirmed. Collectively, however, they are worthy of recognition and inclusion as part of an expanded understanding of Mennonite writing. Read together, these works affirm the centrality of faith in animating writing and publishing by Mennonites in this period. The sheer numbers of self-published efforts, many of which are listed in formal bibliographies at the time, suggest the overwhelming prominence of life writing as a mode of writing by Mennonites in this period, suggesting that perhaps the Mennonite suspicion of fiction, and the correlative emphasis on "plain speaking" and truth-telling, may have made life writing a logical choice of genre for aspiring authors. Especially in light of the turn to life writing as an area of study within the larger humanities, and the recent interest in "documentary" modes of writing specifically within Mennonite studies, these works are collectively worthy of academic attention as a literary phenomenon and are occasionally worth revisiting as individual works of literary value.[16]

Like life writing, children's and YA literature has long been relegated to the sidelines of Mennonite critical inquiry. The 2010 special issue of *Journal of Mennonite Writing* showcasing work for "Young Readers," along with earlier essays by Mavis Reimer (1988), John Daniel Stahl (1981), and a brief but notable treatment of "the child" in a 1990 essay by E. F. Dyck appear to be exceptions that prove this rule. "Children," Dyck suggests with tongue (presumably) in cheek, "are unfit, stylistically, to be Mennonites" (44). Noting a tribute given by Elaine Sommers Rich to Barbara Claasen Smucker at a 2002 Mennonite/s Writing conference, Hostetler's introduction to the 2010 special issue suggests that "Other than that brief moment" between two well-known Mennonite authors of children's literature, "apparently no other serious attention has been given to Mennonite writing for young readers [. . .] despite the fact that the earliest successful literature written by U.S. and Canadian Mennonites was for children." While both children's and YA literature are explicitly set aside in the Mennonite/s Writing bibliography, I found fourteen works of Mennonite children's literature and seven works of Mennonite YA literature published in 1986 alone. One might assume that the logic in explicitly grouping and excluding children's literature is that such work is not worthy of serious academic attention, but if such assumptions are understandable in reflecting the parameters of literary studies when the bibliography was begun in the early 1990s, they are certainly not reflective of the contemporary study of literature. Today, the serious study of children's literature—albeit once "laughable" (Rudd 7)—is widespread and enjoys what the editors of *The Oxford Handbook of Children's Literature* call a "growing body of sophisticated [. . .] criticism" (Mickenberg and Vallone 2).

Like much of the life writing from this period, the Mennonite children's literature is published mostly by Mennonite publishing houses and fulfills a broadly theological and pedagogical function. Several of these books are slim, illustrated volumes for the earliest of readers, such as the "Little Jewel Books" series by the Rod and Staff Christian publishers, which includes Lucy Ann Conley's *The Lost Milk Jar*, *Little Jewel Bird*, and *Two Surprises*, as well as Edith Witmer's *God's Happy Family*. Witmer's second Rod and Staff publication in 1986, *The Anguish of Love*, is aimed at slightly older readers and aims to show how God's will may be fulfilled in challenging times—such as when a widower and widow come together in a marriage that blends their young children into a new family. Other illustrated early-reader texts published this year include Marilyn Holdeman Smith's *Poppa and the Bees* (Rosenort, MB: PrairieView Press), and Ingrid Shelton's *Benji Bear's Surprise Day* (Kindred Press). These simply written and line-illustrated vignettes for beginning readers offer basic lessons in the importance of obeying parents and loving God. The characters are often identifiably "Mennonite" only in their illustrations, as when women in prayer caps and patterned dresses braid their daughters' flowing hair. These works are pedagogical in the doubled sense as being meant to help children learn to read, as well as offering basic models normalizing a highly specific way of life.

One other children's book from 1986 is especially notable in this context. Anna Goertzen's *The Mbambi That Had No Ears and Other Congo Stories* was published by Brunswick Publishing Company. Goertzen is an Oklahoma-born missionary who spent roughly four decades in the Belgian Congo (Zaire), and her sixty-page book contains twenty-two short fable-like stories—she describes them in the opening section as a "parable of the folklore found in Africa" (6)—which look to map a conservative North American Christian morality onto African contexts, stories, and animals. At least one of the stories appears to be a rewriting of one of the best known of Aesop's fables, in which the classic "Lion and the Mouse" becomes "Mungungi the Rat Helps His Enemy." The majority of the parables are straightforward, if abrupt, as in the opening story in which a young antelope, or Mbabmi, disobeys his mother's instructions to stay out of the forest. The antelope is tricked by a sly fox in the forest, who eats his ears but then declares that the antelope never had any ears to begin with. The fox and antelope return to the village, where the judge asks the antelope's mother to settle the disagreement. To the young antelope's surprise, the mother agrees with the fox. "'Yes, this is my son,' she says. 'Truly, he had no ears. I told him not to go into the forest alone, but he did.'" The moral of the story is then stated clearly—"If we do not listen to the Word that God has given to us in the Bible, we may have a fate far worse than Mbambi"—and a scriptural reference provided.

In other stories, however, the stories prove awkward for the theological lessons being invoked. In "Two Young Men (Choose That Which Is Good)," for example, the brothers are invited to ask the village witch doctor for any gift they desire. The one chooses the power of "light and lightning," by which he can "bring all kinds of hardships to any enemy" (15); the other chooses "the magic power of grace and pity," by which he can "take away anger from people, also any evil from the heart" (15–16). Although the scriptural reference provided instructs readers to "Follow not that which is evil, but that which is good," Goertzen suggests that because both brothers "received their power from the witch doctor, a type of Satan [. . . b]oth of these were evil" (16). In "A Field Cricket Races a Rat," an arrogant cricket is challenged to a race and cheats his way to victory, but it is the rat that dies of exhaustion. Both the cricket and the rat, we are told, are examples of Satan's use of pride: "Generally, if two people strive to outdo each other, both are sinning" (33). Finally, a series of stories about a marketplace seem to thoroughly blur the evangelizing lines between Christianity and capitalism. In one, a leopard fails to convince a bird into sharing material to sell, and when the leopard resorts to trying to sell stones against the market's law about selling useful things, he is beat to death by the market owner. The moral? The leopard "disobeyed the market rules and so died for his sins" (38). In another, a twin is stolen from a family and taken to a neighboring village; when the people in that village are unwilling to replicate the twin's vigorous work ethic, he simply returns to his parents. "People who really know Jesus Christ and are born again into the family of God are people who like to work," we are told. "Laziness is the beginning of every evil in the world" (51).

Of course, not all children's literature is aimed at such early readers. Kindred Press, for example, published a number of older children's works and YA novels in 1986, several of which feature Mennonite characters and concerns. Nan Doerksen's novel, *The First Family Car* (illustrated by Kathy Penner), for example, offers simply drawn stories of the Enns family, who are, in the words of its back cover, "struggling to make ends meet during the pioneer days on the prairies." Doerksen's characters are identifiably Mennonite and the writing includes Low German phrases, the thrust of her stories being lightly humorous affairs of conservative family life, equally celebrating simple faith and class mobility. By contrast, Elsa Redekopp's *Dream and Wonder: A Child's View of Canadian Village Life*, also published that year by Kindred, is an episodic account of life in a fictional prairie village that offers a documentarian's account of the disappearing Southern Manitoba villages. It comes complete with line drawing illustrations by Margaret Quiring, a map of Southern Manitoba, and pages from songbooks and handwritten notes. The simple, direct, and enthusiastic narrator makes the youth of Redekopp's intended audience clear, but both its effort and success at immersing the reader within a distinct and fully drawn world makes it notable as a literary work that rewards closer reading. Indeed, the appeal to expert endorsements on the back cover seems eager to establish the work as a literary object: "a child's story, but a most adult book," says a "Dr. Roland Gray, Professor, U. of British Columbia"; "a classic recommended for any course on Children's Literature," says a hopeful "Elizabeth Peters, Professor, U. of Manitoba." Though the desire expressed by such blurbs is clear enough—*please take this book seriously!*—it is a message that appears to have been ignored by its most obvious audience, those of us interested in Mennonite writing.

If the pedagogical, theological, and documentarian function is prioritized in many examples of the year's children's literature, the year's young adult texts are more consistently self-conscious literary efforts. Like Doerksen's *First Family Car* and Redekopp's *Dream and Wonder*, Esther Loewen Vogt's *Turkey Red* and its sequel, *Harvest Gold*, were published by Winnipeg and Hillsboro's joint Kindred Press. First published by David C. Cook in the mid-1970s, Vogt's lighthearted adventure novels celebrate Russian Mennonites' contributions to Kansas agriculture and praise the community's simple faith and are accompanied by striking images by the noted illustrator Seymour Fleishman. *Turkey Red* and *Harvest Gold* are, in every way, stories of assimilation: the German-speaking Mennonites in both novels are initially suspicious of the "English" who live in the surrounding cities and the "Indians" who preceded them in the country, but they come to learn that both are surprisingly helpful. The novels' Mennonites are particularly afraid of their Indian neighbors, and Vogt is surprisingly blunt in grounding their prejudice in the community's complicity in the colonial project: "White men took their land away," notes a character in *Harvest Gold*; "Now we'd better watch out!" (13). The larger book, however, assures readers there is no reason to fear.

As we might expect from the genre and period, the portrait of Indigeneity in the novels are superficial accounts of "noble savages." The single named Indigenous figure in *Turkey Red*, Gray Fox, appears only in order to help the Mennonites live on the harsh land and then promptly disappears. Twice a rattlesnake appears to threaten Mennonites, and both times Gray Fox appears abruptly to offer aid. "'Hold still, white girl!'" he says the first time, swiftly decapitating the snake and disappearing without a word (15); later, when a "rattler" manages to sink its fangs into a careless young Mennonite, Gray Fox emerges from the tall grasses and sucks the venom directly from the wound before disappearing with a "sudden movement" (58). In *Harvest Gold*, however, it is Gray Fox who initially requires physical and spiritual help from the Mennonites. The young Martha finds him badly hurt by the side of a road and, with her parent's help, nurses him back to health. Martha spends her afternoons reading to the injured man from the Bible, and while we are never told he actually converts, it is clear that he is thankful to learn about God. By the novel's close, however, Gray Fox returns to his role as helper: when Martha comes down with a crippling disease, he returns daily with "strange medicine" until the young girl recovers (104). When other Indigenous peoples are mentioned in passing, it is strictly as subjects for outreach, as when Martha wonders "if someday someone would also learn to speak the Sioux Indian language so the Indians could learn of the Gospel" (68).

Vogt is a capable writer and these works are clearly worth inclusion in any bibliography of Mennonite writing. The novels are well paced, their familial dynamics compelling, and their themes consistently (if predictably) drawn. Their most immediate value to the field, however, may be as a relatively early effort to gently stretch the white US Mennonite imagination beyond its isolationist tendencies, while affirming the evangelical framework that had become increasingly influential in the postwar period. The novels' fascinating mixture of assimilative patriotism and evangelical fervor is well summarized in a passage to be found at the close of *Turkey Red*. "Be a Mennonite," Martha is told. "But also be an American. Most of all, always live like a Christian!" (104).

The religious thrust of the Kindred Press YA novels is slightly redirected in the comparable publications from the other major Mennonite press of this period, Herald Press. Where Kindred YA publications emphasize Mennonite setting and characters, those published by Herald are more general in setting, character, and theme, yet more overt in their evangelizing thrust. As Mavis Reimer has argued in a fascinating essay on Barbara Smucker's work (none of which was published in 1986), it would seem that the "question of audience" for Mennonite children's literature has a readable effect not simply on the setting and characters of the writing—Mennonite children should read about Mennonite histories and concerns, while non-Mennonites will not be interested in such specificities—but also on the theological implications of the works themselves.[17] Ruth Nulton Moore's *Mystery of the Lost Heirloom* and *Mystery at Camp Ichthus*, for example, both in the "Sara and Sam" series, are plot-heavy "Christian mystery" novels set in rural Pennsylvania. Even more than in Vogt's *Turkey Red* and *Harvest Gold*, Moore's novels rely on heavily exoticized and romanticized accounts of local Indigenous peoples. In *Mystery of the Lost Heirloom*, the adolescent twins help an "Indian princess" recover her stolen fleur-de-lis pendant. As it turns out, Princess Morning Star's family had converted to Christianity, and her husband, Jim Little Hawk, is an ordained minister; the two are partnering to "bring the Word of God to those who are less fortunate," including "on reservations all around the country" (47). Their prior conversion to Christianity is useful within the evangelistic thrust of the novel, of course, but it also works to lessen fears of the "Indian ghosts" that are important to the plot's progression, and to disarm the concluding gesture, in which the Susquehannock people are so thankful for the twins' help that they adopt them into their "tribe" as "brothers and a sister to our people for as long as [they] live" (141).

Guenn Martin's *Forty Miles from Nowhere*, also published by Herald Press in 1986, replicates the Moore novels in its emphasis on a quick-thinking teenager, but Martin is much more restrained in both tone of prose and in evangelistic fervor. Martin's thirteen-year-old protagonist, Melanie Rose LaRue—notably not a Mennonite—comes of age in a Christian family on an isolated Gresham Island in Alaska. The novel comes to a climax when Melanie's mother develops appendicitis and has to be airlifted to a hospital, leaving Melanie to briefly fend for herself—and to pray fervently for her mother's health—at the cabin during a winter storm. Martin's story has literary aspirations, beginning with epigraphs from Madeleine L'Engle and John Donne that are referenced within the body of the novel, along with the inclusion of poems by the likes of Emily Dickinson, but the prose is plodding and the moral is prioritized in a straightforward manner throughout. The message of the story, lest any young readers had managed to miss it, is usefully summarized in a closing conversation: they are thankful to have learned to "be more dependent on God's faithfulness" (145).

If the YA works published by Kindred and Herald Press overlap in their use of plot-driven fiction to promote religious values, the most explicitly Mennonite and evangelical YA novels released in 1986 were released by Harrisonburg's Christian Light Publications. Mollie Zook's *From Wealth to Faith: A Tear-Stained Journey* tells the story of Hans and Netta Reimer from the safe distance of West Germany, and positions the collapse of the Mennonite world in Russia to be a hard but necessary spiritual lesson in the dangers of materialism. Importantly, this deeply religious novel uses this theologically dubious interpretation of the Russian Revolution as a cautionary tale for its contemporary audience, warning that "America is in many ways ripe for the same things they experienced in Russia" (6). Shirley Boll's *At Every Gate a Pearl*, meanwhile, is a celebratory account of Swiss Mennonite evangelism among Puerto Rican migrant workers in Pennsylvania. Like Zook, Boll makes clear that her book is based on true events, noting that her "prayer" for the book is "that the love of Jesus will shine through the story." Boll's novel tells the story of Rosa Gonzales and her doting husband Luis, who are too poor to formally marry in Puerto Rico. Luis travels to Pennsylvania to earn money through seasonal labor on the Weber's tomato farm but is captivated by the Mennonites' simple and honest faith. What was different about these good people? Luis wonders. "Maybe it has something to do with religion" (30). By the novel's end, the Gonzaleses are married, converted, and baptized, and a Spanish church has been set up in the area to spread the gospel among the other migrant workers. Like Zook, Boll positions international concerns as lessons in faith for Mennonites in rural Pennsylvania, and dovetails its religious and economic lessons throughout.

The missionary focus of Boll and Zook are replicated in several other young adult novels published by Mennonite authors in 1986. Karren Boehr's *Ants in the Sugar Bowl*, for example, published by Concordia House, tells the story of young Trish Witter, a junior high student whose family takes on a missionary post on an unnamed tropical island that is likely Puerto Rico.[18] When Trish confesses early in the novel that she has been praying that the family not be able to leave the United States, her friend offers what effectively serves as the novel's thesis statement. "Trish, how dumb can you get!" she exclaims. "You know that God does what is good for you, not just what makes you happy" (17). Life on the island tests Trish further: not only does she have endless frustrations getting accustomed to differences in language, culture, and living standards; she gets buried beneath rubble in a storm and even briefly decides to stop following God—"I plan to keep believing in Jesus," she says, "but that's it" (102). By the novel's end, however, she has predictably found her faith in God's provenance, as well as hope that the handsome islander who helped to sustain her faith just might be "part of God's plan for me" (165).

One final YA novel is worth pausing over from this year. *Wolfhunter*, written by Joel Kauffmann and published by Nashville's Abingdon Press, is a novelization of a Christian film by the same name. The novel (re)tells the story of a sensitive teenage boy, Josh Sanders, who, with the help of a reclusive woman named Maggie, manages to befriend—and must defend—a dangerous dog in the area. Maggie had lost her faith in God when her favorite student decided to join the military, but Josh's selfless care for the dog helps her "realize it was [. . .] wrong" for her to "get angry at God" (107). Film novelizations rarely make for great literature, and complex plot, nuanced character development, and rich language are hardly the goal here. Instead, like several of the Mennonite YA novels discussed above, *Wolfhunter* is an effort to mobilize a low-stakes adventure plot with teenage protagonists to affirm the Christian values of its target audience. While neither the publisher nor the characters here are Mennonite, the novel's theology might be considered quietly Anabaptist. Kauffmann, best known as the author of the syndicated cartoon strip "Pontius' Puddle," has the characters demonstrate their faith through lived example rather than explicit didacticism and suggests a self-sacrificial dedication to peace as the means to overcome violence—affirming John Daniel Stahl's argument regarding Mennonite children's literature, that "the moral example of action for the sake of others without concern for oneself" has served as a "powerful archetypal story" (63–64). While some conflict is necessary for the plot's development, the larger novel confirms the back cover promise to readers that Josh and Maggie will make a rather paradoxical discovery: "God has shown us another way to 'kill' our enemies—with love."

It would be a mistake to return to the Mennonite life writing, children's, or YA literature published in 1986 with hopes of finding a treasure trove of consistent artistic excellence. Still, it would be a mistake, too, for the field to ignore it outright. A cross-sectional reading across Mennonite life writing from 1986 shows how deeply entrenched Mennonite writers have been in exploring theological elements in their work—whether to celebrate lives in witness to the Mennonite faith, as in *Encircled* and in self-published autobiographies, or to celebrate the individual's ability to rise above the religious community positioned as stifling, as in *Dear God, I'm Only a Boy*. Faith-based Mennonite publishing houses understood YA writing as a pedagogical opportunity, and reading across this literature helps us appreciate the direction and tensions of their educational efforts. In works like *Turkey Red, Harvest Gold*, and *Mystery of the Lost Heirloom*—as in Shirlee Evans's *Tree Tall and the Horse Race* (Herald Press) and Nan Doerksen's *Rats in the Sloop* (Ragweed Press), also published this year—Mennonite authors turned to evangelism as a means of addressing the recognized tensions between their rural communities and the local Indigenous populations. In works like *Dream and Wonder* and *From Wealth to Faith* we see stories of Mennonite cultural, migration, and religious history being animated for a new generation of emerging readers, while in books like *The Mbambi That Had No Ears*, *The First Family Car*, and *At Every Gate a Pearl*, we see how thoroughly religious and economic concerns dovetailed in Mennonite writing aimed at young readers in this period. As Stahl notes of earlier Mennonite children's writing, several of the works published this year—especially those published by Kindred Press—are of note in that they critique and even invert the individualism and gentle rebellions we might expect to find in young adult novels aimed at a more general North American audience, instead celebrating the "ideal of self-denial for the sake of family life [. . .] as leading to growth of character and spirit" (73). "Obedience to God's law [. . .] means freedom" in such works, Stahl continues, "and the conformity to group ideas and values" is the foundation for the individual (73). Given that these lessons are sharply out of line with what we might expect from the Mennonite writing that we usually discuss when we return to the 1980s, one of the enduring impressions of reading across the Mennonite children's and young adult literature published in 1986 is its sheer bulk. It is worth reminding ourselves that what we commonly think of "Mennonite literature" in this period—the highly self-conscious, often experimentally "literary" writing of the 1980s, influenced by feminism, postmodernism, and poststructuralism—is, in quantity if not quality, completely overwhelmed by the writing in genres that we have collectively ignored.

1986: OH, *THAT* MENNONITE LITERATURE

When we turn our critical focus away from Mennonite life writing, children's and YA literature, the remaining collection of works published in

1986 initially reads like a return to familiar territory for the field. Audrey Poetker's first book of poetry, *i sing for my dead in german*, for example, was published in 1986 by Turnstone Press, the Winnipeg-based (but non-Mennonite) publisher widely recognized as playing a central role in the "miracle" of Mennonite writing's florescence in Manitoba during the 1980s. Poetker's work has received limited but sustained critical interest, both demanding and rewarding a close consideration of her use of language that grounds its position in Mennonite literature. As Julia Michael has noted, several scholars have engaged the collection's use of untranslated Low German words, as well as nonstandard English that mimics its diction (275). Poetker's strategic use of syntax had precedence in the Armin Wiebe's *Salvation of Yasch Siemens*, published two years earlier, and others from this period that sought, in Hildi Froese Tiessen's memorable description from a 1988 essay, to deploy "mother tongue as shibboleth" ("Mother"). In form, as well, Poetker's collection powerfully anticipates later work in the field—most notably that of Di Brandt, whose own debut, *questions i asked my mother*, published the following year by the same press, employs a strikingly similar use of nonstandard punctuation, suggesting these writers' shared indebtedness to the larger poetic movements of the period.

Like Poetker's debut, much of the remaining set of texts published by Mennonites in North America in 1986 is, in theme and structure, in keeping with what one might expect from the developmental history of this period. They are mostly published by secular presses; they emphasize ethnic rather than theological elements of Mennonite identity; they are self-consciously literary in form and structure; and, crucially, they prioritize the individual subject while critiquing the community's isolationist faith and its turn toward evangelism. Unlike *i sing for my dead in german*, however, the vast majority of the remainder of the work from this period has received precious little critical attention. If, from a literary historical perspective, the work discussed above helps us appreciate the larger writing context out of which what we usually think of as Mennonite literature was beginning to emerge, the work to be discussed below shows the broader range of texts and authors that participated in the field's emergence as a minority literature. Accordingly, if my willingness to expand the genres to be included in a critical conversation about Mennonite literature can help to explain the critical neglect of the work discussed above, the neglect of the work discussed below is more difficult to understand—perhaps especially where they not only predate but seem to anticipate the more canonical work that was soon to follow.

Several works published in this year fit easily into the field's understanding of this period but are rarely recognized as relevant to the field. Betsy Sholl's seventh collection *Rooms Overhead*, for example, fits firmly in the poetry that would soon come to define the field: it offers lyric meditations on the burden of history, carefully crafted rural images, brief narrative portraits dotted by biblical allusions and a few jolts of sexuality, alongside references to immigrant grandmothers from the steppes. Sholl has an eye for detail and a flair for enigmatic phrasing; lines like "Everywhere the distance opens" (63) and "I want the real, the sound of it cracking" (27) help bring the collection's concerns alive. Louis Braun's first collection of stories, *A Stone Watermelon*, is another case in point. *Stone Watermelon* is notable as the first (and still the only) of Turnstone's books of fiction to be shortlisted for the Governor General's Award in Canada, but it has yet to generate any extended attention from scholars in the field. The collection's relative dearth of stories that directly engage Mennonite concerns may explain something of the field's disinterest, though it is thematically connected to the concerns that would otherwise dominate its discussions in this period. It recounts the lives of rural men and women across Canada and the United States who are frustrated by the narrowness of their options, searching for meaning beyond the clichés of church and popular culture, and haunted by their unspoken regrets. Read decades later, *Stone Watermelon* stands out for its nuanced exploration of gendered relationships: between mothers and daughters, as in "The Edge of the Cornfield" and "Monolith," and, perhaps especially, between men—whether those relationships are tender, as between the four aging men in "A Stone Watermelon," and the two young men in "Maltese Princess," or toxic, as between a macho father and his flamboyant son in "The No Place Bar and Grill." Written in a confident and often lyrical prose, attendant to the consequences of class and education, and full of the type of deceptively "plain" language that only loosely veils its pointed critique of small-town morality, Braun's collection clearly anticipates and holds up well alongside contemporary short fiction by figures like Sarah Klassen and Dora Dueck and is not out of place alongside Sandra Birdsell and David Bergen. Moreover, as Douglas Reimer has suggested in his brief reading of Braun's fiction as "effectively deterritorializ[ing] Mennonite heterosexual metaphysics" (199), the book's quiet exploration of queer lives may offer an important predecessor to the current boom of queer Mennonite fiction.[19]

Though the term "Mennonite" is rare in *Rooms Overhead* or *A Stone Watermelon*, both texts are easily readable as Mennonite texts in keeping with the larger field at this time. By contrast, the absence of several other works published this year from the field's memory can be explained, in part, by their focus beyond the community. Andreas Schroeder's novel, *Dustship Glory*, is one notable case in point. Boasting warm reviews from major figures of Canadian letters such as Timothy Findley and Northrop Frye, Schroeder's novel was published first by an imprint of Doubleday in Toronto and reprinted the following year by an imprint of New York's Ballantine Books. *Dustship Glory* is a harrowing fictionalization of the stranger-than-fiction true story that is the building of the *Sontianen*, a large, ocean-worthy ship, on the bone-dry prairie of central Canada in 1930 by an enigmatic and ill-tempered Finnish immigrant determined to sail it home across the Atlantic. It remains, by my reading, among the best-polished writing of Schroeder's substantial career, moving deftly between comedy and tragedy as he explores themes of longing and belonging in the account of an almost mythic historical figure. While it is written by a Mennonite author, its most immediate comparison texts are outside the field: in focus and tenor, *Dustship Glory* is more likely to remind readers of Margret Lawrence or Fredrick Philip Grove than anyone in the annals of Mennonite writing. The original *Sontianen* ship still stands as a tourist attraction in rural Saskatchewan, but the novel has been largely forgotten.

A similar fate has befallen five chapbooks published this same year: John Weier's *After the Revolution*, published by Turnstone; Fred Redekop's *Cornucopia* and Sam Manickam's *Seeds and Seasons*, both published by Pinchpenny; Keith Ratzlaff's contribution to *Three Winter Poems*, published by Penumbra; and Jeff Gundy's *Surrendering to the Real Things: The Archetypal Experience of C. Wordsworth Crocket*, published by Pikestaff.

The twenty-five poems of *After the Revolution*, Weier's first published collection, shows his promise as they move deftly between reflections on his prairie youth, a hardened father, and various lovers. *After the Revolution* fits snugly among the Mennonite poetry in this period: like Poetker, Weier plays with language and capitalization; like Gundy and David Waltner-Toews, he shows a self-consciousness that often results in self-deprecating humor, as in the love poem entitled "another love poem" (25). Redekop's *Cornucopia* is more ambitious in its themes and allusions than is Weier's effort, but it is significantly less successful. While many of the efforts in Pinchpenny's long-running series shine with the promise of their authors' future success, Redekop's effort, full of awkward philosophical references and stilted wordplay, reads—to my ear, at least—like the early effort it must have been.

Sam Manickam's *Seeds and Seasons* is worth pausing over at a bit more length. The thirty-eight-page collection is ably illustrated in ink by Suelyn Lee, and the creative writing is divided in two: the first section, entitled "Colors," is made up of fourteen poems; the second section, entitled "India," contains two works of short fiction. A single-paged introduction offers something of an apology for the collection, describing it as his "first creative fruits," and identifies India as the author's "native country"; the collection ends with a "Glossary of foreign words" with definitions for "White Sahib," "Rupee," and so on. The poems include several haikus, a sonnet, and a range of more open poems structured by strained rhymes; they are mostly earnest reflections on changing seasons. If the poetry in *Seeds and Seasons* reads mostly like the "first fruits" we are promised, the prose section shows real promise. In "The Khud," an unnamed narrator living in a hostel in Mussoorie, India, has heard rumors that the local Hindus cremate bodies in the forest near to where he has often played with his school friends. He quickly agrees to visit the burning grounds the next day, but his bravado disappears when they discover human remains at the site; the story ends with him fleeing back to the relative safety of the schoolyard. The story is a bit wooden and leans a little steep into gothic tropes—the hostel is described as an "old Victorian structure" (27); the narrator's fevered dream positions him as a buzzard above the bones; the skulls are described as "sightlessly star[ing] into the blue beyond," and so on (28)—but the pace is excellent, the imagery crisp, and its effect undeniable.

In the collection's second story, titled "Arriving," a young boy named Ram is waiting in the Delhi airport. Ram has grown up in England and has visited India with his family just once; now he has arrived alone, self-conscious of the fact that he doesn't speak Hindi, and searching for the "real" India—not the "superficial India that tourists bought and took home" (31). Ram is initially overwhelmed by urban India but is drawn to the countryside by a faint "throbbing" that grows stronger as he leaves the city; it reaches its culmination in a forest clearing where he sits beside a small stream and watches the sun rise onto the Himalayas. "Here is where I end and where I start," he tells himself, as he had found a "place where India still pounded a primal rhythm" (37). Notwithstanding its occasional heavy-handedness and romantic conclusion, the story shows several layers in its prose. Most notable, perhaps, is its sharp portrait of colonial double-consciousness: young Ram infuriates his father by describing London as "the home of the white sahib" (31)—only to be frustrated to find himself treated like a foreigner and "sahib" upon his arrival in Delhi, and embarrassed by his inability to speak the language. *Seeds and Seasons* stands out among the year's Mennonite literary publications as one of the few works by writers of color, in its Indian setting, and for the promise of its prose. The collection demonstrates enough potential that one is left regretting that Manickam, now chair of the Department of Spanish at the University of North Texas, doesn't appear to have continued working in creative writing.

Three Winter Poems, a three-poet collection that includes Keith Ratzlaff's work, and Gundy's *Archetypal Experience* are notable here for different reasons. The former turns out to be, appropriately enough, just three poems in length, all about winter. It is a beautifully crafted chapbook—my copy is hand-noted as number 77 from a run of 235 copies—printed to mark the occasion of its press's office move. Yet given that the booklet includes only three poems in total, and just one from Ratzlaff, it may seem surprising to find this book listed on the established Mennonite literature bibliography, while other works, including much more substantial YA novels and memoirs, are nowhere to be found. Lovely as Ratzlaff's poem is, the inclusion of this collection is a lesson in the institutionalizing power of literary celebrity, such as it is in such a small field. Ratzlaff is now a well-established poet and professor, and it must surely be the presence of Ratzlaff's name that has landed the work on the list. Gundy's *Archetypal Experience* is notable as a ten-poem experiment recounting the adventures of C.W., a fictional "pomehunter." The nuanced theological explorations that are typical of some of Gundy's later work are de-prioritized here, and the concept-album approach stands out as productively experimental, but in other ways this early collection is full of the formal and thematic concerns that Gundy has explored ever since: it offers shifting, witty lyrics that play with the sharp juxtaposition of high and low culture, of natural and artificial worlds, and is characterized by winking self-consciousness throughout. Gundy would include one of the collection's poems, "The Archetypal Experience of C. Wordsworth Crocket," in his later chapbook, *Greatest Hits: 1986–2003*.

Surely the most accomplished work of Mennonite literature published in 1986 is also one of its most enigmatic. Janet Kauffman's third book, *Collaborators*, is the rare example of an explicitly Mennonite novel—Mennonite author, Mennonite setting, Mennonite characters, Mennonite concerns—that has garnered more critical attention from outside of the Mennonite community than from within.[20] Published by Knopf, Kauffman's early novel was lauded in reviews everywhere from the *New York Times* to *People* magazine and was shortlisted for the PEN/Faulkner award. The spare, poetic novel is presented in the first-person voice of Andrea Doria, a Mennonite woman named after an Italian ocean liner that sunk in 1956, and centers on her complicated relationship with her aging mother. "My mother lied to me about everything," the novel begins. "She told me she believed in Hell. She told me she was a pacifist, a good Mennonite, and could never kill" (3). Placing a prison adjacent to the family farm and noting the tourists that come to gawk at her Mennonite family as they work, Kauffman explores a central paradox of Mennonite identity—that they may be invisible as individuals confined within a group identity that is made hypervisible by its cultural distinctiveness—which neatly inverts the celebration of conformity we find in the Mennonite children's and YA literature published in 1986. The fragmentary structure of the novel parallels the disorientation that follows her mother's stroke but also makes it difficult to follow the work's frank discussion of her mother's sexuality. (It seems clear she has had intimate relationships with three generations of men from the same family, for example, but it is not clear if that family is also her own.)

Though *Collaborators* stands out in this period of Mennonite writing for its formal and thematic ambition, and its frank engagement with Mennonite sexuality, class, and gender, it resonates strongly with contemporary and more recent work in the field. The first sustained critical engagement with *Collaborators* in Mennonite criticism found it resonant with contemporary feminist theory and celebrated it as a complex demonstration that "a Mennonite woman, as well as a Mennonite man, can be both a 'profound presence' and a thinking, articulate being" (J. Lapp 624). That essay was published in 1998, and I can find no evidence of an extended engagement with the novel in the field since.[21] One might imagine its prominence and contents would have been sufficient to land it on Beck's "canon" of Mennonite "transgressive literature," but its absence from the larger critical conversation makes its omission from any talk of canons appropriate.

If the dearth of critical attention on *Collaborators* is surprising because of the non-Mennonite interest in the book, the dearth of critical attention to Peter G. Epp's novel, *Agatchen: A Russian Mennonite Mother's Story*, is notable given the work was translated and republished specifically for that community's attention and offered by the Mennonite Literary Society. Epp is a notable, transnational figure in his own right: born in Russia and educated in Switzerland, he earned a PhD from the University of Basel in 1912 for his work exploring the soul in Plato's writings, emigrated to the United States in 1924, and taught at Bluffton College and, later, Ohio State. Epp's novel, written in German and first published in 1932 as *Eine Mutter*, was translated and edited by the University of Winnipeg professor, Peter Pauls, for inclusion in the Mennonite Literary Society's (MLS) series of books on Mennonite life and culture. *Agatchen* is presented as memories of Agatha Epp-Boschman-Neufeld, an eighty-year-old Mennonite matriarch living in a small village in Russia, who offers poignant if sometimes meandering reflections on her large family, her long life, and her community. While the episodic first-person account offers some nuanced portraits of

Agatha's extended family—the titles of the majority of the novel's twenty-six chapters are the names of the primary family member introduced therein—it seems clear that the novel's primary goal is to offer a careful account of the Mennonite world in Russia (and to insert some occasionally heavy-handed commentary upon it).

Pauls, the novel's translator, has elsewhere compared Agatchen to Freida Friesen in Rudy Wiebe's *The Blue Mountains of China*—calling Agatchen an "elderly female narrator [that] perfectly exemplifies the oral tradition," he goes so far as to suggest "Wiebe may owe something to Peter Epp" in his creation of Freida ("Rudy" 71)—but his editorial choices appear to suggest the MLS meant the work to serve less as a literary text than as documentation of a specific time, place, and way of life. In this sense, at least, the more immediate comparison is Arnold Dyck's *Verloren in der Steppe*, published serially in the 1940s in German before being translated and collated as *Lost in the Steppe* in 1974. Indeed, the historicizing gesture of Pauls's version of Epp's novel is clear in that the 1986 edition opens with a detailed genealogy and a map of the Molochnaya colony and is illustrated with nine period photographs and six drawings—illustration meant, in Pauls's words, to "help the younger reader to visualize the world that these words are intended to evoke" ("Introduction" 15). Of course, the translation itself is surely meant to reflect the same intentions and should serve as a reminder of the transition from German language to English language that was still occurring in the prominent strain of Russian Mennonite writing in this period.

One final set of texts published in 1986 serve as a valuable point of connection to the bestselling form of Mennonite literature of our day: Mennonite and Amish romance novels. Though Amish and Mennonites are both Anabaptist communities, they are clearly distinct traditions, and scholars would do well to respect their differences. At the same time, however, there are notable overlaps in the literary tradition that encourage a careful comparative lens. *Rosanna of the Amish*, for example, has been described as marking "the beginnings of Mennonite literature in America" based in part on the fact that its author, Joseph W. Yoder, was born Amish and was a lifelong member of a Mennonite church.[22] Moreover, as Valerie Weaver-Zercher has noted in her authoritative *Thrill of the Chaste*, the Mennonite press dominated the genre of Amish romance in this period, as it did from the genre's surprisingly early beginnings up until it started to become a commercially attractive prospect.[23]

Two examples of the genre were published in 1986, and they could hardly be more different. Sharon Curtis and Tom Curtis's *Sunshine and Shadow*, published via a Bantam romance imprint, tells the story of Susan Peachey, a beautiful but naïve Amish widow who falls into a torrid affair with a cynical Hollywood filmmaker shooting a film near her colony. The Curtises were surely setting out to capitalize on the success of the film *Witness*, which had been released the previous year with a similar premise; they even make reference to that film's lead actor, Harrison Ford (154). The mild and melodramatic erotica of *Sunshine and Shadow* is set against a stiff but sympathetic portrait of the Pennsylvania Amish: Susan, who enters the novel when she mistakes an actor in heavy costume for a real monster and leaps onto the set to defend the nearby Amish children in her care, is impossibly sheltered, and the larger Amish community is presented as a prelapsarian antidote to the film crew's urban cynicism. The novel itself is capably written, its predictable rhythm and various clichés perhaps more reflective of the genre than indicative of the talents of its authors, but it is clearly an early example of the unapologetic commodification that would later characterize Amish bestsellers.

The Curtises' steamy romance sits on the same spectrum—albeit on the opposite end—as Carole Page's romance novel, *Rachel's Hope*, re-released in 1986 by the Mennonite publisher Herald Press. Page's conservative, chaste, and deeply religious novel was first published in 1979, but its republication by Herald Press in 1986 shows the Mennonite press's early interest in the romance genre. Herald Press made the decision to step away from the genre in the 1990s, just as the contemporary phenomenon of Mennonite and Amish romance novels began with the phenomenal success of Beverly Lewis's *The Shunning* (1997). As Weaver-Zercher has pointed out, such novels—sometimes called "bonnet rippers"—remain, without question, the bestselling strain of Anabaptist-themed literature. They have been largely ignored by scholars in the field, likely for the sins of being genre fiction (and thus outside the purview of scholars who emphasize "serious" literature), and, perhaps, for rarely being penned by Amish or Mennonite authors (and thus outside the broadly accepted parameters of the field).

Notable exceptions aside, it is perhaps no great mystery why few of the works discussed thus far have become central to the field's account of its own past. The tendency of literary scholarship to overlook genres of writing such as life writing, children's literature, YA fiction, and romance fiction is well known, as is the tendency of minority literatures to foreground "serious" and self-consciously literary work that can serve as evidence of a community's artistic sophistication while being readable as autoethnography. These critical pressures are intensified by what Moretti describes as the bottleneck of literary history: where close reading methodologies all but ensure the vast majority of published work will promptly be forgotten, it is little surprise to find scholars spending their time and efforts on the work that resonates most clearly within the existing critical conversation. How few scholars! How many texts! A cross-sectional reading, however, gives us the opportunity to review the broader set of texts that have been overlooked in a field to date—not simply to cram more texts into the existing frame in a supplemental logic of encyclopedic histories that look to authorize a minority literature by sheer bulk, but also, as we will see below, to help us rethink that framework altogether.

1986: READING YAGUCHI, TOGANE, VAN VOGT

Before closing this experiment in bibliographic literary history, I want to offer slightly closer readings of three texts from this year that estrange the field in particularly compelling ways: Phyllis Pellman Good's slim anthology, *Three Mennonite Poets*; Mohamud Siad Togane's poetry collection, *The Bottle and the Bushman*, and A. E. van Vogt's final short story, "Prologue to Freedom." *Three Mennonite Poets* is certainly the best known of these three and may well be the best remembered of all the Mennonite literary texts published in 1986. As the title suggests, the anthology includes a series of poems by three Mennonite poets: the American Jean Janzen; the Japanese Yorifumi Yaguchi; and the Canadian David Waltner-Toews (who, at the time of the collection's publication, was living in Indonesia).

Like any anthology, *Three Mennonite Poets* makes an argument, and if the life narratives of these poets overlap in significant ways—all are Mennonite, of course, but Janzen and Waltner-Toews were born in Canada, Yaguchi and Waltner-Toews both studied at Goshen College in Indiana, and so on[24]—it nonetheless stands as a notable effort to establish the field as a transpacific (if decidedly English) phenomenon. The selection of poems by Good, the collection's editor, draws on religious foundations to establish the book's thematic links but, crucially, does not efface the racialized and gendered specificities of its authors and contexts. If its declarative title makes clear we are to understand the collection as constituting the work of three *Mennonite* poets, there are sufficient thematic and formal connections between the poems to link them together, as well: all three evince a preference for the lyric; all are concerned with questions of peace and violence; all explore both theological and sexual concerns; and all wrestle with how the dramatic histories of their forebearers reverberate in the mundane and everyday elements of the present. If the poems excerpted for a "Three Mennonite Poets" promotional section in the pages of *Festival Quarterly* that summer underscore surprisingly few of these overlaps, the book's "Editor's Afterword" suggests their work has been brought together by "an honest, a bare-bones truthfulness, a disdain for pretense," a concern for "the individual as part of a community," and "a wish for peace" (115–16). Good's argument holds up well when rereading the collection decades later.

While these shared concerns help Good's collection hang together, it is clear that Janzen and Waltner-Toews write out of one tradition, and Yaguchi writes out of another. Both Janzen and Waltner-Toews are descendants of Russian Mennonites, and their work is littered with a host of shared historical, geographical, and cultural references. Both directly grapple with their obligations to their ancestors' losses in the tragedy that befell the Mennonites in Russia, both touch on the specific foodways and language of the Russian Mennonites in North America, and so on. Their work, in other words, is immediately recognizable within the dominant critical discourse of the tradition. Yaguchi's work, by contrast, emerges from a decidedly different context, and it is to his work that I am drawn here.

At the time of the collection's publication, Yaguchi was already the pastor of a Mennonite church in Sapporo, Japan. Here as elsewhere, his poetry offers a complex and nuanced theological engagement with hope and joy, as well as frank discussions of doubt and sin. Although Yaguchi attended a Mennonite postsecondary institution in the United States, the poetry selected for inclusion in *Three Mennonite Poets* never deigns to bridge the gap that opens between his own set of cultural markers and those geographic, linguistic, and foodway markers that overlap in the collection's other works. Their impact on the collection is transformative. When Yaguchi titles a poem "How to Eat Loaches," for example, he invokes the Japanese context in which the loach fish is a common dish but also seems to anticipate, by way of its "how to" structure, a non-Japanese audience for the work. When, following the instruction to swallow them alive, the poem concludes by comparing the fish's struggle and death to rodents swallowed whole by a snake or "a minority race / in a society" (51), Yaguchi's poem twists back on the reader: what begins as a lesson readable in the anthology's context as a description of "exotic" foodways is revealed as a stinging critique of assimilatory pressures faced by the minority subject.

Similarly, when another one of Yaguchi's poems tackles the question of nonviolence—absolutely central to Mennonite theology—he does so within a frame that will startle readers accustomed to its treatment in Mennonite writing. Confessing the urge to kill that arises within him when he puts on a soldier's uniform, Yaguchi reminds readers that his native Japan fought and died in a battle with his North American readers. If "How to Eat Loaches" addresses and positions as complicit an English-speaking, implicitly North American audience, "Usually" once again places that audience in the crosshairs. It begins with the poet declaring that although he loves peace, he finds himself gripped by bloodlust when he puts on his military uniform. Wishing that war would break out so he could kill or be killed as necessary, he closes the short poem with references to "the Emperor" and "*our* country" (my emphasis, 50). Together, these closing lines establish a Japanese audience for the poem; if North American readers are to position themselves within the world of the verse, it is as the potential subject of Yaguchi's patriotic violence. In fact, "Usually" is but one example of the collection's invocation of Japanese military history: in another poem he casually notes he often "find[s] himself humming [. . .] a military song" (62); in a third he writes of a friend who committed suicide after seeing his sister "hand in hand with an armed soldier" after the war (73). The editor's closing essay underlines this effect, suggesting that Yaguchi's poetry "knows [. . .] the savagery that changed all Japanese who lived through World War II," insightfully adding that "the tension in his lines allows no extravagance and *almost no forgiveness*" (my emphasis, 116). It is true, as Good argues, that one of the elements that connects the three "books" of poetry collected in *Three Mennonite Poets* is "a wish for peace" (116), but it is also true that a sensitive reader will not be able to avoid the uncomfortable reminder that the establishment of "peace" for one people may come at an unimaginable cost for another. Should we have missed the ironies (but also the beauties) of the American and Japanese authors longing for peace in a post–World War II context, Waltner-Toews's later contribution, "The Peace Poem" makes it clear: "The basis for negotiation," it begins, "is slaughter" (Good 103). *Three Mennonite Poets*, then, is a collection well worth remembering, for it is an early model for a way of thinking about the field that draws on related concerns without denying the often-charged differences that keep the field apart.

Where *Three Mennonite Poets* wrestles with theological questions meaningfully and challengingly from a Mennonite perspective, the collection's framing and its content ultimately affirm that theological perspective. That same year, however, Montreal-based Somali-Canadian Mennonite poet Mohamud Siad Togane offered a markedly different account of Mennonite theological practices in his short book of poetry, *The Bottle and the Bushman*, published by The Muses' Co., in Quebec. Invited, in a recent interview, to reflect on his experiences with "ofay" (read: white) Mennonites—as missionaries in Somalia and as peers at a Mennonite university in Virginia—Togane slides quickly into the tone and tenor of his earlier poetry: The "Mennonites encountered a Caliban," he says, "and created almost, but not quite, a Prospero!" It is a comparison that he employs repeatedly in his 1986 collection. In the introduction to the collection, for example, he invokes Fanon to suggest that his adoption of European languages has created a "'civilized' Somali bushman in [. . .] borrowed clothes," and suggests "it is impossible for Caliban to become Prospero." Similarly, the book's fourth poem, "Caliban," begins with an epigraph quoting Caliban's famous critique of the colonizer Prospero: "*You taught me language: and the profit on't / Is, I know how to curse.*" After describing the "shaming laughter" of his childhood classmates when he misunderstands a question asked by "Mis Gehman, Mennonite Missionary teacher," Togane runs through what he calls a "babble" of broken English rhymes before concluding by fulfilling the promise of his epigraph: "FUCKINOBASTARBILAADIFOOL!" (4).

Togane's collection is a study in colonial contact and its legacy is what W. E. B. Du Bois, in *The Souls of Black Folk*, has called double consciousness. Writing in English while living as a Somali immigrant in Quebec, Togane works across a huge range of cultural referents with speed and ease, positioning himself as a frustrated native "other" who is seen—and, crucially, *sees himself being seen*—through a Western and white imagination. It is worth including the collection's opening poem in its entirety:

You Can't Go Home Again

When I was born,
before my mother could suckle me,
I choked on the holy water of Zam-Zam well &
the creed of Islam was intoned into my ears.

I was Queequeg and Friday
before I encountered Stanley and Livingstone.
I bought the best their world peddled;
the Bible and the bottle.
Possessed with the spirits of both
I grew weary and cursed both.

Back to the ancestral cave and cannibalism;
back to the jungle and mumbo jumbo I'd fain go home. (1)

In just a dozen lines, Togane manages to invoke a host of religious, literary, and historical figures to articulate his subject position as one estranged from himself almost at birth—even "before," as he writes, "my mother could suckle me." The "I" of the poem chokes on both the "holy water" of Zam-Zam (the well within the Masjid al-Haram in Mecca) and, implicitly, on the various "spirits" that come from Christianity and alcohol. Queequeg and Friday, of course, are the subservient natives drawn in Melville's *Moby Dick* and Dafoe's *Robinson Crusoe*, respectively, and it is notable that he locates himself in their position *before* he meets the legendarily stoic and brutal British explorer Henry Morton Stanley (or the lost doctor he famously managed to find in Africa). "I was Queequeg and Friday," he writes, "*before* I encountered Stanley and Livingstone" (emphasis added). The implication, it seems, is that he was enamored with the literary accounts of the colonial project before the reality of it became clear. This reading is supported by the tragedy of the final lines, where the narrator desires to return home but can only articulate that "home" in the derogatory terms of the colonial imaginary—as "cave and cannibalism," as "jungle and mumbo jumbo."

A work of racialized, politicized Mennonite literature, the larger *Bottle and the Bushman* is a crass, subversive account of the consequences of colonialism and evangelism, and serves as a compelling rejoinder to the exoticizing missionary narratives offered especially by Goertzen and Lapp. Mennonites themselves, however, are mentioned directly only in passing. A "Mis Gehman" is identified as a "Mennonite missionary teacher" in the poem "Caliban" as quoted above (4) and is described in the next poem explaining the British legal system, weaving together the religious and colonial narratives of the work (5). The final time Mennonites are mentioned is in the poem titled "Exile 1." "Now it is / the seventh season of sorrow / since I ran away / from home / from my kingdom by the sea / from Somalia," it opens, closing by identifying the Mennonites as the ones to initiate this exile:

when a Mennonite missionary
driven
from his fat farm

in Markham, Ontario
by 'Go ye
therefore and preach the gospel
to every creature . . .'
hounded me
in the benighted bush
for Heaven. (30)

Togane mocks the Mennonite missionary project directly here, calling attention to the missionary's material wealth and—by following the scriptural directive to "preach the gospel / to every *creature*" with the verb *hounded*—emphasizing the paternalizing, even dehumanizing, assumptions that would lead someone to leave their "fat farm" to harass others "for Heaven." This critique of the Mennonite missionary project reverberates through the remainder of the collection as part of a larger colonial apparatus that estranges Togane—literally, linguistically, theologically, and emotionally—from his Somali roots but that also brings him to the United States and, ultimately, to Canada. If I suggested earlier that Yaguchi's poetry stands in stark tension to the "Russian Mennonite" writings of Janzen and Waltner-Toews within *Three Mennonite Poets*, something similar can be said about how the ribald language, the range of cultural referents, and the caustic critique of whiteness and colonialism in Togane's poetry similarly works to estrange the rest of the year's literary publications. Crucially, however, Togane is writing with one foot firmly *within* the community: among the earliest Islamic students to attend Eastern Mennonite University in Harrisonburg, Virginia, he now describes himself as a "Moslem-Mennonite or MoMennonite" (qtd. in Samatar "Scope"). That his project stands in such stark contrast to much of the year's publication tells us much about how the majority Russian and Swiss perspectives settles into a set of norms for the field, but the collection becomes recognizable of its larger moment when placed in a fuller account of the period—not only in offering, with Yaguchi, a critique of North-American Mennonite whiteness, but also the context of Black Mennonite thought, where it is complicated by Le Roy Bechler's insightful and conservative study, *The Black Mennonite Church in North America, 1886–1986*, published that same year.[25]

By way of closing this section of this already lengthy chapter, I would like to turn now to a short story written by Alfred Vogt. Vogt was born and raised in a Russian Mennonite village in Southern Manitoba before moving to Hollywood in the mid-1930s to become a founding figure of American science fiction under the name A. E. van Vogt. Van Vogt wrote nearly forty novels and a seemingly uncountable number of shorter works, and if their quality might charitably be described as uneven, his influence in the genre and the extent of his early popularity remains undeniable. He is best known as the author of the novel *Slan* and *The World of Null-A*, or as the author of the short story that inspired the popular film *Alien*. Although van Vogt's popularity has dimmed today, he was arguably the "most popular science fiction writer in the world" through the middle part of the twentieth century (Ellis 204), and he is routinely invoked alongside figures like Isaac Asimov as part of the "golden age" of science fiction.[26]

Van Vogt's final story, "Prologue to Freedom" (1986), was included in the premier issue of the temporarily revived sci-fi magazine, *Worlds of If*.[27] Described in the table of contents as a "novelette" written by "a master from the Golden Age of SF," van Vogt's story is a far cry from his best work, and most notable, perhaps, as a manifestation of the era's Cold War paranoia. The story's setting is the West Coast of the United States; the year, 2004. A gullible public has believed communist propaganda and passed "Proposition 8," splitting California in two. The southern half of the state has a capitalist government in Los Angeles, while the northern half has adopted a communist government based in San Francisco. In a fascinating and lengthy "prologue," van Vogt notes that Vietnam was his model for the state's division. Two of the story's main characters, Paul and Tim, are hopelessly naïve leftist students who helped to turn the northern half of California into a communist state before turning on each other as soon as they have gained a modicum of power. When the horrific consequences of their capitulation to communism start to reveal themselves, Paul's no-nonsense father, safe in the capitalist South, refuses to receive so much as a phone call from his wayward son. "Tell that S.O.B. to go to hell," he declares. "Although I paid for his way through college, hoping for the best, I haven't had a son since he got mixed up with the radical left in his sophomore year" (40). The work is further marred by a fawning portrait of what we would now call toxic masculinity: Sam Mebley's girlfriend, Stella, is described as a "chunky little woman" (35) who knows that getting Sam was doing "better-than-average for a face like hers" (36). Sam, however, is said to know better than to accept Stella's invitation to marry. His first wife had been a "sex maniac"—"Twice an evening was nothing," van Vogt tells us, and she would drag him into an empty room for workplace trysts during the day—right up until "the wedding bells ceased to toll," after which she immediately began developing the "not-tonight headaches" (48). Italicized quotations by everyone from Plato to John Calvin to Eleanor Roosevelt are dropped into the story without introduction or comment, efforts at profundity that are sharply out of place and succeed only in embarrassing the reader. The writing is stilted, the plot convoluted, and the rhetoric melodramatic. The story's abrupt conclusion, with a grim news report on the many problems of the new communist state, arrives as a small mercy.

"Prologue to Freedom" is far, far from van Vogt's best work, then, but it is notable for a number of reasons, including its role as an important precedence for one of the more surprising and significant new trends in the contemporary field, Mennonite speculative fiction. Indeed, van Vogt's work can be understood as the predecessor to the dozen or so sci-fi novels of Karl Schroeder, alongside the noted fantasy writings of Keith Miller, André Swartley, and Sofia Samatar (the latter of whom I discuss at some length in the final chapter of this study), as well as several others.[28] If the surge in speculative fiction by or about Mennonites is such that it has recently been the subject of a *Journal of Mennonite Writing* special issue featuring nine different authors in what the guest editor, Jeff Gundy, refers to as "something new in Mennonite writing" ("Introduction"), its Mennonite precursors are not limited to van Vogt.[29] In fact, some of the most interesting writing from 1986 is science fiction that was published outside the traditional publishing houses altogether (and thus not included in the extended bibliography numbers). Patricia Ann Stoll's PhD dissertation in creative writing at U of Illinois at Chicago, for example, *The Age of Fish*, is a collection of interrelated science fiction short stories. The first section of the collection, "Black Creek Township," is relatively conventional in that it tells the story of a child looking to move beyond the confines of her rural

Mennonite life. The next section is urban and graphic, full of "baby dreams" that involve corpses and sex, often at the same time. The final story, however, is its most interesting. "The Age of Fish" is a futuristic parable in which scientists looking for a middle ground between the "paradox" that women could not be forced to carry babies to term but also could not have an abortion figure out a way for fetuses to be kept in aquariums, breathing from their "gills" which never fully disappear after they grow up and join the rest of humanity on land. This alternative method quickly becomes the standard form of childbirth in North America (though the story's Amish, it should be noted, are among the few who refuse the new mode of childbirth). The thousands—and, then, quickly, the millions—of "fish," as they are called, are initially persecuted but then admired and copied; only later is their genetic propensity for violence and cannibalism realized with horror. When the government tries to make people go back to the "old" way of birth, 92 percent of the women go on strike and ultimately win rewards for live births, including the promise that the scientific community will begin to take seriously women's other concerns. "The next 40 years were truly the Age of Fish," Stoll writes; "the most tumultuous chapter in our nation's history" (201).

Brenda Weaver's *Nuclear Pie: 14 Fables for Our Time*, self-published this same year, is similarly compelling. Noting in her introduction that "the nuclear threat motivated me to write," many of the short works are science fiction cautionary tales, including "Apathy Kills," about Zang, the "captain of the Survey Ship Starluck" (15); "Rosalie Fletcher and the Child-Eaters of Gumurua," which echoes Stoll's focus on cannibalism; and so on. Though Weaver's book is neither as polished as Stoll's dissertation nor as influentially located as van Vogt's, it participates with them as a reminder not only of the absurdities of the Cold War era in which Mennonite literature has been said to have come of age, but also of a broader and weirder Mennonite literary imagination that was already hard at work in this period.

CONCLUSION

The length of this chapter is evidence enough, I trust, of the challenge that faces anyone looking to open the field of Mennonite literary studies to a broader history. And yet its goal has been relatively modest. The experiment I have undertaken has been to follow the implication of Moretti's arguments, including that one reason for the relative narrowness of Mennonite literary history has been the field's methodological investment in close reading. A cross-sectional reading focusing on work from 1986 estranges, or suspends, the teleological selectivity of conventional literary history, a history that succeeded in helping to establish the field as a minority literature invested in discourses of (white) ethnicity and isolation, but which relied on a developmental, anxiety-of-influence logic that obscured the wider activities of the field in this period. I am hopeful, then, that reviewing a broader range of work published in 1986 not only helps to reanimate texts lost in what Moretti would call the "slaughterhouse" of the field's past but also dislodges a number of the assumptions that may underpin the most conventional accounts of the field's past, including: the conceit that the field was entirely unformed prior to the "Mennonite miracle" of the mid-1980s; that its early work was uniformly earnest and strictly invested in forms of white ethnicity and realism; that it was dominated by Canadian poets; and that its religious foundations are unworthy of serious study. Returning to work by Yaguchi, Togane, and Manickam encourages us to think carefully about what constitutes the "Mennonite" in "Mennonite literature," and offers a genealogy of racialized Mennonite writing for contemporary authors such as Sally Ito, Samatar, Dominque Chew, and others; it also reminds us that concerns about the position of racialized minorities in the North American Mennonite church community active in this period were not uniformly absent from the emergent field of Mennonite literature. Similarly, the number of children's works and YA novels released by Mennonite publishing houses in 1986 should give us pause to explore the importance of genre fiction in the field and should encourage us to reconsider the target audience of Mennonite writing. Evangelical narratives such as those offered in the early reader Little Jewel series or the YA fiction of Doerksen, Vogt, Kauffmann, Boehr, and Boll, suggest something of the broader conceptual and publishing landscape of this formative period. And even that writing which reads as familiar to us from afar, writing that we might have expected from this period based upon our conventional narratives of the field—critiques of prairie life and dogmatic religion of the like that can be found in works like Braun's

A Stone Watermelon, Kauffman's *Collaborators*, Weier's *After the Revolution*, Poetker's *i sing for my dead in german*, and so on—should help us better appreciate the wider quality of writing from this period, much of which we have left underexplored and underappreciated.

In much the same way, a cross-sectional reading of 1986 helps us to broaden the history of the field by reminding us of the organizing and institutional work that had been established in Mennonite literature by this time. Pauls's novel from this year, *Agatchen*, was already the eleventh (*the eleventh*!) substantial book in a series from the Mennonite Literary Society (MLS), which had been established nearly a decade earlier with funds from the chair in Mennonite Studies at the University of Winnipeg—and which, by the end of 1986, had published 160 issues of the literary-minded journal *Mennonite Mirror*. In the opening prefatory pages of *Agatchen*, Roy Vogt, the MLS's long-serving president, and Harry Loewen, the UW's Chair in Mennonite Studies, expressed their hope that such works would be foundational for the new field. "As Mennonite writers continue to develop a Mennonite literary tradition," they write, "Mennonite scholars and translators [. . .] help strengthen it by reclaiming through translation the major works of the past that helped establish that tradition" (Vogt and Loewen). Suffice it to say that their hopes have yet to be realized by the scholarship that has followed, though I look to work in this vein in chapter 2 of this study, where I consider the series' opening volume at length. Similarly, Fred Redekop's *Cornucopia* and Sam Manickam's *Seeds and Seasons* were published by Pinchpenny Press, which was, by 1986, into its seventeenth season, already boasting a backlist of nearly *fifty* earlier works peppered with names that are now well recognized in the field. Mennonite and church-associated publishers accounted for twenty-eight of the additional thirty-five books I was able to add to the existing bibliographies, including church-associated publishers with international bases, including Herald Press (Scottdale [PA] and Kitchener [ON]) and Kindred Press (Hillsboro [KS] and Winnipeg [MB]). In other words, by 1986, well before the Mennonite/s Writing conferences began to formalize a critical discourse for the field, Mennonite literature already had a firm institutional basis in both Canada and the United States, with dedicated publishers and publishing ventures, well-organized literary societies, and thriving chapbook traditions. It would be worth our while to take these projects seriously as part of the field's expanded past.

Several of the works and concerns explored in this chapter are already returning to the critical conversation. *Three Mennonite Poets* remains a touchstone of sorts for scholars, regularly cited as an "important" book, though almost always in passing. Yaguchi and Janet Kauffman have both inspired critical interest, as well. Though Cruz is right to suggest that Yaguchi has largely "fallen off of the critical radar" (*Queering* 153), it is worth noting that one of the first issues of the recently established *Journal of Mennonite Writing* was dedicated to his work. Similarly, Togane's work has risen to some interest in Mennonite literary studies via a notable 2017 essay by Sofia Samatar (whose father, the well-known scholar Said Sheikh Samatar, is quoted by Togane in his collection [40]). Gundy's recent survey of Mennonite science fiction is promising, as well; Valarie Weaver-Zercher's book exploring the phenomenon of Amish romance novels is groundbreaking. Individual critical essays, too, have attended to a broader array of authors and texts than our selective literary histories tend to acknowledge. However, in the iterative world of literary studies—where the canon, and much of a text's critical significance, is established by the number of scholars who engage it—individual efforts to expand the field are, nearly by definition, rarely enough. Cruz makes a convincing case that a surprisingly broad number of authors have been represented in the published critical work that has emerged from the Mennonite/s Writing conferences, and I am hopeful he is right in concluding that "the Mennonite literary canon is more fluid and its boundaries are less rigid than many other canons within literary studies" ("Bibliography" 96).

The point, again, is not to claim that the narrowness of the field's conventional literary history has gone unchallenged but rather to suggest that keeping this past open may require a different version of literary history than we have been relying upon thus far. Understood as a *minor literature* with a substantial but manageable bibliography that can be understood not solely as an expression of an ethnic community or two but as a means of reading literary engagements with or about Mennonites more broadly, the field may be better served by a form of bibliographic or encyclopedic history that opens, rather than narrows, its past—without giving up on close readings altogether. Indeed, while I have drawn on Moretti's articulation of the problematics of conventional literary history, I noted earlier that his method and conclusions are somewhat determined by the very canonical logic that his project sets out to critique. My project here, then, also follows the argument of Françoise Lionnet and Shu-mei Shih in their articulation of minor transnationalisms—namely, that minor fields of study must take seriously the specificities of their own histories not only in content but also in focus and method.

My hope is that this chapter has helped to demonstrate that understanding the field as a minor literature can estrange the operative identity-based assumptions that kept the bibliography problematically narrow in the past, obscuring a range of genres and works that remind us that the field has a broader and deeper past than its conventional, developmental literary history would suggest. Though I am far from the first to make this point—I began with Kasdorf's call for new histories, but as early as 1998 Roth and Beck were admonishing that scholars in the still-emerging field were ignoring "Mennonite literature prior to the 1960s" and the "'popular' literature of earlier Mennonite culture" (vii)—my argument here is that we need to think of history itself differently if we hope for such calls to be effective. At the same time, however, I hope this chapter has also shown that a minor literature frame need not—indeed, *should not*—stop us from continuing to engage identity-based concerns when the writing itself insists upon it. I take up this challenge more fully in several of the next chapters, following Stuart Hall's suggestion to engage identities not as a natural phenomenon but as "produced in specific historical and institutional sites within specific discursive formations and practices, by specific enunciative strategies" (2).

In the next chapter, I want to dig deeper into several of the concerns that I have raised in this opening methodological experiment. If a cross-sectional reading of dozens of texts published in 1986 offers a historical approach that reveals a range of genres, texts, and concerns that have been neglected as part of the Mennonite miracle narrative of the field's emergence, what happens if we slow down to take a close, archival examination of the various versions of a key book from an even earlier period? Was the establishment of Mennonite literature as a form of minority ethnic expression really the unique accomplishment of the "miracle" stage of the field's development, or can we find evidence for this project in earlier generations of writers and critics? What other forms and genres were central to this understanding of the field but have been obscured by later field's investment in "serious" literature? What might we find, that is, in a close reading of a short diary with a publication history that crosses not only genres but also decades, languages, communities, and even continents?

CHAPTER 2

A RUSSIAN DANCE OF DEATH

Mennonite Diaries and the Use of Truthfulness

In 1975, the newly formed Mennonite Literary Society (MLS) was organizing a partnership with the University of Winnipeg to bring out a most curious choice of inaugural projects: a heavily annotated translation of a Russian diary that had been published in Germany in 1921. Under its earlier iteration as "Brock Publishing," the MLS had been publishing the *Mennonite Mirror*, a magazine dedicated to fostering a nascent Mennonite literary arts community, for several years; the diary was to be its first major publication. It was the MLS's fervent hope that the diary, announced as the first of a coming series of publications, would "be of interest to general readers, history classes both in high school and undergraduate university years, and Mennonites who wish to expand the knowledge about and preserve the cultural heritage of the Mennonite people" (Vogt and Duckworth). These hopes clearly reflected the Canadian federal government's sudden interest in funding what it described as the "cultural contributions of the other ethnic groups" in a Royal Commission that explicitly positioned the Mennonites as one of the many ethnic groups it hoped to support.[1] The MLS's initial request for federal funding to support the project was flatly rejected by the Department of the Secretary of State, however, on the apparently reasonable grounds that books "must have Canadian content" to be eligible.[2] Undaunted, the MLS pressed on. Unaware that the original diary—thought to have been composed in

French but originally published in German—had already been published in English translation in California in 1930, they were hard at work translating an English edition directly from the early German edition. In 1977, the Mennonite Literary Society celebrated the publication of its first book: Al Reimer's translation of Dietrich Neufeld's diary of the collapse of the Mennonite colonies in present-day Ukraine. The diary, previously published in Germany as *Ein Tagebuch aus dem Reiche des Totentanzes* (1921), was renamed "Under the Black Flag of Anarchy"; the full book, which also included two of Neufeld's later autobiographical works and substantial contextualizing material, was entitled *Dietrich Neufeld's A Russian Dance of Death: Revolution and Civil War in the Ukraine.*[3] The book came with a note of thanks to the "Multiculture Program" [*sic*] of Canada for its generous support and promptly sold out.

In chapter 1, I undertook a methodological experiment that attempted a cross-sectional reading of every book of Mennonite literature published in 1986 in order to refresh our appreciation for the range of literary work being published by and about Mennonites at a key period in the field's emergence. In this chapter, I want to undertake a corollary experiment in what we might call longitudinal reading, pushing deeper into the field's past by tracing the complicated publication history of a single text across a full century, four countries, three languages, and an ocean. As a Russian Mennonite account of the collapse of the Mennonite colonies of what is now Ukraine, *Russian Dance of Death* is immediately recognizable in the logic of the early field—which, as I have documented elsewhere, has returned time and again not only to this particular group of Mennonites but also to this particular story.[4] My goal here, in part, is to demonstrate something of the expansive transnational roots of early Mennonite writing, but also to put some critical pressure on the way that early critics of this period worked to position the field as a form of ethnic expression. I have suggested that critics working in the Mennonite "miracle" stage of the field's development of the late 1980s and early 1990s were using the language and logic of minority literary studies to establish Mennonite literature as a field of study, but the story behind the MLS and the publication of Neufeld's diary shows this logic was animating an earlier generation of scholars already in the 1970s.

I also want to take Neufeld's *Tagebuch* as an opportunity to consider the role of life writing in Mennonite literature in general, and the form and function of diaries as a literary genre in particular. Drawing on the broader reassessment of life writing within literary studies over the past two decades to explore how diaries function within the logic of minority writing, I argue that reading for edits across versions of a single diary can reveal something of the complexity of both the texts themselves and the literary traditions in which they circulate. What might have led the newly formed Mennonite Literary Society to select this particular diary as its inaugural project? How does the perceived authenticity of a diary function within the discourses of an emergent literary tradition, and what happens when a single diary is published and republished, edited, excerpted, and liberally translated across different contexts? How might we position the particular type of truth claims made by the diary as a genre specifically within the emergence of Mennonite literary studies, which, until recently, has largely ignored personal narratives—even as questions of autoethnography and "truth-telling" were of central concern to its early critics?

MENNONITE LIFE WRITING AND THE AUTOBIOGRAPHICAL PACT

Among the various reasons why the diary has been arguably the "most overlooked and devalued form of writing in the fields of literary studies and history" (Rak, "Dialogue" 16) is the challenge of definition. What, precisely, constitutes a diary? Robert Fothergill's appeal for readers to "be agreed that a diary is what a person writes when he says, 'I am writing a diary'" (3) is straightforward but not particularly useful, except in the manner in which he intends it: to demonstrate the definitional slipperiness and correspondingly wide range of examples of the diary as a genre. Those scholars who have aimed for more precision have tended to emphasize the private (and thus ostensibly open, or honest) nature of the form, as well as its spontaneous nature, taking the convention of dating the daily entries as evidence of their immediacy. Sidonie Smith and Julia Watson's concise definition, for example, suggests the diary is "a form of periodic life writing" that "records dailiness" (*Guide* 266), while Elizabeth Podnieks argues not only that a diary "must be written with no consideration of an audience beyond the writer herself," but also that, "by virtue of being defined as a daybook [. . .] it must be spontaneous" (*Daily* 18).

These same attributes are often taken by readers to suggest that diaries offer a relatively unmediated form of access not only to the thoughts of the author but also to the events they record. In his study *Using Diaries for Social Research*, for example, Andy Alaszewski defines the diary as a "document created by an individual who has maintained a regular, personal and contemporaneous record," and lists its defining features as it being *regular*, *personal*, and a *record of contemporaneous* events—adding that the "entries are made at the time or close enough to the time when events or activities occurred so that *the record is not distorted by problems of recall*" (emphasis added). As Liz Stanley and Helen Dampier argue, the diary is "often thought of—by readers, if not now by most theorists—around assumptions about the temporal and spatial status circumstances of its writing" (25). The "facticity and 'present-ness' of time in a diary are seen to be guaranteed," they suggest, so that they are "treated as relatively free of retrospection and thus as more referential than other forms of life writing" (28). I take from Stanley and Dampier the caution that contemporary life writing theory is deeply skeptical of any diary's claims to immediacy or transparency, but also—crucially—their recognition that diaries often circulate among general readers as a privileged form of referential writing.

It is the way that the diary is "thought of" that is the focus of the genre's most influential theorist, Philippe Lejeune, who insists autobiographical writing in general is "a mode of reading as much as it is a type of writing" ("Pact" 30). Indeed, what distinguishes autobiographical texts, for Lejeune, is primarily the promise they make to the reader of their own veracity. The "autobiographical pact," he suggests, is inherent in all life writing but strongest in diaries, whereby an implicit contract exists between the reader and the author, "guaranteed" by the publisher, attesting to the referential truth of the text. This is why, for Lejeune, the defining feature of a "real" diary is not its privacy nor its immediacy—elements that are routinely imitated in fictional diaries for literary effect[5]—but rather the name on the book's title page, which promises the reader that the book's author, its narrator, and its protagonist are all one and the same. "In printed texts, responsibility for all enunciation is assumed by a person who is in the habit of placing his *name* on the cover of the book," Lejeune writes; this name is the "only mark in the text of an unquestionable world-beyond-the-text, referring to a real person" ("Pact" 11). Even as readers will recognize that diaries must provide deeply personal and thus subjective accounts of the world they describe, the autobiographical pact extends an implicit promise that the author is not intentionally lying and has not returned to edit or revise the account. What is thus most notable about diaries, for Lejeune, is the "type of reading it engenders [and] the *credence it exudes*" (emphasis added; "Pact" 30). This insight is central to my argument in this chapter, and is anticipated by E. F. Dyck's insistence that, in the context of Mennonite literature, "plain-ness is a style as much as is glamour: though the two are different styles, they are incontrovertibly both styles" (44). As we will see, both styles are at play—and often in conflict—in the various editions of the Neufeld diary.

Although literary scholars have been reluctant to invest their efforts in early Mennonite life writing, its ability to exude credence and invite a direct form of reading are strong reasons to rethink its position in the emergence of the field. As Julia Watson notes, drawing on the influential work of John Eakin, "Autobiographical and biographical projects share what he calls 'referentiality,' that is, they refer to an externally existent world, unlike fiction, where the reference is of verisimilitude to a possible world" (Herbe 10). It is life writing's "referentiality"—that is, its ostensible link to the "real" world—that would seem to make it a natural fit for a community that was long skeptical of flights of imaginative fancy and believed it was their biblical duty to let their *yea be yea* and their *no be no*. As Hildi Froese Tiessen suggests in the introduction to a 1989 anthology of Mennonite writing, the emergence of literary writing among the Mennonites of North America was notable in large part because of the community's historical belief that "the play of the imagination was frivolous and worldy; at worst, it was an expression of the cardinal sin of pride" (*Liars* xiii). In naming the anthology *Liars and Rascals: Mennonite Short Stories* to register the illicit status of fiction authors in the community, Froese Tiessen cites the early novelist J. H. Janzen's recollection in 1946 of a bishop admonishing him for his choice of vocations. "He [. . .] tried to make plain to me that 'novelists were fiction writers and that fiction was a lie" Janzen recalls. "I surely would not want to represent myself to him as a professional liar" (22).[6] Froese Tiessen suggests that this attitude "remained to a large degree unchanged until the 1960s and beyond" (*Liars* xii). Subsequent critics have occasionally looked to recuperate such logic into aesthetic critiques of style: in 1990, for example, E. F. Dyck's essay "The Rhetoric of Plain Style in Mennonite Writing" suggests that the "ethnicity that is called Mennonite is figured by a paradox called *plain style*," which "pretends it is the figureless figure of truth" (37). It was, he insists, a "continuing paradox in Mennonite attitudes to literature: the wiles of the devil 'rhetoric' may be used for the glory of the god 'truth'—but for nothing else" (36). Dyck's language makes clear how thoroughly religious discourse and (Russian Mennonite) ethnic concerns were understood to blur together in this early analysis, even where it was the subject of critique. In art, he concludes, the problem is not "plain style itself" but "rather the insistence that the plain style is not a style at all but a moral imperative" (42). As Redekop suggests in the context of a related argument, the Mennonites are a "group that for centuries has polished its image in the mirror as an example of plain style and literalism" (*Making Believe* 72).

Unsurprisingly, then, the twinned promises of access and authenticity were potent in the context of emerging literatures such as Mennonite writing, which were being fostered as direct expressions of distinct ethnic communities. This was central to the logic of the MLS's selection of Neufeld's diary as the first in a "projected series of such translations of Mennonite literature and history" as announced in that first volume (Vogt and Duckworth), and it remained the dominant logic for the duration of the series.[7] Part of my argument in this chapter is that the neglect of diaries and related autobiographical forms of writing is particularly notable in hindsight: not only within the Mennonite context, where we have noted it would seem a suitably "plain" or referential form, but also within the larger study of minority (i.e., ethnic) literary traditions, where it would seem to respond almost directly to what Yoonmee Chang has usefully called the "ethnographic imperative" under which racialized authors have long labored, the often "explicit directives and implicit pressures to create superficially informative and exoticized 'insider's views'" that result in a "body of literature that serves as a simplistic 'tell-all' ethnography" (7).[8] In a parallel argument that recalls our previous caution about literary history's narratives of development, Werner Sollors has suggested that the "historical unfolding of ethnic writing" is commonly understood as a "process of growth," in which literature "'grows' from nonfictional to fictional forms," and, with it, "from 'parochial' marginality to 'universal' significance in the literary mainstream" (241). It was precisely this type of "growth" that was being imagined by many early advocates for Mennonite literary production in Manitoba. The editors of *Harvest: Anthology of Mennonite Writing in Canada, 1874–1974*, for example—the first collection of Mennonite literature, published in Winnipeg in 1974—openly conceded they had adopted editorial strategies that would enable them to engage in writing less for its literary accomplishment and more "for the sake of their authenticity in capturing the Mennonite experience" (G. K. Epp vii). The archive shows the newly formed Mennonite Literary Society advocating for the field in similar terms: in one letter Roy Vogt responds to the "Ethnic Press Analysis" undertaken by the Citizenship branch of the Secretary of State on behalf of the MLS to express his bewilderment on "why it would not be listed among the ethnic publications"[9]; in another, Al Reimer defends the MLS's engagement with a short-lived and controversial Mennonite pavilion at the Winnipeg Folklorama Festival (1980–83), by insisting the community was "fighting for ethnic survival." "Anything that helps to delay our ethnic demise," he insisted, "is to be welcomed" (qtd. in Smucker 22).[10]

There is a rich set of fascinating personal narratives in Mennonite studies that are ripe for critical consideration. Although a comparative analysis of such work is clearly well beyond the scope of this chapter, I should note that these works range from obscure diaries and biographic accounts of local figures to highly polished memoirs by some of the field's most prominent authors. Examples of the former would include much of the life writing in the Hyperion series, along with texts like Gerhard Lohrenz's memoir *Storm Tossed* (published by The Christian Press in 1976) and Peter J. Dyck's diary, *Troubles and Triumphs* (self-published in 1981), while a range of nonpublished life writing can be found in places like the

Mennonite Archives of Ontario, home to diaries by Laura Shantz, Isadore Snyder, Ephraim Cressmen, and others.[11] Examples of the field's more prominent life writing are by definition better known but would include Miriam Toews's fascinating first-person biography of her father, *Swing Low: A Life* (2000); Rudy Wiebe's award-winning *Of This Earth: A Mennonite Boyhood in the Boreal Forest* (2007); Rhoda Janzen's bestselling *Mennonite in a Little Black Dress: A Memoir of Going Home* (2010); and John Ruth's *Branch: A Memoir with Pictures* (2013); as well as a personal favorite of mine, Maurice Mierau's lively *Detachment: An Adoption Memoir* (2014).

Before moving on to the Neufeld diary, I would like to pause briefly over another diary especially relevant in the context of my argument. At the same time that the Mennonite Literary Society was working at publishing Neufeld's *Russian Dance of Death*, the Mennonite Historical Society (MHS) of Canada was busy on a life writing project of its own, which was published in 1985 as *The Diary of Anna Baerg: 1916–1924*. Like Neufeld, Baerg lived through the violent collapse of the Russian Mennonite colonies following the Russian Revolution; like Neufeld, she was a highly literate figure, and an astute observer of the political and religious concerns of the period. As a woman in a patriarchal society who also suffered from a physical disability, however, Baerg did not have the education or opportunities that would be afforded to Neufeld. Notably, much of her enormous diary was written on scrap paper, including the backs of milk carton labels from MCC relief packages that she stitched together by hand into small booklets that can still be found in the archives.[12] The diary's many pages were discovered in an attic in Saskatchewan following her death in 1972, and—like Neufeld's diary—were excerpted in translation for the journal *Mennonite Life*. The full diary was translated from its original gothic German to nearly six hundred single-spaced pages of modern German script by Clara K. Dyck, before being excerpted and translated into English by Gerald Peters for the final MHS edition.

The fact that both the Mennonite Literary Society and the Mennonite Historical Society were focused on diaries in this period reflects the way that diaries often blur the thin line between literary and historical notions of textual value. But where this type of life writing continues to be of interest as complex primary sources for scholars of Mennonite history,[13] it has been largely ignored by Mennonite literary critics. The Baerg journal is a notable exception.[14] Ann Hostetler, for example, makes a convincing case that the diary is among the source documents for Sandra Birdsell's well-known novel, *The Russländer*,[15] while Magdalene Redekop and Pamela Klassen discuss the gender politics of its publication: Redekop takes note of the editorial introduction's claim to be telling Baerg's story in a "balanced [. . .] fashion" and wonders just "who is doing the depicting or balancing here"? ("Pickling" 112), while Klassen suggests that what she sees as a surprising lack of extended introspection in *The Diary of Anna Baerg* may reflect a gendered editorial decision to "delete personal references in favour of more 'important' events" (438). Indeed, the full Baerg diary includes entries from 1916–1959, and the MHS's decision to excise the final thirty-five years of the diary makes clear that the editors prioritized the dramatic accounts of the Russian Revolution in her account. Notably, internal minutes from the Mennonite Historical Society show Peters, the editor, explaining that he has "tried not to make Anna into a heroine," while board members encourage him to make "translation of the diary into a more literary document" (2).[16] These types of editorial interventions stand in rather stark contrast to the approach taken in the historian Royden Loewen's recent selection of early diaries in *From the Inside Out: The Rural Worlds of Mennonite Diarists, 1863 to 1929*, where diaries are treated as a form of primary evidence. Where the MHS was keen to render the Baerg diary "more literary," Loewen assures readers he has "reproduced the selections in their entirety, including repetitious detail," as well as "all the spelling and grammatical errors, inconsistencies and factual errors" (x).

These types of editorial decisions will be at the heart of my analysis in this chapter. Loewen's evaluation of the "errors" and "inconsistencies" as central to a diary's value reflects his work as a historian, and it lies in rather stark contrast with most published diaries, the majority of which are carefully revised, edited, and polished in an effort to make them more readable. Indeed, many of the best-known diaries have been subject to extensive editorializing—both Samuel Pepys and Anne Frank rewrote their diaries with the intention to publish later, for example[17]—without losing their sense of immediacy or authenticity for their more general readerships. At times, journals have been so heavily revised, edited, and polished for publication that it is difficult to speak of an original text, resulting in what Stanley and Dampier describe as a "simulacrum diary," while Roland Barthes has argued that *all* daily journals are "inauthentic" in this sense, "doomed to be a simulation" because every diarist is aware of themselves as writing a diary, and this self-awareness will always be inscribed in their work (493). As we will see, these types of questions and editorial choices—not only those interventions by subsequent editors and publishers but also the author's own revisions that can be traced across publications, translations, and decades—can be read as their own form of literary history.

To date, Mennonite literary studies has largely kept its collective focus on poetry and fiction—on capital "L" literature, as it were—though there are signs that this may be changing. Reviewing the 2015 *After Identity* collection for the *Journal of Mennonite Writing*, Jan Schroeder noted it was "obvious that by 'writing,' most of the contributors mean 'literary writing,'" and suggested a wider consideration of "who is included and excluded by the word 'literature'" is needed in the field ("Who's a Mennonite?" 2017)—an invitation echoed in *Making Believe*, where Redekop suggests that the "body of autobiographical writing by Mennonites calls out for serious scholarly attention" (193). There is reason to believe that such calls are starting to be answered. The eighth Mennonite/s Writing conference at the University of Winnipeg in 2017, for example, took as its theme *Personal Narratives of Place and Displacement*, looking to recognize both the value of, and the relative absence of work on, personal narratives in the field to date. In the opening essay of the subsequent special issue, Froese Tiessen noted "life-writing—as life-writing—among Mennonite authors has received until now only scant critical attention" ("I Didn't" 30).[18] More recently still, a 2018 issue of the *Journal of Mennonite Writing* focuses on what it calls "documentary literature," guest editor Julia Spicher Kasdorf suggesting that "documentary material have had a constitutive and abiding influence on Anabaptist thought—as well as Mennonite fiction, creative non-fiction, and poetry" ("Documentary"). There remain definitional challenges in determining what types of writing and venues will be included as *literary* in such discussions, but it is clear that a reconsideration of what constitutes the "writing" in "Mennonite writing" has begun.

This chapter looks to participate in this larger reconsideration by taking the numerous translations and publications of Neufeld's diary as a case study demonstrating the importance of life writing to the early field. Given the complexity of the simulacrum effect that will inevitably shape autobiographical life writing, careful critical readers must, as Smith and Watson insist, seek to "engage the narrative tropes, sociocultural contexts, rhetorical aims, and narrative shifts within the historical or chronological trajectory of the text" (*Guide* 13). There is, then, a crucial distinction to draw between the conventions that govern the impact and circulation of diaries as implicitly "authentic" accounts of their subjects and the conditions under which they are written and prepared for publication. With Lejeune and alongside Stanley and Dampier, my interest in this chapter is not to define the diary as a genre but rather to explore what we might call the *diary effect*, reading Neufeld's diary not for its (admittedly substantial) historical interest per se but rather for how the strong sense of historical immediacy produced by the diary as a form—how the perceived referentiality extended by the implicit autobiographical pact—is being marshaled and employed by its author and editors to literary effect in different contexts. A close reading of the diary in its various forms shows just how hard Neufeld and the Mennonite Literary Society worked to direct that effect to their desired ends, with important lessons to teach us about the relationship between historical and literary writing. But first, we must begin with the rather dizzying history of the diary itself, which traveled across continents, oceans, and languages before arriving as Mennonite Literary Society's inaugural publication.

TRACKING DIETRICH NEUFELD'S *RUSSIAN DANCE OF DEATH*

The much-traveled Neufeld diary recounts the chaos in the former Mennonite colonies of south Russia (now Ukraine) as they collapse in the aftermath of the Russian Revolution. At their height, the Mennonite colonies of Russia had a population well over one hundred thousand people and were prosperous and autonomous enough that scholars sometimes refer to them as the "Mennonite Commonwealth."[19] It was not unusual for the children of wealthy Mennonite entrepreneurs in this period to leave the colonies for secular postsecondary education abroad, and Neufeld was in Switzerland studying ancient and modern languages when the First World War broke out. He spent much of the war as a "civilian internee" in a small town in Bavaria after being identified as an "enemy alien,"[20] returning to the Mennonite colony of Khortitza in the difficult winter of 1917 just as fighting between various factions of the Russian military, Ukrainian separatists, and anarchists began to sweep through the area. Caught up in the larger violence of the postrevolutionary years in Russia, the network of colonies shattered, launching a desperate mass migration of some twenty-five thousand Mennonites—nearly a quarter of the colonies' population—to North America. Neufeld documented the chaos and fled for Germany in 1920, where he finished his PhD before migrating to Canada. After a brief stint in rural Manitoba, he moved to the United States, teaching at a number of colleges in Ohio and New Mexico before finishing his academic career at Pepperdine College in California.

The dramatic history of which Neufeld was a part has long been a focus for Mennonite writing and scholarship, with historians, authors, and literary critics swinging between hagiographic celebrations and damning critiques of the "Russian experience" and its legacy in the North American Mennonite community.[21] As I recount at some length in my earlier work, many of the early Russian Mennonite scholars working to establish the nascent literary community in Winnipeg saw the trauma of the Russian experience as effecting the "birth" of a Mennonite literary imagination in North America—including Al Reimer, translator and editor of the MLS's edition of the Neufeld diary.[22] Little wonder that they saw Neufeld's account, an eyewitness account to period written in a dramatic and self-consciously literary prose, as an appropriate "first book" for their series. According to the account given within the diary itself, Neufeld wrote the original text in the midst of the action it records, mostly in French, so that it could not be read should it be found by the anarchists (38).[23] Neufeld emphasizes the contemporaneous nature of the writing throughout the work, repeatedly expressing his near despair and uncertainty as to what might come next. "They're here!" begins an early entry, announcing the arrival of the dreaded anarchists (12); "Now they are coming!" concludes another. "Away with my notebook . . ." (25).

As a published diary, however, *Russian Dance of Death* is notable not only for the particular vantage it offers of the past it records but also for its circuitous publication history. The entries of the brief diary begin in September of 1919, when its author had just turned thirty-four, and run roughly six months through to March 1920. Neufeld must have set about translating it almost immediately upon returning to Europe in the fall of 1920, as he self-published it as a thin German booklet entitled *Ein Tagebuch aus dem Reiche des Totentanzes* by late summer, 1921. It appears there was some interest in this initial publication and that it circulated widely: before emigrating to North America two years later, he would self-publish at least two additional autobiographical German-language booklets, one of which opens with a page of favorable reviews of the 1921 diary from Germany, the Netherlands, and the United States.[24] An unused introduction for the later first English edition of the diary—a copy of which can be found in the Reimer archives signed as "Dmitri Novopolye," one of Neufeld's pseudonyms[25]—notes it was first "published in Germany and was translated into Sweedish [*sic.*]" and goes on to suggest that the response he received from "Germany, Holland, Sweden, South America have greatly encouraged me in presenting it to the English reading public" ("Introduction").[26] Later that decade in California, Neufeld would translate his German diary into English and circulate the manuscript widely in search of a publisher; the archive includes a number of letters from prominent readers expressing their surprise—and at times, their delight—at receiving early copies of the diary, as well as a list of well over a hundred people to whom the book was sent.[27] Among the most notable responses in the archive are letters of thanks and even offers to help place the diary from the Pulitzer Prize winners Willa Cather and Zona Gale, as well as some gentle editing advice from Hartley Burr Alexander, past president of the American Philosophical Association.[28] It was ultimately published as *Russian Dance of Death* in 1930 with what looks to be Neufeld's own publishing venture, "Key Books Publishers," under the pseudonym of Dick Gora.[29] Relatively little came of this second edition, however, and the Key Books Publishers venture was abandoned.

After Neufeld passed away in 1958, his diary was posthumously published at least twice. In 1969, fifteen condensed selections from the diary were published over four full pages in the American periodical *Mennonite Life* with the title "On the Banks of the Dnieper." Neufeld had legally changed his name after receiving citizenship in the United States in 1930, and the 1969 selections were accordingly attributed to him under his new name of Dedrich Navall. The *Mennonite Life* excerpts were followed by a warm biographical account of the author written by Lotte Navall, Neufeld's wife. When the Canadian editors at the newly formed Mennonite Literary Society set out to publish the diary as their inaugural book project in the 1970s, however, they were unaware of the 1930 edition in English, and they began translating the work from the first German edition. Reimer was alerted to Neufeld's own English translation midway through the project but evidently preferred his own translation, taking the earlier English translation under consideration as he carried on.[30] In his introduction to the 1977 edition, Reimer describes the diary's complicated translation issues as follows: "To complicate matters, the author originally wrote most of his journal in French, so that both the German and the English editions are to a large extent translations of the original French text. Consequently, they differ from each other somewhat in places. I have carefully compared the author's English translation with my own and have not hesitated to add small details from it which are not contained in the German text" (xi). I follow Reimer in comparing the translations of the diary shortly, where I will return to explore his admitted lack of editorial hesitation in some detail. For now I will simply note that in the final MLS edition, the diary was retitled "Under the Black Flag of Anarchy" and presented as the first of three of Neufeld's autobiographical writings from the period, all collected under the title *Dietrich Neufeld's A Russian Dance of Death: Revolution and Civil War in the Ukraine*.[31] This time the diary found both a publisher and an audience: after selling out of several printing runs by Hyperion Press in Winnipeg, it was picked up by Herald Press of Scottdale (PA) for an American edition in 1980, which sold out as well. In 1988, in response to what the later book jacket describes as "overwhelming demand," the book was reprinted a final time in both Winnipeg and Scottdale.

To review, then: it appears there are five full versions of Neufeld's diary in four languages, three of which have been published in four different countries over nearly eight decades: the original diary, handwritten in French and lost to history, as well as later published translations in German (Emden, 1921, extant), Swedish (Huddinge[?], 1922[?]), and twice in English (California, 1930, and Winnipeg, 1977, both extant). Additional publications include excerpts of the 1930 translation in a 1969 issue of *Mennonite Life* and two reprints of the 1977 translation by Hyperion and Herald Press (1980, 1988). The diary has been published under at least three (and possibly four) author names, two of which are pseudonyms, and in English alone it has been presented under three different titles. This is a diary, clearly, that has been of interest and use to a wide range of readers in a host of very different of times, places, and contexts. Even without the original French and rumored Swedish versions available for consultation, the numerous versions of the Neufeld diary present a wonderful opportunity to practice a different form of literary history. What might we learn about the Neufeld diary—and, by extension, about its various audiences, and about the establishment of a Mennonite literary tradition in North America—by tracing the editorial decisions that have informed the circulation of this most transnational of texts?

"IT IS NO FICTION, WHAT I HAVE WRITTEN": THE NEUFELD DIARY AS HISTORY

I began this chapter by suggesting it was notable that the Mennonite Literary Society chose a diary for its inaugural publication in 1977, and by arguing this choice reflected not only a Mennonite preference for clearly referential writing but also what Chang describes as the "ethnographic imperative" placed upon emergent minority literatures in this period (7). The fact that the Mennonite Historical Society of Canada was also hard at work on life writing projects in this period would suggest that the perceived referentiality of the diary—that is, its status as a historicizing document for part of the larger Russian Mennonite community in Canada—was central to its value. Given my interest specifically in the function of the book's genre, however, it is worth noting that both Neufeld and Reimer drop the term "diary" from the title of their English editions, leaving the German equivalent *Tagebuch* out altogether.[32] The German title, *Ein Tagebuch aus dem Reiche des Totentanzes*—literally, "a day-book from the Realm of the Dance of Death"—becomes simply *Russian Dance of Death* for the 1930 edition, and *Dietrich Neufeld's A Russian Dance of Death: Revolution and Civil War in the Ukraine* on the cover of the 1977 edition, and "Under the Black Flag of Anarchy" within it. Presented without the generic descriptor even in its subtitle, Neufeld's text is not immediately recognizable as a diary and could appear, from its various covers, to be a work of fiction. Although Neufeld repeatedly describes the work as a "diary" in the introduction to his English edition, Reimer resists using the term himself, describing his translation as a "book" (1), a "story" (5), an "account" (5)—or, most often, a "journal" (xii, 3, 4). These discrepancies may be indicative of the definitional difficulties that surround life writing narratives more generally, but they also, as we will see, appear to reflect a tension between historical and literary perspectives on the book.

Let us begin with a consideration of the diary as a historical document. Each of the four English publications of Neufeld's diary include introductory materials that are clearly meant to affirm an autobiographical pact between the diary's author and its audience, working to assure readers that the text is an accurate representation of the historical events it presents. In its 1921 German edition, for example, published in the midst of the unfolding crisis, the immediacy and perceived accuracy of the account is leveraged in a call for sympathy and aid for Mennonites still remaining in Russia. Neufeld begins his foreword with an eight-line rhymed epigraph that presents the larger book as the *cri de coeur*. "The world, she must hear!" he writes. "The suffering of our souls is desperate; Our cry must bring forth a solution!" (3).[33] After several pages of historical context for the diary that emphasizes the Mennonites' suffering at the hands of the notorious Ukrainian anarchist Nester Makhno, he closes his foreword with an echo of his earlier plea for help: "The tragic fate of the innocent Mennonites under Machno's three-month rule in the Chortitza area is unimaginable for a Western European. "'May the cry of this diary awaken the compassion of the Western Europeans in the sense that they feel at one with the people down there, both with those who are suering and those who are lost, in order to be with them, and with them, to be ashamed; because humanity is a whole, and each part is jointly responsible for the whole'" (4).[34] Writing in 1921, Neufeld offers the diary as an eyewitness account to an ongoing tragedy with the hope not only of informing the "Western European" audience of the Mennonites' fate but of shaming them into recognizing a responsibility to intervene.

The goal of the later translations and republications is less immediate by definition, it would seem, but—as we might expect—they continue to emphasize the immediacy and referentiality of the diary, and thus the historical value of the work. Neufeld introduces the 1930 edition, for example, with the insistence that "this diary has been written during those fateful days and months when the tragic fratricide, or call it civil war, was at its climax in Southern Russia" (1), before offering a brief hagiographic history of the Mennonites in Russia and their experiences in the postrevolution anarchy. In the unpublished introduction to this first English edition, he is even more adamant in his assertion of its historical accuracy. "It is no fiction, what I have written in this book," he begins. "It is a true story—'A first hand, historical source,' it has been called by European critics."[35] The brief editorial comments on the 1969 publication of the diary in *Mennonite Life* echo these claims, noting the passages have been excerpted from "an extremely exciting and vivid diary" that recounts "the arrival of the Makhno bandits who plundered the villages and killed the population" (161).

The paratextual materials of the MLS's 1977 edition of the diary, however, are the most substantial and the most interesting to me here. In his 1976 request for funding from the Canadian Secretary of State for Multiculturalism, MLS president Roy Vogt insists that "a real need exists for young Canadian readers of Mennonite origin to obtain these materials," describing the diary as a "first hand account of tragic incidences in the recent history of the Mennonites which would greatly interest the younger generation" (1). Reimer's introduction reiterates Vogt's argument. "The events and experiences described in this book belong to one of the most violent and chaotic periods in modern world history" (1), he begins, moving directly into a lengthy historical account of the Mennonite colonies of Russia and the events that led to their collapse. In fact, it takes Reimer several pages of introductory comments to get to the author of the book itself, finally introducing Neufeld as a "man of unusual courage and foresight" who "kept a secret journal under [. . .] perilous and trying circumstances" (4). Unsurprisingly, perhaps, the history offered by Reimer's introduction reads largely as hagiography—Mennonites are "devout, hardworking, and self-sufficient colonists" (1), the violence that befell them is "among the most terrible ever suffered by a helpless people" (3), and so on—as he positions Neufeld as a "historian" who "felt compelled to record these tragic events for posterity" (4).

It is easy to forget that the 1977 Hyperion edition of the diary was undertaken by the Mennonite *Literary* Society, for the majority of Reimer's editorial decisions appear designed to work to bolster the diary's value as a primary source historical document rather than for its considerable accomplishments as a literary text. He emphasizes the immediacy of the diary as assurance of its value, introducing the document by marveling at what he calls Neufeld's "sharp eye for detail" that enabled him to select "the significant out of a tangle of impressions—no mean feat for a man writing a journal at odd, stolen moments with the threat of arrest and even death hovering over him" (4). In case such a dramatic context might lead us to doubt the veracity of Neufeld's account, Reimer annotates the original diary with sixty-two explanatory footnotes and three maps; the larger book includes another two maps, and three appendixes that offer a chronological summary of its events and brief essays on controversial matters described in the book.[36] Moreover, Reimer positions himself as a historical guide by interjecting in cases where Neufeld ventures too far into hyperbole. When the journal describes an attack on a Mennonite village by anarchists as "a real Massacre of St. Bartholomew" (28), for example, Reimer adds a critical footnote that suggests the "author's grim descriptive phrase is not really appropriate," given that "only three people were killed" (28n23). Along with the paratextual maps, appendixes, and frequent editorial additions or amendments indicated by block brackets, these corrective footnotes—of which he includes at least nine others—clearly function to complement and extend the diary's value as a primary source, resulting in, as he puts it, a "story" that is not simply an individual's account but will work to serve as one of the "headstones or monuments" to the "Mennonite martyrs" of Russia (5).

Each of the publications of Neufeld's diary has relied upon the autobiographical pact in order to marshal what Lejeune identified as the "credence" that is "exude[d]" by life writing. The pact, Lejeune notes, invites the particular "type of reading" that engages the material as referential and relatively accurate ("Pact" 30). There is little question, in this regard, that Neufeld's skill as a writer was helped by the diary format to encourage readers to read the book as an eyewitness account. In one remarkable letter, for example, the well-known American author Willa Cather suggests the book has the "one literary quality which seems to me more important than any other,—sincerety [*sic*]"; she adds that she "cannot doubt that it is the story of an actual experience" (1)—a description of the diary that is included on the back of the MLS's later edition, despite Cather's caution.[37] The sense of sincerity produced by the diary as a genre can be notably juxtaposed to Neufeld's later autobiographical writings from the period, included in the MLS edition as "The Ordeal of Zagradovka" and "Escape from the Maze." As Reimer notes in his introductory comments, neither of these sections are diaries. Instead, the former was "pieced together by [Neufeld] from the reports of eye-witnesses," and is presented in "the more formal, third-person style of the historian and polemist" (65); the later returns to the first person, but, as Reimer writes, it "has something of a fictionalized air about it," and, curiously, is "written from a non-Mennonite point of view" (88). The fact that the MLS chose to publish the three works together under the title of the original diary and with the accompanying documentation suggests the hope is that the "credence" of the opening diary will be extended to the later texts. To my eyes, however, it would seem to have the opposite effect: the fact that the last section is explicitly fictionalized but retains many of the narrative devices of the opening diary suggests to me that the diary itself may have been revised and substantially polished before publication. This is a point to which I will return.

While each of the three major editions of Neufeld's diary are clearly presented as historical documents, then, a comparison across the 1921, 1930, and 1977 editions reveals that the details of this "story" shift meaningfully with each publication, the reader's credence being produced and nudged in specific directions. Indeed, Reimer is admirably frank in his introductory comments regarding his own interventionist approach to translation. Slipping briefly into the third person, he writes, "The translator's aim must be to steer a steady course between literal accuracy on the one hand and imaginative interpretation on the other" (xi). However, it requires a bit of comparative sleuthing to understand what is at stake in the specific "imaginative interpretations" he acknowledges to have taken. Indeed, if the autoethnographic pact of life writing within an emergent minority literary tradition would purport to offer readers authentic insight into the history and culture of a community, a closer look at the form and function of the various publications of Neufeld's diary serves as a valuable reminder of the competing or even conflicting uses to which the autoethnographic pact can be employed. While a full accounting of the various translation and editorial choices across the diary's various publications would no doubt be fascinating, I will have space only to begin a comparative discussion here.

One way to trace how contemporaneous concerns have shaped the contents of these ostensibly "spontaneous" texts is to follow how the introductory description of the Mennonite people in the diary's opening entry shifts with each publication. Following their opening place, date, and time markers—all three list Khortitza, September 15, 1919—all editions of the diary begin by establishing their setting. "*Fünf Tage bin ich nun hier am Dnjepr*," begins the German edition (5). In 1930, Neufeld translates this opening directly, as "For five days I have been here on the bank of the Dnieper" (5), which Reimer echoes in 1977 as "I have lived here on the banks of the Dnieper for five days now" (7). Almost immediately, however, substantive differences begin. The 1921 diary reports that when the author looks down from his house on the hill upon the "*friedliche Kolonistensiedelung*" ["peaceful colony"] on the river's edge, it looks almost as if it had been "*angeschwemmt daliegt*" ["washed ashore"] by the river itself. The image is important for Neufeld, and he takes time to emphasize his meaning in terms that clearly emphasize the community's Germanic heritage: "*. . . ist es mir so, als ob diese Wasser, weither vom Nordwesten aus deutschen Landen kommend, hier ein Zipselchen deutscher Erde abgelagert hätten. Ein Geschlecht ist darauf aufgewachsen, das deutsch spricht, eigen denkt und ähnlichen Gemütes ist wie die Deutschen*" (5). The passage can be translated as follows: ". . . it is as if these waters, coming from the North-West German lands, have deposited a bit of German earth here. A generation grew up on it that speaks German, thinks for itself, and is like the Germans in outlook and disposition." Writing in German for a German audience, the 1921 publication presents the Mennonite colonies of Russia as having been transplanted directly from Germany. Not only are these Mennonites unambiguously "like the Germans," in this opening passage, even *the land* itself is German. When Neufeld translates this passage for publication in California less than a decade later, however—some fifteen years after the United States helped to defeat the German army in the First World War, and with the specter of National Socialism on the horizon—he describes the Mennonite colonies in notably different terms. In the 1930 edition, the Dnieper is described as bringing sediment not from "Germany" but "from a foreign land," and the colonists having arrived from somewhere described simply as "distant western countries" (5): "Now I turn my eyes to the stream quietly flowing on and on; it makes me think that these waters, coming down from far away, have deposited here a bit of that remote country. Here has grown up a generation which speaks its own language and has its own ways of thinking, akin to the foreign stock from which it is descended, though all connection with the parent country was long ago severed" (5). Here the diary loses the specificity of its "original" German edition in rather conspicuous fashion. "German lands," "German earth," and "speak[s] German" have been rewritten as "far away," a "remote country," and "its own language"; if it remains true that the Mennonites of South Russia are of "foreign stock," the 1930 edition is careful to reassure readers that "all connection with the parent country" had long been "severed" (5). More than simply obfuscating his earlier account of the village, the 1930 edition also contradicts it outright, soon suggesting that the community's former homeland was not Germany at all but the Netherlands. Where the 1921 text proudly describes Khortitza as "*die älteſte deutſche Niederlassung in Süd-Russland*" (5) ("the oldest German settlement in South Russia"), the American readers in 1930 are informed that "This colony of Dutch Mennonites is the oldest in South Russia" (5–6). Only pages later will the 1930 text acknowledge the Mennonite community's association with Germany, and even here it is rendered an accusation rather than a historical fact. Yes, the "farmers [. . .] had come from the European West," he concedes, but they had long since become the "most loyal Russian citizens," even though they were now "considered as being of German origin" (9).

It is tempting to read Neufeld's rechristening of the Mennonites as "Dutch" as a cynical deployment of ethnic revisionism in an effort to deflect anti-Germanic sentiments of the period. Certainly, there is something strategic in his decision to reach back to the community's longer connection to the sixteenth-century Netherlands, and to downplay a formative century and a half in the Danzig region that had led to their adoption of German as their church language. In this, certainly, he is far from alone: historians of this period will note that the Mennonites in the Soviet Union were undertaking a similar project of formally presenting themselves as Dutch to the Soviet government in order to avoid laws specifically targeting Germans—a process sometimes called the "Hollandizing" of the colonies. It is a practice that Reimer notes in his final footnote to the diary, where he references it in an explanatory note regarding what he describes as the "notorious Land Liquidation Laws by which all property owners of German ethnic background were compelled to sell off their holdings" (64 n62).

The archive, however, presents a more complicated story behind these alterations. Neufeld's personal letters with Mennonites both in North America and abroad suggest he was thoroughly disillusioned with the politics and rhetoric of postwar Germany. In a 1934 letter to a Mr. Lugebuhl in Ohio, for example, Neufeld begins in English explaining that he will write the remainder of the letter in German as requested but asks that it be noted that he is doing so under protest (1). In a letter to Dr. Rempel the following year, Neufeld describes himself as "so disgusted with the

German situation over there in Europe" that he is considering refusing to teach German altogether and expresses his dismay at what he calls the "Nazi propaganda" that has made its way into German-language Mennonite newspapers (2). As noted earlier, Neufeld would even legally change his name to Navall, a decision that was made specifically in an effort to disassociate himself with the country and was not received well by members of his own family.[38] In a handwritten passage added to the bottom of a lengthy 1977 typed letter to Al Reimer, Mennonite historian David Rempel took note of these shifting designations for the Mennonites in the two publications of Neufeld's diary and suggested they were a direct reflection of the author's earnest politics. "By 1929–30 [. . . Neufeld] had become increasingly apprehensive of developments in Germany and quite bitter anti-Nazi," Rempel reports. He was, in fact, "quite strongly anti-German" (7). While there is little question that the shift from "German" to "Dutch" between the 1921 and 1930 edition is politically motivated, then, it would be simplistic to suggest the revisions are straightforward or cynical. Crucial for me here, however, is the point that the diary *form* exaggerates the stakes of such changes: shifting identity claims that might be simply notable if found across revised editions of a work of fiction, here seem to betray the autobiographical pact established by the form itself, which otherwise asks its account to be received as transparent and unmediated by later revisions.

The Mennonites of Russia were described in Neufeld's diary as "German" in 1921 and "Dutch" in 1930 and would continue to shift in the coming years. When *Russian Dance of Death* was excerpted for publication in the pages of *Mennonite Life* in 1969, the editors sought to sidestep all the confusion about the community's historic identities by adopting the vague language of the 1921 edition's opening paragraph, and then quietly excising nearly three pages from the source text to leap past the troublesome section altogether. By the mid-1970s in Canada, however, when the diary was edited as the initial publication of the Mennonite Literary Society, eager to establish an ethnic literary tradition of Mennonite writing, these Mennonites' Germanic heritage returns to the text with a vengeance. In Reimer's translation, the Dnieper once again has deposited the Mennonite villages from the "distant Germanic lands." The 1930 edition interjects into the 1921 text to assure its readers that "all connection with the parent country was long ago severed" (5), but the 1977 edition doesn't simply remove this addition—it inverts it. Here is the opening of the diary in Reimer's imaginative interpretation:

> I look down on the peaceful settlement. It lies below me as if it had been deposited by the calm Dnieper waters, which flow down from the northwestern plains beyond which lie the distant Germanic lands from whence these settlers came. The spiritual ties with those ancestral lands remain unbroken, although the physical separation took place many years ago" (7)

Reimer began his edition of the diary working from the 1921 German text, where Neufeld had emphasized this particular Mennonite community's historic Germanic roots, but he had access to the 1930 translation midway through his efforts. Did he understand himself as "correcting" Neufeld's 1930 revisions via the 1921 publication? It is unfortunate that the original French edition is unavailable for comparison, but it is clear that Reimer is not simply returning to the first German text here. In describing the community's German heritage as enduring "spiritual ties" to their "ancestral lands," he is expanding upon it with a flourish. The fact that elsewhere on the opening pages Reimer is careful to indicate his editorial interventions through the academic convention of square brackets—"In the course of time they established [eighteen] villages in this area [the so-called Old Colony]," and so on (7)—only serves to emphasize the implicit promise that the rest of these lines are unaltered beyond translation.[39] Similar revisions can be traced across the 1977 edition, as Reimer works to reintroduce reference to the Mennonites' Germanic heritage where the 1930 edition removed it. The most consistent effect of these revisions is not to outright celebrate that heritage but rather to position it as a central part of why the Mennonites were so clearly targeted by the anarchists who roamed the area.[40]

To be clear, my aim in this section is not to "expose" the politically motivated changes that appear across a comparison of these editions of the Neufeld diary. Translation is always a complex process, and I have already noted that Reimer is frank about his plans to "steer a steady course between literal accuracy on the one hand and imaginative interpretation on the other" (xi). The aim, rather, is to take careful account of such changes, and to suggest they are particularly charged in the translation of life writing, where the autobiographical pact implicitly assures readers they are receiving an unedited, unmediated witness account of the past. Such concerns likely matter most in the context of those reading the diary as a primarily historical text, as in Sean Patterson's recent historical study, *Makhno and Memory: Anarchist and Mennonite Narratives of Ukraine's Civil War, 1917–1921*, which relies heavily on Mennonite life writing as historical accounts and suggests Neufeld's "diary and memoir stand out amongst the primary sources" from the period (77). Moreover, Neufeld seemed aware of the charged nature of his diary and the dangers that might come with reading it across time. Early in the diary but well before the violence has arrived in Khortitza, he reflects on how his tolerance for uncertainty and chaos had changed in the postwar years. The German-language 1921 passage, which I have used as the epigraph for this study, reads as follows: "*Aber freilich, alle Begriffe sind nur beziehendlich, sie haben im Werden der Menschheit nur eine bestimmte Dauer. Danach werden sie unwahr . . .*" In my attempt at a roughly direct translation, it reads: "But admittedly, all concepts have context, they have only a limited time of usefulness. After that they become untrue . . ." Appropriately enough, even this poignant passage has been subject to meaningful revision. Neufeld's own translation of the passage for his 1930 edition, for example, reads: "But in speaking of peace, it must be understood, of course, that all conceptions are relative" (7–8), while Reimer's translation for the 1977 edition reads: "One must not forget, of course, that one's ideas and notions of things are relative and subject to change" (9). These are small changes, to be sure, but Neufeld's 1930 (re)contextualization of the 1921 claim specifically to be "in speaking of peace," and Reimer's 1977 narrowing of its insight to "one's ideas" as being relative (rather than *all* concepts), are meaningful in their implications, and, ironically enough, evidence of its truth.

Reading for these editorial changes across the publications can help us see authors and editors turning to the diary form specifically in order to marshal its strong sense of historical immediacy and authenticity—or what Lejeune calls the "credence it exudes"—and to redirect that force toward a range of ends. Chief among those ends when the Mennonite Literary Society chose Neufeld's obscure diary to be its first publishing project, I am suggesting, was the establishment of a minority literary tradition, where life writing's promise of authenticity and immediacy dovetailed with the country's sudden interest in "the cultural contributions of the other ethnic groups." Forty years later, hope for the diary as a "quasi-literary genre" that "expands the historically marginalized voice" via the logic of cultural "authenticity" in a multicultural society remains strong, as the essays collected by Angela R. Hooks in *Diary as Literature: Through the Lens of Multiculturalism* make clear (ix). Given the ways in which the "credence" of authenticity would seem to imply a mode of reading that prioritizes for historical rather than literary value, however, it is worth spending some time reflecting on the "quasi-literary" nature of Neufeld's diary, and to ask whether it is properly considered literature at all.

"VERILY, A SOPHOCLEAN TRAGEDY!" THE NEUFELD DIARY AS LITERATURE

Diary writing was a common practice in the time and place that Neufeld first wrote the pages that would become *Russian Dance of Death*, and its literary possibilities were already widely recognized. Jochen Hellbeck notes that diary keeping "thrived in prerevolutionary Russian culture" more generally, for example, and continued "in the postrevolutionary climate of terror and distrust"; diaries of the revolutionary period by Anna Baerg, Peter J. Dyck, and others show that the Mennonites were no exception to this trend. What is more, Elizabeth Podnieks suggests that by the nineteenth century many "diarists increasingly viewed their habit—or occupation—as a literary one," so that "by the twentieth century, with the publishing of journals an accepted and expanding phenomenon, diarists had an increasing number of models at their disposal" ("Literary"). However, the diary has only recently become considered a form of literary writing by scholars, in part because the very notion of *literariness* seems to undermine the immediacy and spontaneity that is understood to characterize the genre. In his analysis of diaries kept by French soldiers during World War I, for example, Leonard V. Smith describes this paradox as the "fundamental tension between the immediacy intrinsic to keeping a diary and the requirements of narrative." It is necessary, he suggests, to "disentangl[e] diary and narrative," especially in diaries of combat and violence, lest the latter impose a false coherence onto the former. Paul de Man's observation that life writing tests the limits of the "possible convergence of aesthetics and of history" (919) is also relevant here, as it is a limit to which Neufeld showed himself sensitive in the unpublished 1927 introduction to the 1930 edition of his diary. I have already noted the brief essay's rhetorical emphasis on the diary's historical accuracy, but the larger passage is worth returning to briefly to observe how it positions the work's absence of traditional literary conventions—perhaps even its failure as a work of literature—as evidence of its historical immediacy: "It is no fiction, what I have written in this book. It is a true story—'A first hand, historical source,' it has been called by European critics. Therefore, any principles of construction or a 'plot-idea,' as found in fiction, should not be expected here. I could not for this reason introduce humor at will or get the story up to a certain high pitch of tension and then bring in pauses of relief, etc." (1) The phrasing here is crucial. *It is no fiction*, he writes, rather than *It is not a story*, his insistence upon a generic classification doubling as a type of truth claim. And since this is a "'first hand, historical source,'" he continues, invoking an unnamed external expert, we are to take any awkwardness of phrasing, jarring breaks in pace, or other elements breaking the "principles of construction" as proof that he resisted the urge to return to the diary for editing or revision.

Neufeld's argument here recalls for me Royden Loewen's effort to establish the historical value of his collection of earlier Mennonite diaries by assuring readers he has "reproduced" the diary sections "in their entirety," with "all the spelling and grammatical errors, inconsistencies and factual errors" left unchanged (x). Both arguments are clear efforts to establish what Lejeune described as the autobiographical pact, in that they work to establish not only its genre but, crucially, to control the "mode of reading" that will be brought to bear on the text itself ("Pact" 30). If Loewen's argument is supported by the fragmented and error-riddled syntax of the diaries that follow his introduction, however, Neufeld's unpublished introduction is notable for precisely the opposite reason: it calls attention to the fact his diary works hard to incorporate literary elements throughout, with a clear narrative arc, many literary allusions, reliance on hyperbole and metaphor, and so on—to the fact, in other words, the book hardly resembles what we might expect to find in coming to the unrevised notes of a chaotic period. "Diary?" reads a 1930 review of the first English edition of Neufeld's work. "It is in that form, true; but its content is as dissimilar to the daily jottings which that word commonly implies as was the Ukraine of 1919 to peaceful Pomona valley" (Johnson).

Many of the Neufeld diary's literary elements exist in tension with the presumed spontaneity of its genre. Elizabeth Podnieks suggests that a diary "must be written with no consideration of an audience beyond the writer herself," but also that, "by virtue of being defined as a daybook [. . .] it must be spontaneous" (*Daily* 18), and Lejeune sees unvarnished spontaneity as so central to the function of the genre that he refers to the diary as a type of "antifiction," a concept concisely paraphrased by Rak as a "nonfictional form which does not make use of storytelling devices such as plot twists or even invented events, because diarists have no audience but paper, a screen, or themselves" ("Hidden" 87). I noted earlier that the diary is full of phrasing that would indicate its spontaneity—"Whew! I've managed to get back to our house," begins one entry (15); "I can't write any more; I'm too weak," ends another (55)—but such rhetoric is fully undercut by the literary elements of the larger narrative. The opening entry of all versions of the diary, for example, is full of expository details that are fully superfluous aside from their role in providing an anticipated reader with the diarist's cultural and historical context—details, of course, that the author himself would already be well aware. "This is the largest Mennonite colony in Russia," he writes, ostensibly to himself. "After a long, arduous journey trek the original colonists settled down here [. . .] As I look to the valley below I see, in addition to the fine farmsteads, half-a-dozen steam flourmills, several farm implement factories [. . .] These are industrious people" (8–9). The larger work, too, is clearly constructed with an eye to pace and thematic cohesion. In Reimer's translation, especially, the opening entries appear to foreshadow the coming violence, noting that warnings of chaos are coming "with increasing frequency" (9), its author claiming to have a "premonition of events to come which will be even more fateful than those we have already experienced" (11), recognizing that "something has to give" (11), and so on. Even some of the assurances that he is simply recording his daily reflections—"I have just read over what I have written in my journal today," he writes, "and realize that it's hard to keep one's thoughts and feelings away from the political events of our time" (11)—ring a bit hollow to me. This particular example may have seemed awkward to Neufeld, as well, for though he included this assurance in the 1921 edition, he removed it outright from his 1930 edition, only to have Reimer reinsert it for the 1977 publication.

Neufeld's descriptions of his own role and valor similarly strain against the credence that the diary format otherwise works to establish. In one passage, included in all three editions, Neufeld describes himself not only as nobly refusing the offer of freedom from a house where Mennonites are being held at gunpoint—"Could I leave these ladies since their honor stood at stake?" he asks in the 1930 edition (37); "The honour of these females was at stake," he declares in the 1977 edition (19)—but as having the ability to protect them with his "mental" powers. The 1930 edition is most notable here. When he had been "condemned to be shot" a year earlier, he mentions casually, he discovered that "with highest spiritual efforts [he] was able to disarm the malefactors" (37). Now recognizing himself to be in mortal danger once again, he reports "deliver[ing] an attack with weapons of mental concentration. Suggestively I force upon them the thought: 'you shall not kill me!'" (37). This proves sufficient to defuse the "murderous lust" of all but one of their captors, whom Neufeld goes on to disarm by "increas[ing] the tension of the thought more and more: 'you shall not!'" (38). It must surely be passages such as this of which Rempel was thinking when he gently suggested, writing in a personal letter to Reimer following the 1977 publication, that it is "the conjecture of some people who knew Neufeld better than I did during 1919–1920 that he was [. . .] somewhat exaggerating of his heroic role during the Makhnovshchina" (1978, 1), and that there was "also the feeling than the 'notes' were not always contemporaneous with the events as they unfolded, but were added somewhat later" (1978, 1). Rempel is quick to praise Neufeld's book, adding immediately that "this may or may not have been the case," and insisting that "the point is that it is a contemporaneous chronicle in its major events, exceedingly well written" (1). As we have seen, however, the "exceedingly well written" nature of the work may be understood as further argument *against* its historical value, especially where its presentation of the author in the role of heroic protagonist seems to already be stretching the autobiographical pact near its limit.

Nowhere is the debate over the diary's literary value so clear, however, as in the editorial decisions that surround Neufeld's use of the theatre as a trope, or extended metaphor, to structure the text. The only two extended passages that Reimer removes outright from Neufeld's own editions of the diary are its two most self-consciously literary sections. The first is the eight-line rhymed epigraph that Neufeld included above the opening entry in the 1921 edition, which is included again on its own page immediately prior to the introductory essay of the 1930 edition, where it is included in German as the 1930s edition's only nontranslated text—presumably in order to maintain its rhyme and meter. Reimer, however, excises the epigraph entirely, without comment. Given that the poem is straightforward enough in its contents—the writer declares he cannot help but shout his call for help, for the world has to hear of their need (*Die Welt, sie muss es hören!*)—it seems likely that it is the literariness of the material to which he objects.

The second example is more significant. In both the 1921 and the 1930 diaries, Neufeld describes the colonies as a "theatre" for the high drama of history, presenting the Mennonites as performers who "happen to be on stage and must act." Although the section is too long to quote in full, its opening paragraph gives a clear sense of its direction and is worth including at some length. From the 1930 English edition:

> Thus our situation is comparable to a revolving stage which, as indeed it seems, can be stopped no more. One drama after another is being enacted before the eyes of Europe. We here happen to be on the stage and must act. A turn of the stage, an actor appears,

> making a grand announcement; the spectators of the West look curiously to see how we are going to put into practice those high-sounding principles. We do not know how we are going to do it either. We are scattered all over the stage, and I rather guess it is a poor show. [. . .] We are going to play, on and on. . . . It is like that well-known fairy tale where some bewitched dancers have to dance unable to stop even for a moment. (12)

The metaphor of the world as stage is not original, of course, but Neufeld's deployment of it here is worth exploring. Unlike the most obvious intertext for the passage, the well-known "all the world's a stage" passage from Shakespeare's *As You Like It*, here the world is divided into players and audience. The referent for the singular actor who appears to make a "grand announcement" is unclear, though it may be a reference to Neufeld himself. Those on stage—the "we here" who "happen to be on the stage"—are the Mennonites in Khortitza, surely, those who endured the testing of their "high-sounding principles" of pacifism before the "eyes of Europe." The description of the performance as a "poor show" appears to indicate both that the Mennonites are failing the test of their stated theology and, with the actors "scattered" about, that the audience may be misreading the tragedies through the cold lens of aesthetics, rather than considering the ethical and political urgency of the account. In this latter register, it offers a caution to the reader not to be distracted by the aesthetic shortcomings of the diary itself.

Reimer removes the section in its entirety for the 1977 edition, excising several paragraphs in their entirety from the earlier editions of the work, but the image of the Mennonites forced to play a part in a larger tragic drama is more than a passing metaphor in Neufeld's editions of his diary. Not only does the section above continue in this vein for several paragraphs, the passage literally gives the book its title: immediately after comparing the Mennonites' efforts to try and enact their "high-sounding principles" in a time of war as a people being condemned to "dance" for the entertainment of Europe, the 1930 edition declares that "To leave the stage means to leave Russia" (12); it is, in other words, a Russian dance of death.

Several of the diary's later entries clearly echo this theme, including the two occasions he describes the difficulty that children of slain Mennonites have in retrieving their parents' corpses. In the first, he recounts the death of a prominent citizen and notes that the man's sons were chased away as they sought to return the body to the family. Both the 1921 German edition and the 1930 English edition interject a theatrical reference at the close of the scene: "Verily," Neufeld writes, "a Sophoclean tragedy!" (1930, 58). The 1930 edition of the diary returns to double down on the theatrical reference in a revision of the diary's dramatic conclusion. In its 1921 publication, the diary ends on March 5 with Neufeld scanning a list of the 214 Mennonite men killed in the notorious Zagradovka massacre, and finding his brothers' and father's names. "*So kennt der Frevel keine Grenzen?!*" (79) it concludes, a closing line that Reimer translates for the 1977 edition as "Does crime have no limits then? Is there no end to atrocity? . . ." (64). Given that Neufeld offers extensive reflection and commentary throughout the diary, the lack of a summative or reflective passage here is notable, as is the final ellipsis. In an essay entitled "How Do Diaries End?" Lejeune has noted the "problem" of the diary's conclusion, noting that the contemporaneous nature of the form seems to make it "unfinishable from the beginning" (*On Diary* 191)—a problem apparently reflected in the 1921 diary's concluding ellipses. Revising for his diary's 1930 publication, however, Neufeld solves the "problem" of the diary's conclusion in a different way, returning, rather melodramatically, to the theme of a dramatic tragedy that he had established earlier—and literally positioning his diary within the "highest" of literary genres in the process, inviting the most famous of tragic dramatists to pick up where he has left off. After receiving news that his own family members have been murdered, Neufeld ends the entry, and the 1930 diary as a whole, as follows: "Does crime have no limits then? Is there no end to atrocity? Sophocles, you, who wrote 'Antigone,' I yield the pen to you. I cannot proceed farther . . ." (186). The reference to *Antigone*, left implicit in the earlier first gesture to Sophocles, is appropriate inasmuch as the ancient play is a tragedy set in a civil war and recounts the drama of a family member who attempts to bury a loved one and is cruelly punished by the state. However, as a closing it not only refers back to a canonical work of Western literature but also places a neat thematic bow on a metaphor established earlier and returned to throughout the work. The final ellipsis notwithstanding, the conclusion to the 1930 edition reads as the very type of plot construction that seems to belie the diary's generic claims to spontaneity that is otherwise central to its value. All these theatre references are clearly too much for Reimer, who removes the long meditation establishing it as the text's structuring metaphor, as well as both of these later gestures to Sophocles.

Reimer's engagement with the self-consciously literary elements of the diary on behalf of the Mennonite Literary Society is inconsistent. It is clear that Reimer has set out to downplay, if not remove, Neufeld's reliance on the drama as a structuring motif for the diary. At the same time, however, the 1977 edition includes a host of the diary's other literary references unchanged, including the suggestion that resisting Makhno's men would be "as useless as Don Quixote's fighting with the windmills" (17), his casual observation that Gogol had "honored the memory" of the Zaporizhian Cossocks of the area in the "rose-colored light of poetry" (11), and so on. At times, Reimer even allows an extended literary or classical reference to stand, as when Neufeld turns to Cicero in an attempt to illustrate the experience of being held captive by the rough and uneducated anarchists. In his 1930 edition, Neufeld punctuates his frustrations with having to serve "these rude fellows"—he believes himself among the "representatives of a higher knowledge"—by declaring "O tempora! O mores!" comparing the Mennonites' plight to "Carthage's destruction" (87), and describing their pacifism as a refusal to "imitate" the "men of Sparta" (88). Reimer seems to recognize Neufeld's classical allusions, along with his refusal to offer translations or elaborations on the references, as an appeal to his most educated readers and lets them stand in his own translation (37). Later, however, when Neufeld laments "Quo vadis, poor Russia?" (once again without offering a translation, 103), Reimer includes the sentiment but drops the Latin, simply asking: "Where is poor Russia going?" (43). Similarly, while he removes Neufeld's descriptions of the Mennonite experience in Russia as a tragic drama, Reimer uses the metaphor in his own introduction to the collection, using the phrase that gives the diary its title without presenting it as part of the diary itself. After offering a brief history of the Mennonite colonies in Ukraine and the horrors of the revolutionary period, he writes: "On this tragic stage unfolded the *danse macabre* in which Dietrich Neufeld was forced to participate" (3).

Why would Reimer, an English professor who had just published *My Harp Is Turned to Mourning*, his own major novel exploring this same time and place (and with the same publisher), now working on behalf of the Mennonite Literary Society, choose to remove the theatrical interpretive allusions from the diary and otherwise flatten the heightened rhetoric that seem to clearly reflect Neufeld's literary ambitions for the text? Neufeld himself, after all, had worked to amplify those allusions when he retranslated the diary, and the editors of *Mennonite Life*, excerpting only a fraction of the diary, saw fit to include each one of the theatrical passages I noted above, including its most theatrical closing line (161). One reason, I have suggested here, is that the ostensible intimacy and spontaneity of life writing makes it a poor fit for grand literary gestures. As de Man warns about "making autobiography into a genre" and so positioning it within the "hierarchies of the major literary genres": there is bound to be "some embarrassment," he writes, in that "autobiography always looks slightly disreputable and self-indulgent in a way that may be symptomatic of its incompatibility with the monumental dignity of aesthetic values" (919). Indeed, it would seem something similar is at play here. In the introduction to the 1977 edition Reimer notes that the "main deletion" he has made to the full diary "occurs in the first entry of Part 1, which I have reduced somewhat in the interests of narrative pace" (xi). He is more blunt in a 28 June 1977 letter to David Rempel, describing his substantial cut from the opening entry—that is to say, the paragraphs establishing and elaborating upon the diary's theatre metaphor—necessary because the passage was "flabby and overwritten" (2). A 1929 letter from Hartley Burr Alexander to Neufeld shows Reimer was not alone in this view. After complimenting Neufeld on a manuscript draft of the diary, Alexander offers a critique from what he describes a "literary point of view" that directly anticipates Reimer's own edits: "I do feel, however, that there is a sense of effort in the initial picture and (if you will pardon me) that the sense of reality is impaired by your classical allusions, especially that with which you close." It's hard to disagree with Alexander's critique, in the light of which the logic for Reimer's editorial choices seems clear enough. The implication of these choices, however, remains notable as evidence of the ways in which the editorial process engages aesthetic concerns to impact the operation of the diary effect.

Of course, the inclusion of literary tropes, classical references, and even, perhaps, a sense of foreboding that could read like foreshadowing, is not conclusive evidence that the diary was written after the events it records. Fothergill uses the phrase "book of the self" to describe the way that many diarists become aware of their writings *as books*, and, with it, to "suggest the tendency of the diary to lean towards acknowledged literary forms" (52). Surely this is in full evidence in Neufeld's diary, where the author heavily "leans toward" literary forms, and fashions himself the protagonist—more, the hero—of the account. Moreover, the most recent scholarship in life writing studies has begun to analyze how some of the apparently defining features of fiction also appear in life writing, not as betrayals of the form but rather as—in apt phrasing of Smith and Watson's account of metalepsis—as "figures that texture autobiographical discourse" ("Metalepsis" 3). "Metaleptic ruptures," they insist, "do occur in some autobiographical texts, where they produce an effect of instability and estrangement by unsettling reader expectations about the boundary between narrating and narrated I's, as well as the 'out there' status of the referential world" ("Metalepsis" 3). This may well be true, but where the text in question is striving toward the diary effect—that sense that historical veracity provided by an implicit promise to provide an unvarnished and eyewitness account—it would seem to rely on at least the *appearance* of unrevised spontaneity and would be thus undermined by, say, heavy-handed literary allusions, philosophical digressions, and the reliance on Greek theatre as a structuring metaphor.

Is Dietrich Neufeld's diary a literary text? It would seem that the 1977 diary, for the purposes of the MLS's broader assertion of Russian Mennonite ethnic cultural production, needs to be literary enough that it *could* be considered literature but should not beg the comparison to the point of insisting upon it. Given the stated desire in Neufeld's diary to be read as representative of a specific understanding of the Mennonite experience in Russia, perhaps the most pressing question is not whether the self-consciously literary aspects of Neufeld's diary are stylistically regrettable but whether they undermine the diary effect. To judge from the numerous print-runs of the MLS edition in the decade after its publication—an ocean and half a century removed from its original writing, retranslated and heavily edited—it would appear that the work had finally found its mark, the autoethnographic pact working to ensure its function as a work of minority writing during a time of multicultural difference.

WHO WROTE *DIETRICH NEUFELD'S A RUSSIAN DANCE OF DEATH*?

Before concluding this chapter, I would like to address one final question: Who, exactly, is the "author" of *Dietrich Neufeld's A Russian Dance of Death*, published for the Mennonite Literary Society in 1977? The answer is less obvious than one might imagine, and its importance clear, given how much of the book's value is caught up in its status as an eyewitness account to history. Lejeune, we recall, insists that the proper name on the front cover of autobiographical texts bears the "responsibility for all enunciation" within it and is the "only mark in the text of an unquestionable world-beyond-the-text, referring to a real person" ("Pact" 11). "The presence of the author in the text is reduced to this single name," Lejeune writes, that name being the manner in which the author "is linked, by a social convention, to the pledge of responsibility of a *real person*" (11). Given the particular set of social conventions that surround the diary as an ostensibly contemporaneous account of what it records—including, of course, the intimate and immediate response of the writer in question—is there not a sense in which a revised, re-edited, and repeatedly translated autobiographical work disperses the "responsibility for all enunciation" within it across not only the author at various ages but also the subsequent editors and translators?

This question is further complicated in a longitudinal reading of Neufeld's diary. Like a number of other Mennonite authors of his generation, Neufeld routinely wrote under pseudonyms. His diary, remember, was twice attributed to "Dietrich Neufeld" (1921, 1977), but also to "Dirk Gora" (1930), to "Dedrich Navall" (1969), and—in the unpublished draft introduction of 1927—to "Dmitri Novopolye." Lejeune dismisses pseudonyms as unproblematic for the autobiographical pact, insisting that they are "simply a differentiation, a division of the name, which changes nothing in the identity" ("Pact" 12). But are we so sure? These names ultimately refer to the same person, to be sure, but this "diversion of the name" on the title page certainly changes what Michel Foucault influentially describes as the "author-function," giving rise to the types of concerns I have wrestled with in this chapter. As Foucault asks: "Under what conditions and throughout what forms can an entity like the subject [here, the author of the diary] appear in the order of discourse; what position does it occupy; what functions does it exhibit"? (314) Does Neufeld's choice of "Gora" as a surname for his 1930 diary, like his decision to change his last name to Navall around the same time, not reflect the revisions he made to his description of the Mennonites between his 1921 and 1930 diaries? Does it not serve to obscure, if not change, the overtly Germanic heritage of the author, and, in the process to change something fundamental in the "identity" it constructs, and thus the meaning of the work? The original diary was written by Dietrich Neufeld, but the editors of *Mennonite Life* attributed it to Dedrich Navall (Neufeld's later name), while Reimer later returned to his earlier name. What is more, given Reimer's aggressive translation practices—which he openly acknowledges as an attempt to work "between literal accuracy" and "imaginative interpretation" ("Introduction" xi)—perhaps we should not be surprised to find that while Dietrich Neufeld is clearly identified as the author on the cover of the 1977 work, it is indicated in such a manner as to emphasize the role of the translator and editor. Copied directly, the cover of the 1977 book reads:

> *Dietrich Neufeld's*
> A Russian Dance of Death
> Revolution and Civil War in the Ukraine
> *Translated and Edited by*
> *Al Reimer*

Lejeune assumes the name "above or below the title of the volume" will be the same, but here we see the authority—and perhaps also the responsibility, and the accomplishment—of the text being divided between two figures, listed above *and* below the title. Notably, the title and Neufeld's name are in white, while Reimer's name is presented in black, and in a slightly larger font. Lest it seem that I am reading too much into Reimer's name being on the cover, consider that the back cover of the 1977 and 1988 editions of the book include a single large photo and extended bio—not of Neufeld, the diarist, but of Reimer, the translator and editor! Although Neufeld's name stands alone on the book's spine, it is nowhere to be found on the back cover, even in the five sentences given to describing "*The Book*." Instead, his picture and biography are on page xiii of the book, slotted between Reimer's "Preface" and Reimer's "Introduction."[41] The paratextual material of the 1977 and 1988 editions of the diary, then, displace the author-function at least as substantially as do the shifting pseudonyms of the earlier editions.

Perhaps the best way to answer the question of who authored *Dietrich Neufeld's A Russian Dance of Death*, however, is to extend Gilles Deleuze and Félix Guattari's well-known argument that in the context of minor literatures, "what the solitary writer says already constitutes a communal action" (17). In the minority literature framework in which Mennonite literature was emerging, we might say, there were no solitary writers—not even solitary diarists. Individuals may write in isolation, but whenever they are identified, published, and promoted as part of a minoritized literary tradition, their text—and, through the logic of the ethnographic imperative, the authors themselves—become interpellated into a collective project. This authorial interpellation is clearly amplified in a case such as the Neufeld diary, where the text in question is a deeply personal narrative, and where the purported value of the text seems to oscillate between its historical value as a primary source and its literary qualities as a compelling narrative. When the text in question has been long out of print, as is the case with Neufeld's diary, these pressures grow stronger still, with the text's republication clearly responding to a contemporary set of concerns that can be traced across translations and publications. After all, what one chooses to recover from the slaughterhouse of literature will tell us at least as much about who we are, and what we value, as it does about the nature of the past itself. Diaries may be located in a specific past time by definition, but this is not quite the same as suggesting they are entirely *of* the past. "When diaries are read later," Julie Rak notes, "an aspect of pastness in diaries becomes activated, for the present" ("Hidden" 87). The question I have tried to answer here, then, is *what aspect is being activated* in the 1977 edition, and to what end?

CONCLUSION

From letters to diaries to biographies and memoirs, life writing was absolutely central to the establishment of a literary culture among North American Mennonites in the twentieth century. For early aspiring Mennonite creative writers, life writing provided a mode of imaginative expression that was reassuringly referential within a theological context suspicious of—if not outright hostile to—the literary arts; it also offered a mode of writing that was immediately recognizable within the later multicultural context rewarding autoethnographic expression. Far from it being strange that the Mennonite Literary Society was interested in a diary in 1977, the context in which Mennonite literature was emerging would seem to make Neufeld's book an entirely logical choice as its first major publication: the republication of *A Russian Dance of Death* in 1977 is clearly a case of a diary activating the past in service of the present. Of course, returning our scholarly gaze to the heydays of interest in autoethnographic interpretation does not mean we need to embrace its logic, nor need these early examples of life writing—even the most referential of works—be understood in straightforwardly referential terms. We can, I think, look to move "beyond autoethnography" in the sense articulated by Eleanor Ty and Christl Verduyn: attending closely to its expression not in order to unthinkingly endorse or reject its logic but with a critical eye to better understand its operation (3–5).

If it was possible, from 1921 through 1977, for the shifting identity claims in Neufeld's diary to function across languages, decades, and continents, and if it were commonplace, even as late as 1986, to see writers earnestly invoke and explore Mennonite identity in a range of genres, minority literature's emphasis on identity would soon produce its own critique. Indeed, even as the "Mennonite/s Writing" critical conversation was forming in the early 1990s, popular and academic discourses around identity were rapidly changing, so that the foundations on which the field was being built were shifting. In the next chapter, I want to explore how authors of Mennonite descent quickly began to respond to the ethnic framework through which their writing was being received, attempting to rebuff the earnest demands of identity-based reception to their work while still looking to wield its undeniable power and appeal. My argument will be that although it is true that contemporary literary studies has explicitly rejected the type of reified ethnic identities that once were imagined to be the foundation of minority literatures, it does not mean that such identities can no longer be found in the contemporary pages of Mennonite writing. To the contrary, I trace in contemporary Mennonite writing in North America an essentialized and decontextualized Mennonite identity—what I am calling the "Mennonite Thing"—that is self-consciously invoked, exposed, and explored, a process through which it is reanimated as identity for an ostensibly post-identity age.

CHAPTER 3

THE MENNONITE THING

Identity in a Post-Identity Age

There is a well-known joke in Mennonite circles that begins with the already-a-punch-line-of-a-question *Why don't Mennonites have sex standing up?* The humor of the answer—*Because it might lead to dancing*—lies in the suggestion that in the absurdly uptight world of the Mennonites, rules and regulations have become more important than the religious principles they once reflected. An essay in the 2013 "Mennonite Sex" special issue of *Rhubarb* magazine identifies this as "likely the first joke any Mennonite child understands about our shared heritage" (C. Redekop 64), while Jeff Gundy has christened it the "ur-Mennonite joke" (*Walker* 193).[1] Its widespread circulation reflects, in part, the fact that it does not refer to any particular group or denomination of Mennonites[2] but rather appeals to a generalized and abstracted notion of a conservative Mennonite identity writ large, but also the fact that it offers something less a pointed critique of that identity than a playful affirmation. The implied original rule (*No dancing, as it might lead to sex!*) may be inverted (*No sex, as it might lead to dancing!*), but the result in behavior is exactly the same (*No dancing! No sex!*). The rule itself may be held up to ridicule, but the animating principles of modesty, abstinence, and so on, are left untouched, just like the bodies in question.

Drawing on Slavoj Žižek's work on the inversion of ideology and the fetishistic structure of the "Ethnic Thing," I want to suggest that the structure of the above joke—or, more specifically, the function of Mennonite identity within it—reflects the role that Mennonite identity currently plays for much of the larger field of Mennonite literary studies. To this point in the study, I have been exploring how a developmental model of literary history may be tying the field of Mennonite literary studies to the logic of its emergence as a form of ethnic minority literature. I have suggested that the framework of a "minor transnationalism" can estrange some of the field's methodological assumptions and may offer support to the wide-ranging work taking place in the Mennonite literary studies today. In chapter 1, I looked to interrogate the canon-forming logic of conventional literary history by undertaking a cross-sectional reading of every Mennonite literary book published in English in 1986 to try and uncover what type of writing had been left behind in the "slaughterhouse" of the field's neglected past; in chapter 2, I undertook a longitudinal reading of a single work of life writing, following the circuitous publication of the Neufeld diary across more than fifty years to argue for the significance of life writing as a genre that fostered the early field's emergence as a minority literature by bridging—or by attempting to bridge—the discourses of history and literature.

In this chapter, I want to move toward more contemporary work to suggest that a version of the strategic deployment of identity I traced across Neufeld's diary's iterations can also be read in more recent work, except that it has become playfully self-conscious. By the late 1990s, postcolonial critiques of minority literatures (including Mennonite writing[3]) had made clear the limits of the identarian logic that had been central to their establishment, but this did not mean that identity stopped being of central concern for many readers—and writers. Here, I focus on a prominent strand of contemporary writing that has routed its engagement with the most conventional aspects of Mennonite identity—what I am calling the Mennonite Thing—through a variety of distancing gestures, strategically mobilizing notions of cultural authenticity and cohesive group identity in such a way that it continues to function without being directly readable as autoethnography.

THE MENNONITE THING

Mennonite literary studies may have emerged in a period where it was commonplace to celebrate minority literatures as expressions of distinct identities, but scholars quickly interrogated those assumptions and have widely accepted that identities are better understood to be hybrid, shifting, constructed and contingent, less as reified "things" in themselves than as positions or locations that can be temporarily occupied and—perhaps—strategically mobilized.[4] At the same time, identity-based area studies have proven remarkably resilient, continuing to emphasize race, ethnicity, gender, and sexuality as primary avenues for engaging literary texts. I see nothing particularly surprising about this enduring critical focus on identity, as recognizing the constructed multiplicity of our identities, along with the clear need to continue grappling with the questions of individual belonging and collective meaning that remain powerful forces in contemporary life, seems to make the discussion around identity more compelling, rather than less. What is more, if it is true that Mennonite literary criticism has sometimes misread literature as social history, it is also true that much of what circulates as contemporary Mennonite literature continues to directly invoke and explicitly explore Mennonite identity as one of its central concerns.[5] Such work rewards an informed reading, especially as scholars have noted that the nature of its engagement with that identity has changed. In 2003, for example, Ann Hostetler took note of an "ironic reference to Mennonite touchstones of identity" that marked the work of "a younger generation of writers" (*A Cappella* 181); in 2005, Jeff Gundy warned that within a narrow emphasis on the aesthetics of Mennonite identity in writing, "obvious and easily manipulable cultural makers like Lowgerman and Zwieback seem to become central" (*Walker* 49). How are we to read the ongoing invocation of these markers of cultural authenticity in our ostensibly post-identarian times?

One way to understand how identity functions in such a context is to turn to a passage of Slavoj Žižek's *Sublime Object of Ideology*, entitled (appropriately enough) "The Ideological Quilt." Žižek suggests that identity is constructed and maintained as a "structured network of meaning" through ideology, as the "multitude of 'floating signifiers,' of proto-ideological elements, is structured into a unified field through the intervention of a certain 'nodal point'" (95–96). If "Mennonite" serves as the ideological "nodal point" holding together a discourse of Mennonite literature, however, this would be no reason to begin searching for the particular group or definition of Mennonites to which it corresponds. "The element which holds together a given community cannot be reduced to the point of symbolic identification," Žižek writes elsewhere. "The bond linking together its members always implies a shared relationship toward a Thing" (*Tarrying* 201). For Žižek, the various elements that one might point to as giving structure to a community—its shared history, rituals, theology, kinship ties, and so forth—will always prove insufficient to explain its constitutive element. "The Thing is not directly a collection of these features," he writes; "there is 'something more' in it, something that *is present* in these features, that *appears* through them" (*Tarrying* 201). I find Žižek's account of the identity as Thing helpful in examining the function of identity in much of contemporary Mennonite writing, though I hasten to add that he seems unable to escape the political implications that come with his insistence on the ostensible unintelligibility of identity as Thing—a point to which I will return to at the close of this chapter.

In *First as Tragedy, Then as Farce*, Žižek builds a similar argument regarding the role of ideology more generally. In response to the suggestion that ideology can no longer function in the context of today's cynical populations, Žižek insists that it is the very belief in the absence of ideology that demonstrates just how deeply imbedded we continue to be within it. Ideology continues to function, he suggests, but it does so today through the appearance of its rejection. He goes on to offer a number of brief but telling illustrations of this process at work, including two that are of particular interest to my discussion here. In the first, he notes the mockery of pseudo-oriental spiritualism in the popular film *Kung Fu Panda* and argues that despite "constantly being undermined by a vulgar-cynical sense of humour [. . .] this continuous self-mockery in no way impedes on the efficacy of the oriental spiritualism—the film takes the butt of its endless jokes seriously" (50–51). In the second, he recounts an anecdote about the Dutch physicist Niels Bohr, in which a scientist visiting Bohr's house expressed dismay at finding a horseshoe nailed above the door. "The fellow scientist visiting him exclaimed that he did not share the superstitious belief regarding horseshoes keeping evil spirits out of the house," Žižek writes, "to which Bohr snapped back: 'I don't believe in it either. I have it there because I was told that it works even when one doesn't believe in it'" (51). For Žižek, such stories exemplify the cynical logic at play in contemporary ideology, where "nobody takes democracy or justice seriously, we are all aware of their corrupted nature, but we participate in them, we display our belief in them, because we assume that they work even if we do not believe in them" (51).

The Mennonite Thing, as I am formulating it here, is simply the conceit of an essential, static, and authentic Mennonite identity that is expressed through (but is not reducible to) stereotypical markers of Mennonite culture, language, and faith. Conventional markers of the Mennonite Thing often become associated with Mennonites for historical reasons, but through the exoticizing logic that reifies and commodifies them into easily consumable tokens of cultural difference, the most immediately recognizable aspects of a broadly defined "Mennonite culture" such as quilts, borscht, head coverings, *zwiebach*, and so on become overdetermined signifiers of an essentialized Mennoniteness that exists nowhere but as an abstract ideal.

My description of the conceit of reified ethnicity as "Thing" is meant to gesture to Žižek's work, of course, but in sketching out the Mennonite Thing I am also picking up on a term that has been in circulation for some time. In the 1985 collection *Visions and Realities*, for example, Margret Loewen Reimer and Paul Gerard Tiessen make use of the term in their interview with the "young poets" Patrick Friesen and David Waltner-Toews. "Don't you think both of you are sentimental and romantic in bringing forward the 'Mennonite' thing?" they ask, following up on a discussion about *The Shunning*. "You have found in the 1970s and 1980s this marvellous homogeneous culture, and isolated stable culture [. . .] A cohesive, sharply defined thing" (251). Both poets initially demure—Waltner-Toews first responds by flatly denying such a thing could exist—before conceding that yes, they've wrestled with just such a "thing" in their work, Friesen in *The Shunning*, and Waltner-Toews in his Tante Tina poems. Around this same time, David Arnason, an early editor at Winnipeg's Turnstone Press, attempted to distinguish between writing by Mennonites, and some other, vaguely defined aspect of Mennonite literary identity. "We have no interest whatsoever in Mennonite history or anything particularly Mennonite," he insisted. "We are interested in good fiction, good poetry, and it just happens that a lot of Mennonites are writing good fiction and good poetry. But again I want to make it absolutely clear that we have very little interest in 'the Mennonite thing'" (213). This may well be true, but it is equally true that the broader fascination with "the Mennonite thing" was enabling Turnstone at the time. Elsewhere, I put it this way: "The socio-political contexts that encouraged a generation of Mennonite authors to write out of their experiences as 'ethnic Canadians' are the same contexts in which it became culturally compelling and economically viable for a small press to begin publishing book after book of and often about a rural, separatist, deeply conservative Christian community, and to be able to reasonably expect a 'mainstream literary market' to respond enthusiastically" (*Rewriting* 43). Arnason, even more than Loewen Reimer and Tiessen, is using the term derogatively, but it more commonly circulates as an affectionate shorthand, as in John Barber's *Globe and Mail* review of *Irma Voth*, succinctly entitled "Miriam Toews: It's a Mennonite Thing," or in the Mennonite Artist Project, a New York–based web initiative launched in 2009 connecting some five hundred Mennonite artists in its stated effort to "find other people who make art and get the Mennonite thing."[6]

In this chapter I am most interested in works that seem to engage with Mennonite identity as Thing not only strategically but self-consciously, looking to interrupt the type of autoethnographic reading that, as I explored in the last chapter, was so central to the establishment of the early field as a form of minority writing. As I hope will become clear, however, it is not always easy to determine where the line between irony and stereotype can be drawn. In fact, this is one reason why I turned to Žižek's work to help explore the function of identity in these texts, rather than, say, Spivak's work on strategic essentialism, or Rey Chow's work on coercive mimicry, despite their obvious similarities: Mennonite literature's engagement with its own essentialized identity is rarely as politically motivated or tactically deployed as the former would suggest, nor is it as subjugated or as racially determined as the latter. Žižek, too, is not a perfect fit here: for all the circuitous complexity of his writing, Žižek can be maddeningly reductive, and the role of identity in Mennonite writing is not strictly ideological in Žižek's sense of the term. I want to suggest that in key ways, however, it is strikingly similar in its *function*, and that, as I will argue at the close of this chapter, some of the dangers of the endurance of the Mennonite Thing can be recognized in the limitations of Žižek's own work. For now, let me qualify that by "ideology" I mean simply an ordering framework that structures thought and experience through an overarching principle or concern, similar to Kasdorf's use of the term as the politicized "name [for] the set of ideas that shape expectations, actions, and goals, and that get reproduced within the group as normative" ("Mightier" 46). "At the point of contact with the dominant world view," Kasdorf writes, "ideological difference becomes evident and signifies—even clarifies—identity: 'just what we do' escalates into 'what it means to be us'" (46). Žižek relies heavily on Lacan, but one need not fully adopt a Lacanian understanding of subjectivity to acknowledge the ways that desire and identity are closely intertwined in literary studies, or the ways that ideological difference is ripe for reification.

Žižek's work is helpful in the context of this study because it provides another way of engaging Mennonite literature's ongoing investment in identity without falling immediately back into reductive questions of authenticity or accuracy. It is more than two decades now since Ann Hostetler and Hildi Froese Tiessen each drew on Stuart Hall to caution critics against the dangers of essentialized notions of Mennonite identity,[7] and it has long been common practice for critics of Mennonite writing to avoid defining the field's parameters in anything but the broadest of terms. More than one prominent author of Mennonite descent has publicly denied being a "Mennonite author"—including both Friesen and Waltner-Toews in the interview I mention above—and, as I traced at some length in my introduction, critics have been warning of the field's potential collapse since before it was established.[8] Is it not possible that, lacking a clear, coherent, and static understanding of the "Mennonite" in "Mennonite literary studies," the wider field has been sustained in important ways simply through a shared commitment to its existence, aided by a collective willingness to actively defer the definition of its central concern? And if the sustaining feature of identity in Mennonite writing is not some clear set of practices or beliefs but rather our shared investment in its endurance, the question of whether or not a text's representation of Mennonite identity (as opposed to Mennonite history or even specific Mennonite communities) is "true" or "accurate" is not only secondary to understanding the role of identity in the field, it is to fail to recognize that this indeterminacy has been a central aspect of its function. In a critical context where the identity in the field's disciplinary signature is deeply unstable, and where this instability is overcome largely by a shared willingness to forge on without a stable referent, it does little good to respond to Mennonite literary texts by railing against the loss or misrepresentation of a true, essential identity, one characterized by a history and vision with clear origins and parameters, which we must protect at all costs, and so on. To make this argument in the context of much of contemporary Mennonite literature, it would seem, is to push against an open door.

HOW TO READ CONTEMPORARY MENNONITE WRITING

Perhaps the best example of how Mennonite literature has come to strategically engage identity as Thing is one that is also deeply self-conscious about the process at play. In 1986, Jeff Gundy—whose poetry, unlike his nonfiction, rarely directly addresses his Mennonite background—wrote a brief essay for *Mennonite Life* entitled "Being Mennonite and Writing Mennonite." "For someone like me, whose immediate background is largely without the colorful, obvious markers of Mennonite identity, it is not all that easy to decide how to go about making my work distinctly Mennonite," he writes. "Do I dredge up any scraps of 'heritage' I can, like the dim memory of the great-aunt asking 'Sprichen sie Dietsch?'" (11). Several years later, he returned to this topic with a prescriptive parody, "How to Write the New Mennonite Poem." Under the guise of instruction, Gundy's poem critiques the instrumentalization of Mennonite identity in contemporary poetry, but its critique is complicated by the fact that the poem closely follows its own advice. It makes sure to "Get the word 'Mennonite' in at least / twice, once in the title," for example, and it deploys each of the markers of Mennonite identity that it suggests are problematically tokenized. "Choose two from old Bibles, humbly beautiful quilts, / Fraktur, and the *Martyr's Mirror* in Dutch," it begins, going on to encourage authors to include "zwiebach / vareniki, borscht, and the farm, / which if possible should be lost now" (86).

If Gundy's poem critiques the use of what he earlier called the "colorful, obvious markers of Mennonite identity" in poetry, it does so precisely by raising each of them in turn, capitalizing on their exoticism even as it exposes and disavows this process. Both Shirley Showalter and Julia Spicher Kasdorf point to Gundy's poem as perceptively critiquing the dilemma facing the contemporary Mennonite author. Writing in 2009, Showalter describes the poem as Gundy's "gentle prod to himself as well as to other poets," noting the particular challenge facing authors who engage Mennonite identity in their literature today. "The problem of being a Mennonite writer is that you cannot be one completely un-self-consciously anymore, and too much self-consciousness has ruined many a writer," she observes. Showalter turns to Gundy's poem as evidence that "perhaps awareness of the paradox itself is the only answer to this dilemma." Kasdorf, meanwhile, suggests Gundy's poem "pokes fun at the overly self-conscious 'new Mennonite' poet who has internalized society's desire for cultural stereotypes and who clutters his poems with signs of authenticity" (*Body* 54). But if the poem does address an aspiring poet—"You, of course, are a backslidden, / overlearned, doubtridden, egodriven / quasi-believer," it reads (86–87)—its primary reference remains something called "the new Mennonite poem." It is this slight distance, from a *poem about identity* to a *poem about identity in poetry*, that enables Gundy's work to capitalize on the very process of exoticizing that it critiques, so that the ostensible object of the poem's concern (i.e., a discredited, reified form of traditional Mennonite cultural identity) is able to continue its function as the work's animating force. What is more, by embedding this account of Mennonite writing in a poem, rather than an essay, Gundy not only identifies but demonstrates how the critique of essentialized identity does nothing to prevent its ongoing function in literary texts.

Just how powerful is the Mennonite Thing? Well, Gundy has published at least seven books of poetry, in addition to several hundred poems in various journals, and "How to Write the New Mennonite Poem" is one of his only poems to explicitly address Mennonite identity. He has called the poem an "exception" to his larger body of work (*Greatest* 8) and concedes he wrote it "mainly as a sort of joke" (*Walker* 122), if "partly out of frustration at being turned down by a Mennonite magazine because [his] poems lacked particular cultural markers" (*Greatest* 8). In spite of this—or, as I'm arguing here, because of it—"How to Write" quickly became one of his most discussed and reproduced poems. After first being published in the inaugural issue of *Mennonot* in 1993, it was promptly reprinted in the *Mennonite Weekly Review*. Gundy himself selected it as the only one of his own poems to include in his 1997 review of US Mennonite poetry for the *Mennonite Quarterly Review*, an essay later republished in his award-winning collection *Walker in the Fog*, where the poem is reproduced in full[9]—as it was when he included it in his 2003 chapbook, *Greatest Hits: 1986–2003*. Kasdorf, meanwhile, reproduced "How to Write" in full in her 2001 collection of essays, *The Body and the Book*, while Ann Hostetler selected it as one of six poems by Gundy for inclusion in her 2003 anthology, *A Cappella: Mennonite Voices in Poetry*. The poem's enduring popularity is surely due, in no small part, to its reproduction of the most clichéd representations of Mennonite cultural authenticity. But if it succeeds because of its ambivalent adherence to the logic it critiques, this stands as further testament to the precision of its argument: readers want that Mennonite Thing. Gundy sometimes speaks dismissively of the poem—writing that "its rather fussy and (I thought) comic instructions have been taken more seriously by critics than by other Mennonite poets," and adding that he "stand[s] with the poets" on this point ("Doubt" 342)—but I want to reiterate the poem's significance, for its logic is far from unique. In fact, I would risk suggesting it is but the clearest example of a leading paradigm in the field.

Gundy's poem reads in direct conversation with a number of other poems explicitly engaging Mennonite identity, including Kasdorf's much-anthologized poem, "Mennonites."[10] In one sense, Kasdorf's poem, first published in her acclaimed debut collection, *Sleeping Preacher*, is a fitting object for Gundy's critique. Not only does it bear many of the identity markers parodied by Gundy, and there is little question that it has circulated, at least in part, because of the capital it gains within the multicultural exoticization of ethnicity. Kasdorf herself notes that when the poem was anthologized in Stuart Hirschberg's multicultural reader *The Many*

Worlds of Literature, it came complete with what she calls a "wildly embellished" biographical blurb about her own Mennonite past, one that effectively "wrapped [her] in a quilt" (*Body* 57). More recently, Froese Tiessen has compared the poems and finds it "interesting" that "both Kasdorf and Gundy implicitly conflate 'Swiss' and 'Russian' Mennonite experiences here (as well as American and Canadian experiences)." Though Froese Tiessen suggests this is reflective of a former era of identarian logic—"In a former paradigm," she writes, "it was convenient and acceptable to do so" ("After" 217)—I am suggesting that, acceptable or not, this "paradigm" remains prevalent today.

In my reading, Kasdorf's poem—like Gundy's—is far from a naïve replication of an essentialized cultural identity, and it strikes me that its cross-cultural engagement with Mennonite identity is done for reasons other than convenience. In fact, the poem's enigmatic first line, "We keep our quilts in closets and do not dance," is notable in that it raises the specter of the Mennonite Thing through its disavowal, opening with an archetypal Mennonite object only to immediately close the door on it. In his concise critical reading of the poem, Gundy points to its description of Mennonites as rushing to "clean up [God's] disasters," its positioning of Nazi soldiers as "heroes" for helping Mennonite refugees, and its closing image of the Mennonite singing voices "lift[ing], as chaff lifts toward God," as evidence of the poem's "understated but radical irony" that raises "primary markers of Mennonite identity" only to have them threaten to "dissolve, to be inadequate against the gathering sense of lack of worth or identity" (*Walker* 99). This is in line with my own reading, and I would add that it may be because of the rural, pastoral, and "simple" connotations of the Mennonite Thing that such markers of irony or ambivalence are at risk of being misrecognized by those who come to such texts expecting earnest expressions of cultural authenticity. According to Kasdorf, not only has her poem been widely misread as straightforward autoethnography, there have been some for whom the poem's ambivalent ending is so out of keeping with their expectations that they have simply assumed she does not understand the meaning of "chaff" (*Body* 69). Similarly, readers' responses to the poem's central question, posited midway through the piece, will largely depend on how they have read the poem's engagement with Mennonite identity. "This is why we cannot leave the beliefs," the narrator declares, after recounting the persecutions of earlier generations of Mennonites. "Or what else would we be?" (129). This question seems to have been taken as rhetorical by many readers,[11] but in my reading it seems to present a radical invitation for us to reconsider the foundational narratives and markers of our collective identity. Gundy's interrogation of a clichéd Mennonite identity in "How to Write" is obviously much more explicit, but Kasdorf's "Mennonites," too, seems to offer its markers of Mennonite identity self-consciously, invoking a "traditional" Mennonite identity as part of a larger effort to both animate and interrogate her readers' expectations.

For an apparently earnest critique of what is at stake in Kasdorf's representation of Mennonite identity, it is worth turning briefly to David Wright's poem, "A New Mennonite Replies to Julia Kasdorf."[12] Although Wright's poem engages most obviously with Kasdorf's work, it also seems to play off of Gundy's piece, turning the "New" of Gundy's title from a literary narrative (a new Mennonite poem) into a conversion narrative (a newly converted Mennonite). Wright's poem suggests that appeals to the conventional markers of a traditional Mennonite cultural identity implicitly exclude members of Mennonite churches who were not born into the Swiss or Russian communities. "As best I can tell, most of our quilts here were inherited," Wright's poem begins. "Not much borscht, / few shoofly pies at potlucks—instead it's / hummus, free range chicken, carob brownies." The poem speaks of the "Many new and remade and restless / and not-quite Mennonites" who "cannot play / the name game," and who "park ourselves in pews / next to women and men who know better / what real Mennonites really are" (5). If Gundy's poem takes up identity via representational issues within Mennonite writing, Wright's poem can be understood as extending this concern to Mennonite identity in and of itself. In fact, the ironic repetition of "real"—"what real Mennonites really are"—questions the function of the Mennonite Thing not in literature but within the pews of the church itself.

Wright's poem makes an important argument about the exclusivity of a certain form of Mennonite identity and engages with these markers of cultural authenticity in order to disturb their normativity and blend them into an expanded vision for the community. It places a productive pressure not only on the easily fetishized objects of a conventional Mennonite identity (quilts, borscht, and so on) but also on the divisiveness of a certain form of Mennonite theology, one that leads church members to "seem amused," "grieved," or "simply angry" at the prospect of an expanded vision that would include touchstones from other cultures or denominations. However, it would be a mistake to read the poem as straightforwardly didactic. Take, for example, the narrator's confession, midway through the poem, that he "need[s] the book / on 606" (5). On the surface, such a confession serves to emphasize that the narrator feels himself to be outside the conventions that govern the Mennonite church. But by leaving the reference to "606" unexplained, Wright deploys it as a shibboleth of sorts, exercising something near to the type of insider knowledge against which much of the poem rails, and quietly reinscribing the narrator within the boundaries of the community.[13] As in its closing image of a Mennonite woman in a "heavy head covering" eating at China Buffet (which is coupled with a sly reference to ethnicity and passing), the poem quietly signals its awareness that the line between insiders and outsiders is less firm than it may appear. Moreover, its largely earnest theological critique is destabilized, at least in part, by how closely Wright's poem follows the prescription offered by Gundy's parody: it, too, is sure to "Get the word 'Mennonite' in at least twice, once in the title," as Gundy recommends, and it, too, references quilts, borscht, and shoofly pies, as well as a character from the *Martyrs Mirror*. There is even a Mennonite mother (although, unlike per Gundy's recommendation regarding grandmothers, she is alive and doesn't appear to have suffered). Much like Gundy's and Kasdorf's poems, then, it seems the success of Wright's "A New Mennonite" depends in part on the very Thing it sets out to interrogate.

Quite apart from the legitimate question of how readers position themselves in relation to texts like the above poems, it seems important to reiterate that the referent for the various identity markers they invoke and engage is far from a clearly defined specific ethno-religious community. That is, the question of whether or not a reified and exclusionary Mennonite identity like the ones constructed by these poems truly exists—and it clearly doesn't, for all three poems showcase an amalgamation of Swiss and Russian Mennonite history and identity markers—is largely irrelevant to the *function* of Mennonite identity within them. Isn't the argument of Gundy's poem, lodged at work like Kasdorf's "Mennonites" and Wright's "A New Mennonite," precisely that the Mennonite identity being invoked and circulating in such works is simply the *idea* of an authentic conservative Mennonite identity, one expressed through (though not reducible to) stereotypical markers of Mennonite dress, language, and belief? And yet even as these poems carefully distance themselves from an essentialized, decontextualized Mennonite identity, they also constitute fine illustrations of how that identity continues to function in contemporary Mennonite literature, each having become important "Mennonite poems" in their own right. Not only did Hostetler include all three of these poems in her influential anthology of Mennonite poetry, for example, she positioned them as the first poem for each author. And little wonder: paraphrasing Žižek, we can see how each of these poems takes the butt of its own joke seriously, showing how identity continues to function even when we claim not to believe in it.

I want to close this section with one final example of a contemporary poet playing self-consciously with Mennonite literary identity as Thing. Like Wright, G. C. Waldrep was not born into a Mennonite community but chose to join a Mennonite church later in life. Where Kasdorf and Gundy write in response to what Kasdorf has called the "autoethnographic demand"—that is, they are wrestling with the knowledge that readers will expect their work to express their Mennonite heritage in some recognizable manner—Wright and Waldrep wrestle with the knowledge that their own work, lacking the immediately identifiable markers of the genre, is unlikely be immediately recognized as "Mennonite poetry" at all. Waldrep's 2009 prose-poem exploring these issues, "Mennonite Poem," begins with what is immediately recognizable as an effort to engage the Mennonite Thing. "Every Mennonite poet has to write a Mennonite poem," it begins. "But I am not a Mennonite, and so instead this is a poem about a frieze portraying a small band of oboe players" (25). This immediate rejection of the frame invoked by its declarative title, followed by its ironic invocation of oboe players, throws the reader's assumptions about what they might find in "Mennonite Poem" into sharp relief. And yet if much of the prose poem does, indeed, consist of speculation regarding a missing oboe player whom the poet imagines to have been caught in traffic, it cannot resist digressing briefly into disavowals of the Mennonite Thing itself. "If this were a Mennonite poem there would be some invocation of the prairie, the grasses—the insolubility of an ablative sky—but since it's not, I'm going to place it inside a forest," begins the second stanza. Imagining the trees humming along with a lost oboe player in the fourth stanza, Waldrep suggests they "sing in four-part harmony, as they most certainly would if they were Mennonites, or at least the sort of Mennonites most likely to appear in a Mennonite poem" (25).

In her cogent analysis of this poem, Magdalene Redekop's correspondence with Waldrep resonates with my description of Mennonite identity as Thing and echoes Gundy's account of the motivations behind "How to Write the New Mennonite Poem." She writes, "When I emailed Waldrep about 'Mennonite Poem,' he said that it began as 'a response to the commodification of Mennonite heritage' that he observed in a group of poems published in an American journal called *Mennonite World Review*. Those poems, he said, 'dramatized the distance I felt from the 'heritage' thrust of Menno-lit.' As a convert, he explained, he found 'arguments of "heritage" and culture divorced from faith . . . not only problematic, but also exclusive: indeed, they perform an erasure'" (qtd. in Redekop, *Making Believe* 312). Like Wright's "New Mennonite," Waldrep's "Mennonite Poem" clearly means to critique the exclusivity of the role that Mennonite identity as Thing has come to play in literature—"the sort" of Mennonite identity, as Waldrep puts it, that is "most likely to appear in a Mennonite poem." Where the poems by Gundy, Kasdorf, and even Wright fold back onto themselves by their appeals to the very markers they set out to critique, however, Waldrep largely manages to resist the temptation to re-inscribe his poem within the recognized parameters of the field. He raises the specter of prairie grasses and four-part singing, to be sure, but there are no ironic disavowals of bonnets, ethnic food, pacifism, quilts, or German, or any other clichés that would firmly ground the poem in "Menno-lit" by means of its conspicuous rejection. Instead, while the poem begins in certainties—"Every Mennonite poet has to write a Mennonite poem," he writes, "But I am not a Mennonite"—it ends in a deep and productive uncertainty. The lost oboe player, knowing that he has missed the rehearsal, imagines his fellow oboe players searching the horizon and drifts into a meandering speculation: "this, the missing oboe player thinks, is probably a lot like being Mennonite, though whether by this he means himself, or his colleague on the dune, or the act of seeing, or being seen, or possibly his other colleagues who are by now driving home, having meals with their families, shopping, etc., things Mennonites do, or even the automobile, perfectly serviceable, perfectly stationary, engine idling, inside of which his body comfortably rests, neither the forest nor the music is sure" (25). What does it mean to be Mennonite, he wonders? Is "Mennonite" the subject of this poem or its object? Is it more like the "act of seeing, or being seen"? Is it perhaps like a "perfectly serviceable" but "perfectly stationary" car, comfortable and useless? Or is Mennonite literature more like a frieze of oboe players, a frozen tableau of artists unable to make music, locked in a moment of time, unaware that one of their members is missing? And what, ultimately, does a "Mennonite Poem" look like? With these unanswerable questions, Waldrep refuses to allow the signifier "Mennonite" to settle into place. But with the declarative title that insists this is, indeed, a "Mennonite Poem," he claims a space of his own within the field.

Once we recognize how the Mennonite Thing functions in contemporary Mennonite writing, we can find examples of it strewn across the field. We can see it throughout much of Kirsten Eve Beachy's recent edited collection *Tongue Screws and Testimonies*, for example, in which it seems that many of the Mennonite writers and artists who took up Beachy's call to engage the *Martyrs Mirror*, a sixteenth-century martyrology that is an iconic text in the Mennonite tradition, do so in order to carefully distance themselves from it. We can see it in Alayna Munce's *When I Was Young and in My Prime*, with its young urban protagonist struggling to repurpose the most traditional elements of her family's heritage as part of her attempt to negotiate the shifting contours of a transgenerational, collective Mennonite identity.[14] We see it in highly self-conscious works like Stephen Beachy's *Boneyard* and Nathan Dueck's *He'll*, each of which—as I briefly note in chapter 5 of this study—distances itself from its own account of Amish and Mennonite characters by presenting itself as a "found manuscript." And we can certainly see it in much of Miriam Toews's work, in which, despite her clear critiques of readily identifiable communities, she also seems eager to expose the simulacrum of identity as Thing. In *A Complicated Kindness*, for example, teenagers work in a heritage village standing at the edge of East Village, Mennonites dressing up as "Mennonites" to meet the expectations of the tourists who arrive to gawk. In *Irma Voth* (discussed at length in the next chapter), a Mexican Mennonite colony is literally turned into a film set, yet the eccentric filmmaker makes it clear that he is uninterested in the Mennonites themselves. "I don't care about the Mennonites as a group," he insists. "I'm interested in the fact that nobody would understand their language and that they were uniform. There's no distinction, one from the other, and so they are props, essentially, for pure emotion" (243). Here the Lacanian logic of the Mennonite Thing reaches its peak: while "real" Mennonites self-consciously perform their Mennoniteness, the signification of Mennonite identity is completely emptied, signaling nothing but the idea of otherness itself.

Even I am suggesting that Mennonite writing that engages identity as Thing is particularly prevalent today, self-conscious literary engagements with Mennonite identity are not entirely new. In a previous project, I traced the emergence of what I called the "Mennonite exotic" as part of the tokenizing logic of multicultural discourses of otherness, noting that early Mennonite critics such as John Ruth and Peter C. Erb had cautioned that "Mennonites don't need [. . .] evidence that we, too, can be packaged and sold in the marketplace of literary sensation" (Ruth 68), and that Mennonites were in danger of "preserv[ing] their ethnic peculiarities, as they do canned goods, to sell when the best market conditions arise" (Erb 205).[15] Ruth and Erb were concerned about the tendency of literary writers to slide into stereotypes, and both note the economic reward incentivizing such work. There is, however, evidence that even earlier writers were engaging those stereotypes self-consciously. Consider, for example, Elmer Suderman's 1974 poem, "Directions for Celebrating the Centennial of the Coming of the Low German Mennonites from the Steppes of Russia to the American Prairies." "It is best to be a Birthright Mennonite and have / grandparents who came from the Molotschna in / the 1870s," it begins, admonishing readers to "Avoid / laughter unless you can laugh in Low German" (2). It closes with a warning that folds back upon itself with precisely the type of self-conscious declaration through disavowal that I am discussing in this chapter:

> Above all, and you must remember this, so pay
> very careful attention: Don't write poems about
> being a Mennonite. No poems. A poem, remember,
> is a lie, is a lie. No poem, please, not even a
> prose poem. (2)

Suderman's prescriptive poem is almost eerie in its clear anticipation of Gundy's "How to Write" by nearly twenty years, suggesting something of the longstanding function of the Mennonite Thing in the field, as well as the persistent frustration poets have felt regarding the autoethnographic imperative in Mennonite writing. If the function of irony in Gundy's "How to Write" is somewhat more complex than it is in Suderman's relatively straightforward affirmation-through-ironic-disavowal, the nuances of "Directions for Celebrating" should not be overlooked. Note, in just the closing lines quoted here, the repetition ("poem" is included five times; "remember" and "is a lie" are included twice); several sets of internal rhymes (the long vowels of O ["so" / "don't" / "no" / "prose" / "poems"], E ["please" / "remember" / "even"], and I ["write" / "lie" / "Mennonite"]); and alliteration ("poems. A poem" / "poem, please" / "prose poem"); as well as its establishment of an internal dactylic rhyme ("remember" / "attention" / "Mennonite" / and "is a lie"). Read on the page, the irony of Suderman's poem is complemented by the use of line breaks that make clear the straightforward diction is meant to be read as poetry; read aloud, the aural playfulness of the argument comes to life, with the deceptively plain language choices leaping with repetition, rhymes, alliteration, and rhythm.

A decade later, in the 1983 poem "Roots," David Waltner-Toews playfully describes Rudy Wiebe, already well known as a Mennonite author, as digging through a potato field. Although Wiebe is unable to find his "roots"—the genealogical urge in Russian Mennonite culture being the poem's primary trope—he does stumble upon an unidentifiable bone that gets up and walks to Winnipeg and back before ending up in his mother's potato soup. Much as in his popular Tante Tina poems (in which

Waltner-Toews takes on the heavily accented voice and persona of a conservative Mennonite woman, and which he occasionally performs in drag), "Roots" raises the most conventional markers of Mennonite ethnic identity—from *rollkuchen* and borscht to stories of the Russian colonies—strategically, his ironic tone establishing a distance from the material even as he engages it sympathetically. And, much like Gundy's "How to Write," Waltner-Toews's "Roots" self-consciously capitalizes on the very form of identity it is ostensibly interrogating. Nowhere is this clearer than in the poem's italicized first line, which, in declaring the poem to be "*not about Rudy Wiebe, but for him*" (75), neatly encapsulates the inversion of identity I have been wrestling with in this chapter. Just as it is possible to write an entire poem about "Rudy Wiebe" and declare that it is not about Rudy Wiebe, Mennonite identity is able to function throughout contemporary Mennonite literature, much of which continues to be about "Mennonites," even where it has stopped being about Mennonites.

While the majority of critical engagements with the idea of Mennonite writing—from Ruth's *Mennonite Identity and Literary Art* (1978) to Harry Loewen's *Mennonite Images: Historical, Cultural, and Literary Essays Dealing with Mennonite Issues* (1980) to Froese Tiessen and Hinchcliffe's *Acts of Concealment: Mennonite/s Writing in Canada* (1992) and Reimer's *Mennonite Literary Voices: Past and Present* (1993)—have been thoroughly earnest affairs, a more playful, self-aware engagement with identity can also be located in the nonfiction tradition. This is obviously the case, for example, in books like Emerson L. Lesher's 1985 *Muppie Manual: The Mennonite Urban Professional's Handbook for Humility and Success*, and J. Craig Haas and Steve Nolt's 1993 *Mennonite Starter Kit: A Handy Guide for the New Mennonites (Everything They Forgot to Tell You in Church Membership Class!)*, two how-to-be-a-Mennonite texts, the latter of which includes a pseudo-academic article entitled "Identifying an Identifiable Identity" (27), which gently mocks Mennonite frivols and clichés in order to restore the notion of Mennonite identity. Less obvious, perhaps, it the way in which the Mennonite Thing can circulate un-ironically in our more earnest critical efforts—as in my own decision to open this chapter with a discussion of the "ur-Mennonite" sex joke. Is there not a sense in which my discussion of the joke also functions as a form of disavowal? As if the act of analysis somehow diminishes the fact that I began my critique of the Mennonite Thing by animating it as forcefully as possible? I would argue that many critical works operate in this manner, deeply indebted to identitarian logic even where they claim to set it aside. Perhaps it is true, as Maurice Mierau writes in a slightly different argument about Mennonite writing, that "the quintessential Mennonite position" is to be "detached and obsessively attached at the same time" ("Why" 78).

The circulation of the Mennonite Thing in literature and criticism is not entirely new, then, but what does seem different today is its prominence and the fact that so many of the field's authors now seem willing to engage with elements of it as a primary mode of identity rather than as a mode of critical commentary. Suderman and Waltner-Toews may be caricaturing Russian Mennonite voices to reduce the sting of their otherwise earnest critiques, but contemporary writers of Mennonite descent are much more likely to write with a meta-fictional awareness of the impossibility of ever truly "fixing" the tradition in any meaningful way.[16] Today, when the very aspects of Mennonite identity that would make it recognizable in literature are the ones most heavily overdetermined, a common response has been to engage this identity indirectly, through some form of critical distancing, so that the Mennonite Thing is disavowed, even as it is invoked and animated. In simultaneously satisfying and disturbing their readers' expectation for the Mennonite Thing, writers such as Gundy, Kasdorf, Wright, and Waldrep, like Suderman and Waltner-Toews before them, effectively engage the conventions of Mennonite identity without fully occupying its predetermined position.

OTHER MENNONITE THINGS

To this point I have been mostly following the convention of Mennonite literary studies as a form of minority literature, in that I have been focusing on how a conspicuous disavowal of Mennonite identity has enabled conventional markers of traditional Russian and Swiss Mennonite heritage to continue functioning in writing *by* Mennonites. There is no reason, of course, that these same markers cannot be deployed by those approaching

Mennonite characters and concerns from outside the field as it is commonly understood, and turning to such works helps us recognize how thin the line is between ironic distance and essentializing embrace. The rampant (and clearly effective) use of Mennonite and Amish identity markers as selling points for romance fiction—"You slap a bonnet on the cover and double the sales," as one marketer told *Newsweek* (qtd. in V. Weaver-Zercher 4)—offers one particularly lucrative example. Comically exaggerated versions of conservative Mennonites abound in popular culture, often serving as either comic relief or as a shorthanded effort to sharpen contrast with the subject matter at hand. The popular Canadian television show *Letterkenny* is a case in point. The series focuses on the problems of Letterkenny, a fictional small town in Southern Ontario, and it includes a running subplot about the main characters' Mennonite neighbors, Noah and Anita Dyck. The Dycks are a hodgepodge of Mennonite stereotypes, Russian Mennonite by their last names but Old Order (Swiss) in their clothing and use of horse-and-buggy, and apparently Amish in their adherence to *Rumspringa*. When the Mennonite joke gets its inevitable moment in *Letterkenny*—the impossibly naïve Mennonite patriarch refers to dancing as "a vertical expression of a horizontal intention"—it, like the majority of the show's dialogue about the Mennonite characters, fails to rise above simple innuendo.[17] The Italian filmmaker Luca Guadagnino's film *Suspiria* (2018), by contrast, invokes the Mennonite Thing as a means of linking its demonic plot to a vaguely defined fundamentalist religious community.[18] In this remake of a 1977 cult classic, an untrained Mennonite dancer from rural Ohio named Suzie (played by Dakota Johnson of *50 Shades of Grey* fame) manages to score a place in an elite dance school in Berlin that turns out to be run by a literal coven of witches. In a truly bizarre closing scene, the young dancer is revealed to be none other than Mother Suspiriorum—one of the "Three Mothers" that have ruled earth for centuries. Along with a demon-like aid, the young Mennonite dancer oversees a mass murder of half the coven before the film closes with her taking over the school. Even starring roles by Tilda Swinton and a soundtrack by Radiohead's Thom Yorke can't save the film, though it does manage to offer an original twist on the old question of why Mennonites shouldn't dance.

Perhaps the most notable recent example of the Mennonite Thing in popular culture, however, can be found in the two seasons of the television crime drama *Pure*. First produced by Canadian Broadcasting Corporation, *Pure* was heavily promoted as a six-part series based *very* loosely on the true story of a Mennonite crime ring that smuggled cocaine from Mexico into Canada. The first season's plot showed an effort to engage Mennonite concerns and even the long arc of Anabaptist history, with individual Mennonites grappling with their faith and pacifist beliefs, and a dramatic finale that is clearly meant to invoke the Mennonite martyr narratives of the sixteenth century. Beyond these broad strokes and its central conceit, however, the show managed to be both sensationalistic and patronizing while being littered with factual errors. Panned by scholars across Canada as being a "jarring misrepresentation" (Gingrich and Fast 280), "highly problematic" (R. Loewen "More"), and "exploitative" (V. Thiessen), the show was canceled after a single season. In a fascinating example of the transnational nature of the Mennonite Thing, however, it was promptly picked up by the American network WGN. WGN invested in a full second season, even bringing in Alyson Hannigan (of *How I Met Your Mother*, *American Pie*, and *Buffy the Vampire Slayer* fame) for several episodes. WGN took the exoticizing logic implicit in the CBC's first season of the show to an extreme, promoting its second season on social media by inviting Twitter users to play a game that required them to discover which Mennonite-looking ornamental cookie tin contained bags of drugs, and on the streets of Los Angeles by encouraging tourists to take free "buggy" rides and pose for photos in a pop-up "barn" alongside bricks of faux cocaine, stacks of money, and women dressed up in stereotypically "Mennonite" attire.

Although the promotional campaign for season two of *Pure* is an extreme example, it is not difficult to find other cases where the line between what is often a strategic and self-conscious deployment of identity as Thing slips into an essentialized Mennonite ethnic identity. The recent establishment of a formal "Mennonite Heritage Week" by the Canadian federal government would seem a case in point. Put forth by British Columbia Conservative (and proud Mennonite) Member of Parliament (MP) Ed Fast, the private members' business proposed the following: "That, in the opinion of the House, the government should recognize the contributions that Canadian Mennonites have made to building Canadian society, their history of hope and perseverance, the richness of Mennonite culture, their role in promoting peace and justice both at home and abroad, and the importance of educating and reflecting upon Mennonite heritage for future generations, by declaring the second week of September as Mennonite Heritage Week."[19] The prospect of a Mennonite Heritage Week offered a rare moment of near political consensus in the House. An MP from Southern Manitoba, Candice Bergen, happily rose in favor of the bill and even quoted extensively from the popular Mennonite satire website *The Daily Bonnet* in making her case to her colleagues in the Canadian parliament. "If you're Mennonite, you're going to get these headlines, I won't try to explain it," she noted, before offering "Sound of Knacking Zoat Used as Mennonite Mating Call" and similar headlines to what appear to be empty chairs, with a few MPs guffawing off screen. When the Speaker bent to the "unanimous consent" of the House to allow her to continue beyond her allotted time, Bergen responded by collapsing the community's religious and ethnic elements completely. "*Dankeschön*," she said. "That's Mennonite for [thank you]."[20] By a vote of 275–6, the Canadian government formally established the second week of every September as "Mennonite Heritage Week."

Outside the halls of government, the response was predictably different. A *Winnipeg Free Press* article on the proposal took stock of the response from church and academic leaders, quoting the Chair of Mennonite Studies, Royden Loewen, as describing himself as "appalled" at the proposal, and Karl Koop, professor at Canadian Mennonite University, as suggesting that even the discussion of the matter in Parliament was "an embarrassment" (qtd. in Longhurst). The directors of the Canadian Conference of Mennonite Brethren Churches and of Mennonite Church Manitoba, respectively, both chimed in to point out the week relies on an erroneous conflation of ethnicity and theology (Longhurst). "We were all a little stunned and a lot embarrassed earlier this year to see Members of Parliament from across all party lines get up in the House of Commons and sing our praises," added S. L. Klassen, who writes a popular online blog under the pseudonym "The Drunken Mennonite." "It was a rare moment of cross-partisan consensus that just goes to show that unity of purpose is most easily attained when there is general ignorance about the subject at hand. And when the stakes are low" ("How to"). At a time that Mennonite scholarship is elsewhere exploring the most regressive examples of Mennonite ethnocentrism, this state-sanctioned embrace of Mennonite ethnicity seems awkward at best.[21] It should also serve as a reminder of just how easily the self-conscious irony of the Mennonite Thing can be lost when it is pressed into service of the most conventional forms of stable identity claims.

Part of my argument in this chapter is that the exoticizing logic in evidence within the most reductive and stereotypical portrayals of the Mennonite community in popular culture is not always easily disentangled from the strategic and self-conscious deployment of essentialized identity markers common in contemporary Mennonite writing, nor are they necessarily far removed from the corridors of political power. I am not willing to follow Žižek fully through to his politicized conclusions about ideology, but the questions prompted by his work are nevertheless worth asking as we consider the circulation of the Mennonite Thing beyond the narrow confines of the field as it is conventionally understood. What role has the abstract idea of a distinct, reified Mennonite identity—one that may be founded in but is often extrapolated far beyond the lived experiences of Mennonite communities—come to play in the structure of these communities, institutions, and churches? To what extent has the threat of the disappearance of the Mennonite Thing, or what Di Brandt calls "the myth of the vanishing Mennonite" ("In Praise" 129), become indispensable to the shoring up of the community's borders? Is it even possible that, rather than a communal heritage and theological tradition under threat, much of what endures and circulates today as distinctly Mennonite in North America is best understood as the product, rather than the object, of such a myth? If so, how might this process have limited, rather than protected, the Mennonite community?

Perhaps, following Žižek, we ought to consider if the distance-taking I have been tracking in the literature is a form of "inherent transgression," in which "the very emergence of a certain 'value' which serves as the point of ideological identification relies on its transgression, on some mode of taking a distance towards it" ("Inherent" 3). In such a context, it becomes increasingly difficult to distinguish between invocations of conventional identity markers as strategic and ironic, and those that function as regressive and essentializing, inasmuch as they begin to look like two sides of the same coin. In the first chapter of this study, I drew on Stephen Greenblatt's caution regarding the strategic use of conventional literary history by minoritized fields of study, where he warned that scholars might "believe that they are appropriating traditional forms, but it may well be the forms that are appropriating them" (59). Might something similar be at play with the Mennonite Thing?

My concern with the blurry line between how Mennonite identity functions as ironic Thing and as regressive essentialism reflects what I see as a limitation with Žižek's own work. For Žižek, the ostensible ambiguity or unknowability of what constitutes identity as "Thing" is central to its animating force. "The element which holds together a given community cannot be reduced to the point of symbolic identification," Žižek insists. "The Thing is not directly a collection of these features," he writes; "there is 'something more' in it, something that *is present* in these features, that *appears* through them" (*Tarrying* 201). Žižek will argue that this "something more" is, in fact, the enjoyment one gets not from the actual items or practices, nor even the belief itself, but rather from the tautological experience of believing that others believe in it: "'I believe in the (national) Thing,'" he writes, "equals 'I believe that others (members of my community) believe in the Thing'" (*Tarrying* 201). Yet is it necessarily true that the "Thing" itself is, in fact, empty of signification? Žižek has been criticized elsewhere for sliding into essentializing logic even as he claims to be moving beyond it, as in Che Gossett's reading of what he calls the "transcendentalizing of sexual difference" in Žižek's fumbling attempt to critique what he calls "transgenderism."[22] Here, a related issue arises as he attempts to dismiss the concrete identity markers in the name of an ostensibly empty ideological "nodal point." Such an argument, I worry, sidesteps the painfully obvious: that the invocation of essentializing elements of highly specific and visible forms of Mennonite identity while mystifying their significance as something "other" than, or "beyond" concrete markers of white Mennonite ethnic difference risks affirming that identity in almost transcendental terms. The point, emphatically, is that markers like bonnets and *summa borscht* are neither empty nor mystical, nor are they a simple "multitude of 'floating signifiers,' or protoideological elements" magically fixed into meaning by the term "Mennonite." To the contrary, they are markers of highly specific Euro-Mennonite communities, which, if they have been historically dominant in the North American Mennonite tradition, should not be mistaken as the defining terms of a broader Mennonite identity. The key here, then, is that though an essentialized Mennonite identity may be *functioning* as Thing in the pages of contemporary Mennonite literature much as Žižek suggests—as a type of mystical nodal point holding together a field of floating signifiers—we must be careful to not allow self-consciousness or other distancing gestures to obscure us to the risk of an apophatic or ironic re-entrenchment of specific markers of white Mennonite ethnicity as the normative parameters for Mennonite literature itself.

CONCLUSION

In the next chapter, I will turn to Miriam Toews's novel *Irma Voth* as a response to Carlos Reygadas's film *Silent Light*, reading the two as offering a fascinating debate about the reification of Mennonite identity as Thing, and following North American Mennonite writing beyond literature and into Mexico. Before moving on, however, let me return, briefly, to the joke with which I began this chapter. In *Dancing Naked: Narrative Strategies for Writing Across Centuries*, Brandt describes the "new Mennonite writing" of the early 1990s as undertaking a "kind of striptease, taking off the clothes of the official story, layer by layer, stripping away the codes we have lived by to get to the stories underneath of our real, aching bodies in the world" (36). After offering examples from poems by Michelle Hildebrandt, Heidi Harms, and Patrick Friesen, she continues: "What the new Mennonite poets are doing is *yup*, confessing, taking their clothes off in public all right, but they're doing it standing up, and yes, the old joke was right, if you do it that way, it turns into a kind of dancing" (41). Twenty-five years later, Mennonite writers continue to take their clothes off in this sense of an ontological striptease, though they seem increasingly self-conscious about it, as if they are now well aware of the particular audience that gathers when Mennonites get naked. Today, when authors and critics of Mennonite descent choose to engage Mennonite identity in their writing, many begin by anticipating their interpellation into an exoticizing discourse of cultural authenticity, a process they set out to counter through a series of distancing gestures that leaves them at least a little clothed. In simultaneously satisfying and disturbing their readers' expectations for the Mennonite Thing, writers such as Gundy, Kasdorf, Wright, and many others before and since, manage to engage the conventions of Mennonite identity without fully occupying its predetermined position. Far from lodging simple critiques of an outdated model of Mennonite identity, however, such works have become a constitutive mode for the field.

How are we to read the varied invocations of an essentialized Mennonite identity that continue to circulate in academic, popular, and political discourses well into our ostensibly post-identity age? The answer I've tried to suggest here is that it requires a form of reading that attends not only to the strategic deployment of identity *within* the field as it is conventionally understood, but also to the larger contexts in which such works circulate. Recalling our discussion from the introduction, it requires an understanding of Mennonite literature not as a canon of clearly defined works but rather as "a mode of circulation and of reading," to redirect Damrosch's phrasing. The point is not simply that *any* discussion of Mennonites in literature can be read as participating in and perpetuating the field's longstanding focus on Mennonite identity, though that is certainly true. Nor do I mean to suggest there is a clear distinction to be drawn between an ideological function of identity as Thing and some implicitly "real" or "authentic" identity that can fully and accurately manifest the contemporary Mennonite experience. Such a desire for the "real" is what produces the conceit of identity as Thing in the first place. More broadly but also more simply, I am suggesting that a partial disavowal has become a primary means through which a widely discredited form of reified or essentialized Mennonite identity—which I have named the Mennonite Thing—not only continues to function in the field but remains one of its central animating forces. Moreover, I am suggesting that the ways in which the conventional parameters of the field as focusing on works strictly *by* (rather than also *about*) Mennonites can also work to limit our appreciation of the larger contexts in which these works are circulating and producing meaning. Affirming the field as a case of minor transnationalism allows us to track these wider concerns across borders and contexts in order to appreciate that it can be surprisingly difficult to make the type of clear distinctions we might want to draw between the ironic invocation of essentialized identity markers as a form of literary strategy and the exoticizing function of those same markers as they circulate in popular and political culture.

CHAPTER 4

IRMA VOTH WRITES BACK TO *SILENT LIGHT*

On Faith and Fantasy in Mexico

Early in the twenty-first century, a fascinating debate about the representation of Mennonite cultural difference has played out over borders and across media, bringing New Latin American cinema and Canadian fiction together in an unlikely setting: an isolated Russian Mennonite colony in the deserts of northern Mexico. A small network of such colonies dots the state of Chihuahua, home to the descendants of a mass migration of Mennonites who left the Canadian prairies in the early twentieth century in an effort to maintain their separation from the secular world. They brought with them a literal interpretation of the Bible that includes a theological commitment to simplicity, modesty, and a deep suspicion of the arts. They also brought *Plautdietsch*, or Low German, an oral dialect understood almost exclusively by their fellow colonists. In 2007, an eccentric Mexican director managed to film a movie about adultery among these Mennonites, shooting on location and in Low German, using mostly local colony members as actors.[1] This most implausible project—"somehow willed into unlikely existence," as the *New York Times* put it, "by the extravagantly talented Carlos Reygadas" (Dargis)—went on to premiere at the Cannes Film Festival, where it shared the 2008 Jury Prize under the title of *Stellet Licht* [*Silent Light*]. Three years later, the film's lead actress—the celebrated Canadian Mennonite author Miriam Toews—published a novel about a young Mennonite working as a translator for an ethically dubious

Mexican director attempting to film a movie about adultery in a colony in northern Mexico. Knopf released Toews's entertaining novel, *Irma Voth*, in 2011; it quickly became a bestseller.

As should be clear from even this quick summary of the two works, Toews's *Irma Voth* is a careful and strategic retort to Reygadas's *Silent Light*, restaging the film's plot and key scenes while systematically undermining its politics. For Reygadas, the isolation and potential unintelligibility of the conservative Russian Mennonites in Mexico are not obstacles to be overcome but rather key attributes to be exaggerated as part of his effort to present a drama that is paradoxically meant to be both utterly authentic and completely otherworldly. He is far from alone in taking this view. As Magdalene Redekop writes in a conversation about *Pure*, the "radical Anabaptist stance of separation from the world"—which she suggests can be understood as "our foundational gesture"—seems to be the feature of the community that "fascinates non-Mennonites." "To a casting director," she continues, "it must look as if the 'people apart' are ready-made for theatre, already dressed in costume" (*Making Believe* 75). Few have taken up this gesture with the relish of Reygadas, and Toews responds to the film's effort to capitalize on the exoticism of the colony setting by self-consciously locating the Mennonites within a broader social and historical migratory context, affirming the flawed agency of individual colony members and critiquing the community's efforts at self-isolation as a catastrophic failure of the imagination. While both works conclude by suggesting a miraculous rebirth is required to save the community, they disagree profoundly on the nature of that rebirth, and—perhaps—whether such a miracle is possible.

In the introduction to this study, I noted that the critical conversation around contemporary Mennonite literature in North America has routinely imagined the field in transnational terms, but it has focused almost exclusively on the work of Mennonites from Canada and the United States. This geography reflects the history of the field's emergence, of course, and, as I noted earlier, it follows the practice of many Mennonite institutions such as the Mennonite World Conference.[2] However, it is also one of the methodological assumptions that could be productively estranged by reconsidering Mennonite literature in North America as a case study in minor transnationalism. Here, too, Mennonite literary studies lags behind other fields of Mennonite studies—including, most obviously, Mennonite history[3]—but there are promising scholarly developments here as well, including a recent special issue of the *Journal of Mennonite Writing* that is focused on Mennonite Women in Mexico (guest edited by Abigail Carl-Klassen). In this chapter, I want to join this conversation by asking what the points of connection and tension between Reygadas's film and Toews's novel may have to tell us about the complexities of representing Mennonite cultural difference across media and beyond Canada and the United States. How do the divergent media and geopolitical contexts for these works—Mexican cinema and Canadian fiction, respectively—inform their intertextual dialogue and shape their respective portrayals of the Mennonite community? And how might an understanding of the theology and history of this specific group of Mennonites—an understanding almost completely absent from the non-Mennonite critical commentary on these works to date—help us understand the successes and failures of these two very different projects?

MIRACULOUS REALISM IN *SILENT LIGHT*

Silent Light opens with a single, extraordinary cross-faded shot that starts with a chorus of nocturnal insects and a black night sky that rotates almost imperceptibly as a host of stars slowly focus into view. It takes a full minute for the camera to pan down and level onto the darkened silhouette of a tree-lined horizon. A second minute sees an orange-red sunrise gather and clear; a third minute passes as the camera inches forward between two trees and a lush grain field is revealed in the graying light. The first cut of the film occurs at the four-minute and forty-second mark, first to a simple farmhouse and then quickly to its interior, where a large family is praying silently over breakfast. Much has been made of the film's opening, widely celebrated as "astonishing" (de Luca, *Realism* 73) and "spectacular" (Redekop, *Making Believe* 105), and there is little question that it is as beautiful as it is technically impressive. Here, however, I am most interested in how it reflects Reygadas's broader effort to estrange, rather than introduce, the Mennonite community that will be its subject. Together with the even longer sunset scene that returns viewers to the heavens at the film's close, the opening shot frames the film's narrative by presenting the Mennonites as profoundly, almost existentially, isolated. As José Teodoro reports, viewers "begin as if lost in the cosmos" (48), with a swirling night sky and no contextualizing details to help them ground themselves in a specific place or time.

The framing shots' dramatic rejection of spatial and temporal context extends throughout the film, as Reygadas refuses any information that might help viewers locate themselves in the highly specific historical, geographic, and theological context in which the story will unfold. The agricultural landscape of the opening, where nearly all the action of the film takes place, is undeniably beautiful, but it is also generic enough as a setting that it could be anywhere with wheat fields and gentle hills. Moreover, the austerity of colony life makes it similarly difficult to place the film in time. Although the Old Colony Mennonites of the film do not reject all technology, their modest use of electricity and dated automobiles or tractors simply position the film in the latter half of the twentieth century. The fact that almost every character in the film wears the homemade clothing in the convention of the colony—ankle-length patterned dresses and head covering for the women, dark slacks and hat for the men, and so on—and is speaking Low German only further complicates any effort to locate the film in place and time. It is an effort clearly signaled not only by the framing imagery, but also in the early moment where the patriarchal figure at the heart of the film reaches up to stop a ticking clock.

After the extended opening that serves to estrange, rather than introduce, the subjects of the film, Reygadas drops his audience into the midst of a marital crisis: Johan, a middle-aged farmer, is guilt-ridden but unable to end his affair, which has become common knowledge on the colony. Johan's wife, Esther, is stoic but devastated by his betrayal. She ultimately dies of a broken heart, only to be miraculously resurrected from her coffin at the film's close by a deep kiss from Marianne, her husband's lover. Just as viewers are never told where or when the film is set, there is no context provided for the intimate relationship at the heart of the film: we are never shown how Johan and Marianne met or how the affair began, and we are given no indication of what might happen after the film ends. And, just as significantly, we are given no explanation for the sudden intervention of the supernatural at the conclusion of a film that is otherwise characterized by many of the tropes of documentary-style realism.

Before we move on to explore the *effect* of Reygadas's directorial choices, it is worth pausing briefly over his own commentary about his choices in the film. "The idea for choosing the Mennonites as a context for the love story was that I wanted something as timeless and placeless as possible," he explains in an interview with Jonathan Romney. He continues:

> If you drive around on Mennonite land, you wouldn't know where you are or what era you're in, if not for cars. I also chose the Mennonites because they're a uniform society: you wouldn't be distracted by whether one man is successful at his work or another is rich, or whether one of the women is very beautiful and has breast implants. I wanted to keep out all those things like interest, ego, jealousy, to keep only the archetypes, as in fairytales or myth. The language was also very important. [. . .] When I did the Spanish subtitling I tried to keep it as neutral as possible, using a style you wouldn't be able to identify as Spanish, Mexican or Argentinean. ("Sheltering" 43)

I will have more to say about this presentation of the Mennonites as a "uniform society" devoid of beauty, ego, and jealousy shortly, but here I want to observe Reygadas's emphasis on the function rather than the content of Mennonite cultural difference. Although the film lacks the ironic self-awareness that I have suggested is characteristic of many strategic deployments of Mennonite identity as Thing, *Silent Light* reflects a similar desire to invoke and deploy the community's cultural distinctiveness as we have seen in works such as *Pure* and *Suspiria*. Magdalene Redekop is surely right, then, to suggest in her compelling examination of *Silent Light* and *Irma Voth* that Reygadas's camera "sees the Mennonites but does not know them," and that "These Mennonites welcome the camera into their homes, but the community filmed remains inscrutable, somehow opaque"

(*Making Believe* 102); I would add only that this is clearly an artistic choice on the director's behalf. As Jonathan Foltz writes, the "film is clearly invested in the aesthetic value to its audience of [the Mennonites'] unfamiliarity" (165). Reygadas avoids contextualizing details, in other words, precisely because he intends the setting to be otherworldly, and the Mennonites' primary function in the film is to evoke a sense of cultural difference without specificity, logic, or history—indeed, to provide a highly specific setting that seems to be outside of history altogether.

Nowhere is Reygadas's effort to invoke Mennonite cultural difference for the "aesthetic value of its unfamiliarity" so clear as in his decision to shoot the entirety of the film in Low German, a dialect spoken almost exclusively by decedents of this particular group of Mennonites. Asked how he knows that the actors recited the proper lines, Reygadas responds by insisting it doesn't matter. "I don't," he admits. "Maybe I said, 'Say hello,' and they said, 'Ice cream.' I hope not. But who cares? If you feel it's right, it's right" ("Sheltering" 43). Reygadas, of course, is relying on the assumption that the film's audience will be unable to understand the language as well, so that the effect will be, as Tiago de Luca writes, that the dialogue has "a purely citational" or "material quality" (*Realism* 77)—to be *signifiers*, we might say, that are fully disconnected from their specific *signifieds*. Indeed, it is clear that the filmmaker is brazenly confident that his viewers will be similarly unable to understand his dialogue: not only do the accents of his two lead actresses (the only non-native speakers of Low German in the film) shift widely throughout, but the film offers what are often comically loose translations in its subtitles. Redekop, who identifies Low German as her mother tongue, describes her "shock" that the "words coming out of the actors' mouth sounded like gibberish," adding the "subtitles were ridiculously inaccurate," suggesting the language is "estranged" but "in ways that make little sense" (*Making Believe* 107).[4] One way to make sense of this estrangement, I am arguing, is to read it as a type of crude shibboleth. As Froese Tiessen observed in an early essay, Low German has often been used in writings by Russian Mennonites in Canada as a means of "re-delineating the [. . .] barriers between insider and outsider," and providing "a source of resonance for the insider" ("Mother"). Here that same shibboleth is being used to evoke dissonance, except in order to establish a barrier that both presumes and positions all of its viewers to be *outsiders*. It is this gesture, I want to suggest, that Toews responds to most forcefully in *Irma Voth*.

The critical reception of *Silent Light* has been substantial, with scholars working to recuperate the film's decontextualized setting as part of an expanded Mexican cultural identity, claiming it "stretches the Mexican imaginary" (Tompkins 185) and "challenges the essentialist, monolithic view of Mexican identity as often espoused by government propaganda" (Manickam, "Other Mexico"). Joanne Hershfield, meanwhile, suggests the critical emphasis on fantastic elements in Reygadas's work simply reflects scholarly ignorance about Mexico (38). However, the overtly miraculous elements of the film and corresponding lack of contextualizing details leads the majority to recognize the film's engagement with the Mennonites of Mexico as intentionally otherworldly: even as Manickam celebrates the film's diversification of Mexican identity, he recognizes that Reygadas places that diversity within a "simpler, prelapsarian world," while Sheldon Penn argues the "isolation and difference of the Mennonite community from perceived national norms or characteristics produces an otherworldliness that removes the story from ideological inscriptions of time and space" (1160). Francine Prose's review of Reygadas's later work for the *New York Review of Books* makes a similar claim in somewhat less academic terms: the Mennonites of *Silent Light*, she writes, are "craggy, pale, and ghostlike" characters who appear "to have wandered in from a painting by Hans Memling, or to have traveled to Central America by spaceship from some medieval German colony on Mars."

Indeed, the operative assumption of the film seems to be that the general ignorance about the Mennonites is so vast—their language so unintelligible, their rejection of individuality, modernity, and consumer capitalism so complete—that they can functionally transcend not merely the specifics of life in Mexico or even the more general conventions of life under contemporary capitalism but the messiness of reality itself. Reygadas fully embraces the pathetic fallacy, for example, having Esther, the scorned wife, literally die of heartbreak after stumbling away from her husband into a raging thunderstorm—a scene Jonathan Romney describes as "daringly staged in defiance of cliché" (Reygadas, "Sheltering" 42). At other times, he pushes further still: after Johan and Marianne have sex for what Marianne insists must be their "last time," for example, an autumnal leaf drops ominously from the ceiling of their small room; and at the film's close, Esther is brought back to life at her own funeral when her husband's lover leans into her coffin for a deep kiss. Viewers have been quick to note the film's indebtedness to Carl Theodor Dreyer's 1955 film, *Ordet*, and the funeral scene is clearly the culmination of this homage. Reygadas, however, has suggested himself that he views it as "closer to *Sleeping Beauty*" than to Dryer's classic film ("Sheltering" 44), and others have agreed—although with varying degrees of appreciation. While De Luca notes this as the scene's use of "a fairy tale trope" ("Carnal"), for example, a more skeptical review in *New York Magazine* describes it as "Tinkerbell dropping into a Lars von Trier picture" (Edelstein). In either case, however, the thorough decontextualization of the community would seem to strip the scene of any shock it might have otherwise produced in its transgression of the strict heteronormativity of this deeply conservative community, with the kiss functioning instead to simply affirm the film's archetypal and "mythic" mode.

It is important to note that Reygadas's ostensible disinterest in the Mennonite community exists in a productive tension with an opposing aim, firmly established through both plot devices and technical choices, to present the film as an unedited documentation of colony life. Indeed, the film clearly reflects Reygadas's self-described distaste for fantasy's willingness to demarcate firmly between a "real" and an "unreal" world, and showcases instead a corresponding exploration of how "we go back and forth in our own heads" between the two ("Impossible" 12). The result is a kind of doubled vision: even as *Silent Light* embraces elements of fantasy or fairy tales, competing elements of documentary filmmaking can be found throughout, including the film's notable lack of non-diegetic music and a corresponding emphasis on background or natural sounds (such as insects buzzing and cattle lowing); the many technical "imperfections" that reveal the presence of the camera, such as sun flares, rain on the lens, and so on; and the almost awkwardly long extended shots, which often focus on relatively mundane experiences that stand outside the narrative thrust of the film. Similarly, the stiffness of the untrained actors who stumble through lines and occasionally glance directly into the camera is fully recuperated via the documentary mode as evidence that the story is "true-to-life." And of course, the decision to shoot the film on location in the colony and to use colony members as actors ensures that many of the minor details of Mennonite life in the film present as accurate, furthering what Romney calls the film's "ethnographic-documentary feel" (17), or sense of unedited or unmediated access into a heretofore-closed world. Not unlike the autobiographic pact extended by works of life writing, the documentarian tropes and modes used by Reygadas proclaims, implicitly, that *Silent Light* is—if perhaps not quite *nonfictional*—somehow "authentic."

Notably, the film's documentarian features were central to Reygadas's ability to reassure reluctant colony members of the value of the project, who participated on the grounds that it would serve, effectively, as a historical document. Rebecca Janzen has learned from her subsequent visits to the colony where the film was set that "some Mennonites felt that he had used them": "The crew suggested they were looking for assistance with a documentary," she reports, and the children's parents were accordingly "aghast when they realized its plot revolved around adultery" (127). Reygadas, however, has continued to argue for the film's value on these terms. "*Silent Light* could be seen as a better documentary on Mennonites in Mexico than one produced by National Geographic," he insists, arguing that conventional documentaries might "tell you the whereabouts and indexes of Mennonites in Mexico, but you'll never see them making love, having an intimate conversation, bathing with their families in a pool, or dying" ("Carlos" 77). Those documentaries are presumably even less likely to show us Mennonites rising from the dead, but it is precisely the film's competing claims to be both fairy tale and documentary that make it such a compelling viewing experience and make its more fantastic elements succeed in such an unexpected manner. Stripped of any contextualization within the film itself, the earnest realism of Esther's resurrection manages to avoid descending into farce or cliché only to the extent to which Reygadas has succeeded in transforming the Mennonites' theology into fantasy—a point to which I will return shortly.

Critics noting what I am describing as a tension between the film's fairy tale and documentary elements have suggested it positions *Silent Light* within cinematic traditions that similarly entangle real and imagined worlds. Cynthia Tompkins, for example, suggests that "the fusion between fiction and the documentary" in *Silent Light* is indicative of its emergence within the technical context of the New Latin American cinema, wherein such a fusion is typical (18). Rick Warner, by contrast, sees this fusion as exemplary of postwar "contemplative cinema" (67), while Michael Cramer views it as Reygadas's ongoing effort to realize something akin to Jean Epstein's cinema of being, in which film enables a complete overcoming of human subjectivity to present us with "the real," only to find it frustrated by the "weight of history" (247). As necessary and valuable as these efforts to locate the director's approach within larger cinematic or national traditions may be, I worry that such discussions risk further marginalizing or outright ignoring the most immediate subjects of the film itself. I am partial, instead, to Niels Niessen's description of the film as a work of "miraculous realism"—a description picked up by Travis Kroeker in his cogent discussion of the work's theological implications (94). "The problem of the (Mennonite) images in the film," Kroeker argues, "is that they are not 'lived' but rather abstract 'props' for a 'miraculous realism'" (94). Redekop quotes Roger Ebert's suggestion that the amateur actors succeed in presenting an "almost holy reality" with some surprise, countering with another critic who describes them as an "obviously unprofessional cast" who are unable to "believably convey even the *idea* of emotional anguish" (Gonzalez qtd. in Redekop, *Making Believe* 106). Without disagreeing with Redekop's assessment on this point, I wonder if we might also hear in Ebert's description of the film's "holy reality" an echo of Niessen's account of it as "miraculous realism," in that both phrases register something of the film's proximity to magic realism while seeming to acknowledge that here it emerges through the community's faith tradition.

Silent Light differs from the vast majority of artistic engagements with the community produced by non-Mennonites in its engagement of Mennonite isolation through its miraculous realism, then, but it does not manage to fully avoid the descent into ethnic voyeurism or exoticism that characterizes many of the popular representations of the community. Indeed, the film's voyeuristic dynamic that can be read in its documentarian promise of unmediated access into a closed community has left a number of critics registering their discomfort. Romney notes that one "can't help wondering what it means for a Mennonite man to play a character caught in the throes of an extra-marital romance" (17), for example, while Foltz goes so far as to suggest that critical viewers will need to "recognize and reflect upon the parasitic voyeurism of aesthetic consumption" (163). Redekop, too, notes the "voyeuristic discomfort" she experienced the moment the film shifted from its opening sunrise to enter the Mennonite house (44) and accuses Reygadas of wielding a "predatory camera" (*Making Believe* 105). Nowhere is the film's voyeurism so clear, however, as in its lone sex scene, an extended single shot in which Reygadas places the viewer in Johan's position atop a supine Marianne for nearly a full minute of thrusting and climax. Lacking non-diegetic sound and with no nudity, the scene is not stylized and cannot be considered explicit; indeed, placed beside the graphic sexuality in Reygadas's other works, it is clear that he has shown restraint. Nonetheless, understood as the culmination of the larger voyeuristic dynamic of the film and in the context of the deeply conservative religious community it depicts, the length and camera positioning of the scene feels gratuitous, even pornographic. Earlier I suggested that the otherworldliness of *Silent Light* is successful because Reygadas reinterprets the community's history and theology as fantasy, a point to which I will return shortly. However, when he presents the audience the point-of-view experience of having sex with a Mennonite—one cannot call it "making love" because, as scholars have noted, the two non-professional actors are clearly "not entirely at ease" with the scene (de Luca, *Realism* 55), and it is "not a joyous erotic encounter" (Janzen 142)—he seems to offer a different kind of fantasy, pushing his miraculous realism past its breaking point. Understanding why the scene feels so out of keeping with the larger film, and what is at stake in Reygadas's strategic engagement with Mennonite cultural difference throughout—as well appreciating the form and focus of Miriam Toews's subsequent anti-adaptation of his film—requires an understanding of the social, theological, and historical contexts for the Mennonites that the film works so hard to efface. And so it is to that most conventional form of history to which we must turn now.

MENNONITE HISTORY AND OTHER FAIRY TALES

General audience members can be excused for knowing little about the Mennonite community represented in *Silent Light*. If it is true that the film encourages a whimsical and even voyeuristic ignorance about the community, it is also true that this encouragement succeeds, in large part, because this particular group of Mennonites *is* a small and isolated community, and it *does* have a long history of intentionally separating themselves from the larger world. In a very literal sense, Reygadas's deployment of Mennonite cultural difference as otherworldly can be said to succeed because the film adopts, exaggerates, and capitalizes on the very elements of that difference that are the direct and intentional consequence of these Mennonites' beliefs and way of life. A basic understanding of this context is necessary not simply to identify the film's limitations but also to appreciate its full accomplishments, as the film's representation of the community as cosmically isolated succeeds in large part by extending the history and theology that it effaces.

The Mennonites featured in Reygadas's film are the descendants of a loose affiliation of Dutch Anabaptists, part of the "Radical Reformation" in sixteenth-century Europe, who eventually consolidated into groups holding strong beliefs in adult baptism, pacifism, and the separation of church and state. Most notably in the context of this chapter, many Anabaptists espoused a commitment to nonconformity and separation from nonbelievers, taking literally the scriptural commandment to "come out from among them and be separate," to be "in the world but not of it." The earliest influential articulation of this principle can be found in the first Anabaptist confession of faith, the 1527 Schleitheim Confession. "We are agreed on separation: A separation shall be made from the evil and from the wickedness which the devil planted in the world; in this manner, simply that we shall not have fellowship with them," the article begins (249).

Today, of course, the larger North American and the global Mennonite faith communities are wide and diverse, the vast majority of them assimilated into the mainstream of their various contexts. The Mennonites featured in *Silent Light*, however, are members of a highly specific subsection of that community that developed a strong sense of itself as a distinct ethno-religious community through a series of mass migrations. Fleeing persecution to the relatively liberal city-states of Prussia (now Poland) in the seventeenth century, they adopted German as their church language while holding strongly to the Low German dialect for everyday conversation; in the late eighteenth century, many of these Mennonites migrated again to settle in separate colonies in South Russia (now Ukraine), where they were granted both land and the isolation to practice their faith and freedom from military service. Here, the marks of these Mennonites' cultural difference—their unique dialect, their isolated colonies, traditional dress, tight kinship ties, and suspicion with some aspects of modern technology, and so on—began to be self-consciously fostered and deployed in an effort to maintain a separation from the larger, non-Mennonite world.[5] In the late nineteenth century, several thousand of the most conservative of these so-called Russian Mennonites migrated once again, this time to "reserves" set aside for them on the Canadian prairies, now sometimes known as "Kanadier" (as descendants of the first "Russian Mennonites" to migrate to Canada), or as the "Old Colony" Mennonites (as descendants of the first, or "Old," colony in Russia).

Early in the twentieth century, as the Canadian state began to rescind their initial promises of military exemption and attempted to bring Mennonite education practices in line with the general public, many of the Kanadier Mennonites negotiated with President Alvaro Obregón for the purchase of arable land and comparable privileges in northern Mexico. Some seven thousand of the Russian Mennonites migrated again, en masse, establishing the first Mexican colonies in the 1920s at roughly the same time as a second wave of mass migration was bringing more than twenty thousand Mennonites fleeing the aftermath of the Russian Revolution into Canada (whose history is partially recounted in Neufeld's diary as explored in chapter 2 of this study). Today, a broader collective migratory history and intentional resistance to assimilation have resulted in what scholars variously refer to as a "trans-statal" (Bottos) or "supranational" (Gingrich and Preibisch 1502) community of Low German–speaking Mennonites spanning the Americas, roughly one hundred thousand of whom remain in Mexico. As Abigail Carl-Klassen notes, the strict isolation of the early Mexican colonies is now far from complete, and it is not unusual for "colonies with modern dress, cars, Internet, and schools accredited by the Mexican education system to exist within close proximity of colonies with much more strict and traditional regulations concerning dress, education, and technology" ("Art"). And yet if it is easy to overstate the extent of their isolation—many speak Spanish, for example, travel into the United States and Canada regularly via seasonal labor routes and are connected to local economies—the Mennonites in Mexico often continue to be understood as a distinct people set apart from their immediate sociopolitical contexts.[6]

Even this cursory history should make obvious that *Silent Light* does not so much impose its portrait of cosmic isolation upon the Mennonites as much as it draws it out from the community itself. The reason the Mennonite colony in northern Mexico lends itself so effectively to the "miraculous realism" of Reygadas's film is that they are the product of a half millennium of migration animated, in part, by a theological desire to be "in the world but not of it"—they have, in other words, actively and intentionally sought to manifest precisely the form of separation and distinctiveness that the film literalizes as "otherworldly." The isolated desert colonies, the nonwritten Low German language, and the unique clothing and nontraditional lifestyle are all intended to produce and maintain a barrier between the Mennonites and the larger world, to set them apart. When Reygadas presents the Mennonites as free-floating in the cosmos, he is, intentionally or otherwise, literalizing one of their central theological tenets, effectively reinterpreting—and affirming!—their theology as fantasy.

As a film that is written and directed by a non-Mennonite auteur from Mexico, *Silent Light* pushes up against the conventional boundaries of Mennonite literary studies in North America. Understanding Mennonite literature as a minor transnationalism—that is, as a mode of informed reading that traces a work's engagement with Mennonite concerns and histories across media, genre, and national boundaries—not only provides a logic and frame through which to extend our appreciation to Reygadas's work but also encourages us to review our appreciation of similar concerns by authors working from within the tradition. Unlike the romanticization or exploitation of Mennonite isolationism routinely evinced by non-Mennonite artists drawn to the community's cultural distinctiveness, those authors working from within the Mennonite community—including those whose works have sometimes been described as "transgressive Mennonite writing"[7]—have more often been caustic in their critique of this same practice. In Miriam Toews's award-winning novel *A Complicated Kindness* (2004), for example, a young Nomi Nickel rails with frustration about growing up in a Mennonite town in Manitoba that "exists in the world based on the idea of it not existing in the world" (64). Nomi turns to literature as part of her efforts to escape her community's isolation, but she is careful to note her distaste for authors such as J. R. R. Tolkien and Ursula K. Le Guin. Much like Reygadas would later do in *Silent Light*, Toews has Nomi recast Mennonite theology as a type of fantasy, but Toews presents it as a delusion from which village members must strive to escape. "I'm not a fan of fantasy," Nomi says. "There's so much of that being crammed down our throats every day in this place. The mark of the beast? Streets paved in Gold? What? Fuck off. I dream of escaping into the *real* world" (8).

Ironically enough, Reygadas has suggested it was Toews's author photo on the back of a copy of *A Complicated Kindness* that convinced him to cast the Canadian author to play the part of Johan's wife in *Silent Light*. It is perhaps not entirely surprising that it would take several months before he was able to convince Toews—who had never acted, never heard of Reygadas, and didn't speak *Plautdietch*, and who, like the vast majority of Russian Mennonites in North America, was very much assimilated into the broader mainstream culture—to agree to don a flowered dress and kerchief to act in a film set in a conservative Mennonite colony in Mexico. It is even less surprising, perhaps, that she would later reflect upon her experience filming *Silent Light* in a novel of her own.[8]

"PURELY BUT SOMEWHAT OUT OF CONTEXT": *IRMA VOTH*

Irma Voth begins in present-day Chihuahua, a Mennonite colony in northern Mexico, where a nineteen-year-old Mennonite woman named Irma is arguing with Jorge, her Mexican (and non-Mennonite) husband. Readers will soon learn that the Voth family fled the Canadian prairies for the Mexican colonies just six years earlier, and that one year before the novel began, Irma shocked her family by marrying a Mexican who turns out to be involved in the drug trade; after Jorge abandons her, she has agreed to work as a translator for a film project about adultery that is implausibly being set on their land by an eccentric filmmaker from Mexico City. After several misadventures on the set, Irma and her younger sister, Aggie, decide to flee the colony and their violent father; in a narrative twist that made me gasp aloud, their mother responds to their whispered plans by insisting they take the family's infant daughter, Ximena, with them. The three sisters eventually make their way to Mexico City, where, years later, Irma and Aggie watch the premiere of the film that they had once worked on, now titled *Campo Siete* [Camp Seven]. The novel closes with Irma standing alone outside the door of her childhood home, uncertain of the reception she will receive on her first return to the colony for a visit.

Toews never mentions *Silent Light* or Carlos Reygadas by name in *Irma Voth*, but there can be no doubt about her intention to establish a direct relationship between her novel and the film. Not only does the book take up the larger premise of the film in its setting and its own fictional film's plot, it also restages several of the film's scenes and, at points, incorporates its dialogue directly. Across these scenes, Toews's most consistent method of direct engagement with *Silent Light* is to ironically undermine the essentializing logic of the film, even as she celebrates its accomplishments and power as a work of art. She has the filmmaker Diego Nolasco—a clear caricature of Reygadas—repeatedly pay off cynical Mennonites in order to use their land (69–70), for example, and depicts the filming process as a dark comedy of errors. In one of the most-discussed scenes in *Silent Light*, Johan's family bathes in an irrigation pond, surrounded by lush greenery and warm sunlight; critics have described the scene as a meditative portrayal of the "age of innocence" (Manickam). In Toews's restaging, however, the lush pond is shown to be an "old, slimy swimming pool" owned by an "ancient Mexican woman in a Nike t-shirt" (60); the day after filming all the actors are sick from the pool's "dirty water" (64). Similarly, a passionate hillside kiss between Johan and Esther in *Silent Light* is restaged in *Irma Voth* to disastrous results: the Mennonite lead actor, Alfredo, proves so hopelessly inept at mimicking passion that Diego gives up and walks off the set; in response, Alfredo cracks open a beer, pulls out a gun, and threatens to shoot the filmmaker's beloved pit bull (102–3).

Toews's rewriting of *Silent Light* goes well beyond undermining specific scenes in the novel. Less directly but more interestingly, *Irma Voth* calls attention to the way in which the filmmakers aim to capitalize on the isolationist history of the community. When an audience member at a fictional film festival asks Diego why he chose to make a movie about Mennonites, for example, his response is a nearly verbatim account of Reygadas's answers in similar circumstances: "I don't care about the Mennonites as a group. Not at all. I'm interested in the fact that nobody would understand their language and that they were uniform. There's no distinction, one from the other, and so they are props, essentially, for pure emotion. Even their setting, you don't know what era it is or where, blonds in Mexico, it doesn't matter, ultimately, when all you want is to communicate an emotional truth" (243). Where Reygadas works hard to estrange the Mennonite community and language in *Silent Light* in order to render them archetypal figures, however, Irma consistently undermines Diego's attempt to employ Mennonite cultural difference as unintelligible: when the novel's filmmaker tells Irma that it "didn't really matter what the actors were saying because nobody watching the film would understand their language anyway" (24), Irma responds by feeding the actors increasingly outrageous mistranslations of his script. Rather than tell Alfredo's wife that she is to assure Alfredo that "she loves him," for example, Irma instructs her to "tell him quietly that you're tired of his bullshit" (50). Later, in Toews's rewriting of the emotional scene in *Silent Light* where Johan tells his wife that he is unable to stop himself from loving another woman, Irma instructs the actress playing the betrayed wife to respond in Low German by asking "Is it because my vagina is so big after having all these babies?" (120) The effect of these mistranslations is comical, certainly, but they also clearly represent a serious, gendered critique of Reygadas's film and, by extension, of the patriarchal Mennonite community itself. At the same time, Toews reasserts the historical specificity of Low German itself, even as she mocks the patriarchal logic that presents Johan to be a victim in his own adulterous affair.

There can be no question as to Toews's intention to engage Reygadas's work, but the vast majority of *Irma Voth* is concerned with the life of its young Mennonite protagonists. Redekop describes Toews's approach as a "comic strategy of reverse adaptation" (*Making Believe* 112) and astutely suggests that even Toews's first-person narrative works to undermine the film's ostensibly disinterested gaze (110). We might extend this reading by noting the neat inversion of the way that Mennonite context and history are effaced in *Silent Light* as part of Reygadas's effort to use the community in archetypal terms: the content of the fictional film in *Irma Voth* is of markedly little concern in comparison to the struggle and adventures experienced by the real-life Mennonites. By foregrounding the artifice of the filming process, the transformation of the Mennonite colony into a film set becomes an ironic commentary on the paradox of the ways in which the community's isolation efforts have rendered it hyper-visible via a cultural identity whose expression includes a visible performance of difference.

In much the same way, Toews's account of the colony members acting in *Campo Siete* neatly inverts Reygadas's use of nonprofessional actors in *Silent Light*. If, as I have argued, the effect of using local colony members as actors in *Silent Light* is to lend the film an aura of authenticity via its documentary mode, in *Irma Voth* the effect is to raise the self-conscious specter of identity as Thing, reminding readers that the cultural distinctiveness of "real" Mennonite identity is always already deeply performative. Numerous characters explicitly attempt to adopt or shed a Mennonite identity through the strategic deployment of visible markers of cultural difference. The first interaction between Irma and her future Mexican husband, which takes place in the novel's opening pages, is a primary case in point. Irma's mother has risked taking the children to a rodeo, and Irma strikes up a conversation with Jorge by asking if he is there "pretending to be a cowboy" (3). When Jorge responds by asking if she is imitating a Mennonite—"Are you pretending to be Mennonitzcha? he said"—she misses the joke and earnestly insists she "really" is one. As the novel continues, however, it becomes harder for even Irma to make these sorts of categorical statements. When she is asked to help the foreign German actress brought in to play a lead role in the film—a position that Toews herself held as one of the only non-colony actors in *Silent Light*—the two women awkwardly acknowledge the thin line between film's "costumes" and the Mennonites' daily attire. "She told me she felt like shit in the dress she was wearing," Irma says, "and then looked at mine and apologized and said that it was weird that her dress was a costume and mine was just a dress" (64). Later, a Mexican film hand buys a pair of jeans and a plaid shirt and declares himself a Mennonite (I always "wanted to be one," he says [39]), and Diego has a "pale Mexican substitute" dress in "Mennonite clothes" for an intimate scene in which the Mennonite women refuse to participate (102). Finally, immediately after the two sisters flee, they buy new clothes that exaggerate their decision to leave not only the colony but also its conventions: in Acapulco, Aggie buys a white bikini with the words *RICH BITCH* emblazoned in gold across the top (152), and in Mexico City they change from their traditional dresses into sweatshirts and pants and leave the store "self-consciously [. . .] like astronauts stepping out onto the moon" (162).

Like Reygadas, then, Toews recognizes the representational and cultural power of the Mennonite colonies in Mexico, but she differs dramatically in her response. Where Reygadas emphasizes the community's efforts at isolation by refusing contextualizing details, Toews works hard to counter this isolation by locating the community within a specific geography and a broader set of competing histories. Where *Silent Light* begins by losing us in the cosmos, the opening pages of the novel offer a set of clear landmarks to help situate the colonies in a specific region of Mexico: Irma carefully notes that the colony is near Rubio, Mexico (2); that one passes the city when driving between Chihuahua City and the border cities of Ciudad Juárez and El Paso (7); and that the distant hills in the west are the Sierra Madre mountains (7). In marked contrast to the hermetically sealed colonies in *Silent Light*, people come and go from the colonies in *Irma Voth* with surprising regularity: the Voth family arrived from Canada six years earlier, for example, and their father visits colonies in other countries; Irma and Aggie take the truck into town to see a rodeo early in the novel (2) and flee for Mexico City midway through it; Jorge sneaks onto the farm to date Irma; the Mennonites sell cheese in the neighboring cities; and so on. And, of course, a film crew from Mexico City lives on the Voth property for months on end.

Toews is similarly insistent on situating the colony within the larger history of the Mennonites in Mexico. Early in the novel, she offers a comedic two-paragraph history of the Mennonites, first recounting their negotiation with the Mexican government for land "where they wouldn't have to send their kids to regular school or teach them to speak English or dress them in normal clothing," before explaining how the martyrdoms of the Anabaptists first set the Mennonites "mov[ing] all around the world in colonies looking for freedom and isolation and peace" (12). In a passage used by Julia Spicher Kasdorf in her theorization of the "autoethnographic announcements" that are common in minoritized literatures, Irma continues in a passage worth quoting at length[9]:

> Different countries give us shelter if we agree to stay out of trouble and help with the economy by farming in obscurity. We live like ghosts. Then, sometimes, those countries decide they want us to be real citizens after all and start to force us to do things like join the army or pay taxes or respect laws and then we pack up our stuff in the middle of the night and move to another country where we can live purely but somewhat out of context. Our motto is from the "rebuke of worldliness," which is from the Biblical book of James: *Whosoever will be a friend of the world is the enemy of God.* (12)

However pithily, here Toews is offering precisely the historical contextualization and theological logic for the Mennonites' isolation in Mexico that Reygadas is so careful to avoid. For Toews, as we will see, an understanding of this history and theology is necessary in order not only to understand its consequences for individual Mennonites but also to start working toward a possible solution.

Irma Voth acknowledges and historicizes the isolationist practices that attracted Reygadas to the Mennonites for *Silent Light* but refuses to endorse them or to disarm them as simple fantasy. Although there are much more sympathetic ways to interpret the Mennonite historical practice of separation—some recent scholarship has even celebrated the principled rejection of consumerism, individualism, and technology practiced in these Mennonites' even more conservative daughter colonies in Bolivia and Paraguay as a form of anti-modern "genius" with much to offer Western society[10]—Toews's caustic portrait of colony life is squarely within the critical tradition of so-called transgressive Mennonite writing. The colony in *Irma Voth* is undeniably human, full of world-weary teenagers, religious hypocrisy, violence and abuse. Where the colony in *Silent Light* is positioned as cosmically isolated, in *Irma Voth* its position near the US border has entangled the colony members in the cocaine trade. The Mennonite women, in particular, struggle against a violent patriarchy upheld by this limited education and isolation: Irma's father whips Aggie when he finds out she has visited the film crew and refuses to allow Irma to leave the colony after her marriage. Irma's terrified mother not only encourages Irma and Aggie to leave the colony, she is so desperate that she gives them her newborn to take with them as they flee. This shocking request is rendered understandable when we later discover that the Voth family's initial emigration to the colonies, made under the guise of the larger community's retreat from worldliness, was in fact an attempt to avoid persecution under Canadian law. Irma's father, we are told, murdered her older sister when she tried to leave the village in Manitoba, running her down on the highway behind the family's barn.

In *Irma Voth*, the Mennonites of Mexico are decidedly of this world, then, both geographically and morally. None of their failures is so consequential, however, as their collective failure of the imagination. In Toews's account, the community's efforts at separation from the world have left them trapped in isolation and in the past. As Jane Smiley points out, the parents in *Irma Voth* "have no moral purpose, only moral habits": Irma's mother encourages her daughters to rebel but is unable to leave herself; even Irma's dogmatic, violent father is clearly trapped in the part he feels he must play. It is against these stifling habits of thought that Toews presents the arts as offering a powerful opportunity for the community. Irma's sister, Aggie, is an artist, and her installations and paintings become powerful moments of beauty and optimism in the novel; Irma herself sets out to write her story, using the pen and pad given to her by the filmmaker early in the novel. The novel's commentary on the power of art reaches its climax near the end of the narrative, with Irma and her sister attending an early screening of *Campo Siete* in Mexico City. Aggie enjoys the film, but Irma weeps throughout—even when watching the German actress earnestly speak the comedic mistranslations she had been fed. "There was something that I was beginning to understand but I didn't know what it was," Irma explains when she later reflects on the film. "It was like watching my own life. It was a pathway into myself" (239). The movie presents Irma with what the critic Paul Tiessen recognizes as "a vantage point to recognize opportunities for re-engaging with her family" ("Watching" 53), demonstrating "the potential for epiphany and transformation that a great art film, like any significant work of art, can introduce into the lives of even the most uninitiated and ordinary folk" ("Watching" 52). And in this, *Irma Voth* explains a paradox of another kind: how *Silent Light*'s engagement with the Mennonites can be deeply problematic as a cultural project and yet remain a tremendous artistic success directly linked to this particular group of Mennonites' history and theology.

Toews is not the first to attribute the challenges faced by the Russian Mennonite community to a failure of the imagination. In 1988, for example, Magdalene Redekop suggested that the "single most significant cause of neurosis in the Mennonite community is the stifling of the imagination" ("Through" 240). Arguing for the promise of a then-emergent body of writing by Canadian Mennonites, Redekop continued: "Imagination is redemptive not only because it helps us to construct enclosures and identities but also because it helps us to break out of them, accepting life as an exuberant disguise" (248). While invoking the redemptive power of art and the imagination will always risk descending into cliché, Toews embraces that risk—not unlike Reygadas's embrace of the pathetic fallacy in *Silent Light*. Indeed, in *Irma Voth*, the redemptive power of art is given a credibility that emerges from the specificity of the Mennonite world in which the novel is set: in a context where the imagination itself is considered dangerous, books, films, and paintings are invested with an inherently transgressive and potentially redemptive possibility. It is against the Mennonite father's fervent insistence that "films [are] like beautiful cakes, filled with shit" (17)—that in fact, all "art is a lie" (18)—that the various artistic endeavors in the book, including not only the flawed film but also Irma's efforts at life writing and Aggie's paintings and installations, all become believable as urgent and necessary escapes into a different mode of thinking.

Although Reygadas's film and Toews's novel are very different works, they end on a strikingly similar note. Each work returns, in their final scenes, to the starry skies of the colony and the possibility—but not promise—of redemption. In *Silent Light*, the concluding sunset and night sky directly follows the resurrection of Esther, closing the representational circle on the Mennonite world by reminding the audience of the placelessness and timelessness in which the action has taken place. In the final image of *Irma Voth*, an expansive night sky spreads out above Irma as she stands outside her parents' house, where she has returned in hopes that in meeting once again she and her father "will both be brought back to life" (253). If the resurrection of Esther in the closing minutes of *Silent Light* is ethereal and ambiguous, a logical consequence of the director's reinterpretation of the community's faith as fairy tale, the possibility for rebirth in *Irma Voth* is messy and personal, as improbable as it is necessary. However unlikely these rebirths may seem, the possibility of resurrection is one that the novel, much like *Silent Light*, ultimately endorses. It is, after all, Toews herself, playing Esther, who was herself reborn at the close of Reygadas's film.

Given the religious imagery of both Reygadas's film and Toews's novel, it is perhaps little surprise to find that at least one scholar in Canada has seen in *Silent Light* and *Irma Voth* an opportunity to "turn Miriam Toews into a theologian" (T. Kroeker 89). In a brief but dense and productive essay, Kroeker explores the parallel resurrection scenes in Dreyer's *Ordet* and *Silent Light* before turning to Toews's novel and suggesting that the latter two works are "bound together in a figural relation to the Gospel of John's sacramental hymn to the incarnation that focuses on the scandalous revelation of messianic authority" (90). Kroeker's reading of the novel emphasizes its penultimate scene, where Toews teases a conclusively happy ending by showing Irma join her family in a "wild, joyful embrace" before revealing it to be a figment of the anxious woman's imagination (254). Describing the scene as "Irma's *imagined* ending" that may or may not "be *made true*" (97), Kroeker reads it as a gendered revision of the biblical story of the prodigal son and suggest it offers "the promise of a non-magical and yet iconic incarnational realism," a kind of "song" that "a Mennonite theology of incarnation needs to hear in order to live again" (97). Tiessen, too, returns to this scene, anticipating Kroeker's reading by suggesting it offers a "reversal of roles of the prodigal son/daughter story" and describing it as "Irma's beautiful fantasy" ("Watching" 70). For Tiessen, the scene accomplishes a less theological form of rebirth: it may be revealed to be as "only a fantasy," but it also shows us the "possibility of someone from the shunned world returning to her original home," and should be read within the novel's larger suggestion that meaningful "encounters with art can [. . .] initiate life-changing renewal" (70).

Notably, Tiessen's and Kroeker's overlapping readings of the novel's concluding scene are supported by a parallel scene midway through the novel, the outcome of which would seem to suggest a promising outcome for the novel's conclusion. In the earlier scene as in the conclusion, Irma is standing outside the family house beneath a "blanket of stars." Here, she is listening to her family sing hymns; when she realizes she can't hear the voices of her sister or father, she rushes in and sees her father beating her sister for disobedience (95–96). Just as the closing scene has Irma imagining a positive outcome for her return, here she first reports that she confronts her father and they lock eyes; his are "wild with fear and despair" and then "he began to cry and he asked me to forgive him." Just as in the closing scene, we quickly learn this is only an act of her imagination. "That's a lie," she concedes immediately. "But it's true that we looked hard at each other" (96). It may be a "lie" of sorts, but this is a context where art itself has been considered a lie. This early moment of imagining *otherwise* proves central to Irma's realization that things can be different, and it enables her decision to flee. It might not be exactly the resolution Irma imagined, but it proves to be the resolution she needs. It also seems to suggest the novel's closing moment of imagination will be similarly productive—even as it warns that the specifics of her warm welcome is a fantasy unlikely to be fulfilled.

CONCLUSION

In taking up the Mexican film *Silent Light* in her own novel, *Irma Voth*, Toews invites us to read across the boundaries of media, language, and geography. Just as a cross-sectional reading of 1986 gives a sense of the scale and range of the field's underappreciated work, the cross-boundary reading encouraged by Reygadas and Toews invites a broader engagement with the place of Mexico in the Mennonite artistic imagination. Of course, understanding *Silent Light* as a work of Mennonite writing requires us to accept "writing" in the broadest sense of the term but also to extend our critical focus to work that is not simply *by* Mennonites but also *about* them, for Reygadas is not Mennonite himself. (Indeed, the fact that this Latin American filmmaker turns to descendants of a white, European group of Mennonites as archetypes in an ostensibly universal story is a telling commentary on the normalized centrality of whiteness in cinema.) At the same time, the film is shot on location in a Mennonite colony, using almost exclusively Mennonite characters, and with Low German dialogue throughout. Understanding Mennonite writing as a critical frame rather than as ethnoreligious expression—in functional rather than ontological terms—offers a means of suspending (but not ignoring) the question of authorial or directorial biography to undertake a careful and informed engagement with the film's representation of Mennonite characters, setting, terms, and concerns. It enriches our appreciation of Reygadas's accomplishment in the film and helps us better understand Toews's project in *Irma Voth*.

How might we move forward with these types of examination? Well, there is no shortage of literary and cinematic work that engages the Mennonite experience in Mexico waiting to be examined in a critically informed frame. In Yuri Herrera's Pen Award–winning novella, *The Transmigration of Bodies*, for example, a ruthless fixer named simply "The Mennonite" roams the nearly empty streets of a Mexican city in the grips of a mysterious plague. In Canada and the United States, television shows like *Pure* may sensationalize the Mexican context, but celebrated young adult and children's literature such as Trilby Kent's *Once in a Town Called Moth* (2016) and Maxine Trottier's *Migrant* (2011) offer nuanced discussions of the Russian Mennonite migratory lines that run across the three countries of North America. Work by authors and artists more closely connected to the Mexican colonies is more rare but includes the poetry of the Texas-based writer and researcher Abigail Carl-Klassen, as well as work in collaboration with, or by, colony members themselves, including Carl-Klassen's *Darp Web Project*, a YouTube series chronicling the lives of Mennonites in the Mexican colonies; bilingual books of narrative folk art such as Sarah Unger de Peters's *Mennoniten in Mexiko / Mennonites in Mexico;* and Miriam Rudolph's *David's Trip to Paraguay: The Land of the Amazing Colours / Davids Reise: in das Land der vielen Farben*. Among the more compelling and promising examples of such writing is Anna Wall's long-running online memoir, *Mennopolitan*, which recounts Wall's experience immigrating to Canada from the Mexican Old Colony village of her youth. Notably, Wall singles out Toews's *Irma Voth* as her favorite book. "It reminds me of myself," she writes.

The next and final chapter of this study will return north of the Mexican border and to the fiction of Canada and the United States, in order to consider a tentative reinvestment in the ideals of Mennonite community that is being inscribed in several recent works of Mennonite writing. The chapter begins with a return to the problematics of narrative history that I explored in the introduction and chapter 1, before offering a parallel close reading of two very different texts. Where *Silent Light* and *Irma Voth* beg a comparative reading by their shared characters, plot points, and themes, and by Toews's active involvement in both projects, Casey Plett's *Little Fish*, about a group of vibrant but vulnerable trans women in Winnipeg, and Sofia Samatar's "Fallow," about the divergent paths of two sisters in a distant galaxy far in the future, might appear to have little to bring them into conversation. Both novels, however, offer compelling explorations of the limits of conventional Mennonite history and—together—offer one of the more surprising gestures of recent Mennonite literature in North America: a willingness to fight for a broader Mennonite future.

CHAPTER 5

ENDURE

Little Fish and "Fallow"

Let's begin with another set of eleven Mennonite literary titles: *Walking to Mojácar; Songen; Years, Months, Days; Once Removed; All That Belongs*; "My Name Is Magdalena"; *He'll*; *boneyard*; *Riding Sidesaddle**; *Little Fish*; "Fallow." The texts in this list are linked not only as works by or about Mennonites in North America published over the last decade or so but also, I want to suggest, by the fact that each work insists upon the value of the past and the need to reconsider how it informs a collective present. The first three titles, all collections of poetry, each work to reimagine traditional German Mennonite hymns, with their authors—Di Brandt, Patrick Friesen, and Amanda Jernigan, the latter of whom works self-consciously from outside the tradition—insisting on the value of these hymns, as well as not only the need but also, startlingly, their authority to rewrite those hymns in service of the present moment.[1] The fiction from this list similarly invites readers to revise elements of the past, but in a slightly different register: in Andrew Unger's *Once Removed*, for example, a quixotic ghost-writer of Mennonite family histories undertakes a massive but clandestine research project in an effort to preserve the fast-disappearing heritage of a Southern Manitoba village. In Dora Dueck's *All That Belongs*, a retired archivist turns her professional gaze to the mysteries of her own family, and Dueck's short story, "My Name Is Magdalena," reads like an archive: it is comprised of thirteen numbered paragraphs, each a first-person memory of a hard life, followed by an italicized paragraph explaining the paragraphs as "*notes for* [the author's] *obituary*" that have been compiled by an editor identified simply as "J" (53). The opening notes in Nathan Dueck's *He'll* and Stephen Beachy's *boneyard* have dubious author-figures who tell readers that the volumes are found manuscripts discovered in terrible disarray and later reconstructed: the pages of *He'll* were ostensibly first found in a rat-eaten package of loose papers, and Dueck invites the reader to "place this earthy 'oeuvre' [. . .] in any order you will" (4); the pages of *boneyard*, we are told, were first burned by its author, with "easily 50 percent of the text of the charred 'original' [. . .] missing" (15). Miriam Suzanne takes these types of gestures to their logical conclusion in *Riding Sidesaddle**, which is self-described as "a novel on 250 interchangeable index cards" meant to "explore[] the construction of narrative and the authority of the novel form." A digital version of the book, with the cards presented in different order upon each visit, is available online for anyone worried they might lose a page or two in the shuffle of their library.[2]

As individual works, the titles listed above are complex and wide-ranging examples of contemporary Mennonite writing, but they also make a collective gesture that will be the focus of this final chapter. In beginning this with a list of titles, I mean, of course, to gesture to the methodological experiment of chapter 1, where I undertook a cross-sectional reading of 1986 to suggest something of the range of texts, contexts, and interests that lie in the field's past that complicate our easy accounts of that history. In that early chapter, I aimed to pick up the work that we had collectively left on the floor of what Moretti calls the "slaughterhouse of literature," and bring it back into our collective purview. I hoped to estrange the selective memory of the field's developmental model of literary history in order to better serve the field's expanding present. What fascinates me about the list of recent texts with which I began this chapter, by contrast, is the way the texts themselves parallel the larger revisionary gesture I suggest the field is undertaking at present, insisting upon both the value of the past and the need to reconfigure it—usually in the hope not of replacing the old narratives with a new, "right" version but rather of leaving that past incomplete, scattered, and open to new futures. Nor am I alone in hearing this backward-looking but forward-thinking resonance among the contemporary work. In the generous closing pages of *Making Believe*, Redekop reflects on her overflowing MennoLit bookshelves and suggests that if she was forced to identify a common concern among the recent work, it would be "anachronic renaissance: the urge to go deep into the past, confronting skeletons and talking to ghosts, and the desire to savor the sweetness of new growth as you move forward and begin all over again" (209).

This restructuring gesture can, I think, be read alongside what I've elsewhere described as the scholarly field's "metacritical tradition" of reconsidering its own history and parameters.[3] For this final chapter, I want to focus on two of the most compelling examples of this revisionist urge: Casey Plett's 2018 novel, *Little Fish*, and Sofia Samatar's novella, "Fallow" (from her 2017 collection *Tender*). Plett's debut novel is an intimate portrait of a trans Russian Mennonite woman struggling to build and maintain her communities in contemporary Winnipeg; Samatar's speculative fiction novella is about a space colony of racialized Mennonites fighting for survival on a toxic planet billions of miles away from Earth. Neither novel is set in the past, strictly speaking—*Little Fish* takes place over two months in a recent but nonspecific Winnipeg winter, while "Fallow" takes place in a far-removed future—but both novels insist that a reconsideration of Mennonite temporality itself will be necessary to enable the possibility of a broader, more inclusive future. Together, these very different projects present a compelling account of the complex need to recall and revise the past, rather than simply reject or replace it—and, in the process, offer models for a tentative reinvestment in the future for Mennonite writing.

LITTLE FISH: LOOKING TO THE PAST FOR A FUTURE

It took a landmark "LGBT Fiction" panel at the 2015 Mennonite/s Writing conference at Fresno Pacific University, organized by Daniel Shank Cruz and consisting of authors Casey Plett, Jan Guenther Braun, Andrew Harnish, and a standing-room-only crowd, for the growing number of works published by and about queer Mennonites to be conceived of as a subgenre in its own right.[4] Although this trend has surprised readers who might have preconceived notions of the Mennonite community as uniformly heteronormative, Cruz's expansive political understanding of queerness enables him to argue "queer Mennonite writing is in some ways a natural extension of the Mennonite spirit" (*Queering* 11), and to suggest that the arguably queer elements of the sixteenth-century *Martyrs Mirror* means "the queer Mennonite literary tradition is nearly as old as the Mennonite literary tradition itself" (Cruz, "Reading" 285n7). In her contribution to the Fresno panel's subsequent publication, Plett makes a similar argument, suggesting there is a surprising amount that "queer literature and Mennonite literature hold in common" ("Natural" 287). Where Cruz establishes this link via shared Anabaptist/queer commitments to radicalism, Plett argues there are also shared thematic concerns, including the "loss of family, the loss of community," as well as "displacement," and "the destruction of stability" ("Natural" 287). Several years after the panel, Plett would publish her much-celebrated debut novel, *Little Fish*, where she would explore the overlapping concerns in depth, testing their possibilities, and, perhaps, looking to move beyond them.

Little Fish consists of twenty-seven chapters, divided into two sections labeled by month. Plett establishes the novel's overlapping thematic concerns immediately, with two epigraphs invoking noted figures from both Mennonite literature (Sandra Birdsell) and trans art (Lexi Sanfino), and its first section title, "November," gesturing toward what will soon be revealed to be a related interest in questions of time. The novel proper begins with a brief two-page chapter that brings these concerns together in memorable fashion. Wendy Reimer, the novel's trans Russian Mennonite protagonist, sits in a Winnipeg bar with three of her trans friends. Wendy's friend Sophie, another Mennonite woman and the novel's most thoughtful character, is reflecting on the subjective nature of time. As an introduction to my reading of the novel, it is worth quoting the book's opening paragraph in full:

> 0
>
> The night before her Oma died, Wendy was in a booth at the bar with Lila, Raina, and Sophie. It was eleven p.m., and they were all tipsy. Sophie was saying, "Age is completely different for trans people. The way we talk about age is not how cis people talk about age." (11)

Presented as chapter "0" and beginning with the proleptic clause "The night before her Oma died," the carefully crafted scene establishes the novel's larger exploration of Wendy's experience of time, and of pasts both Mennonite and trans.[5] Plett is careful to signal that if the death of Wendy's grandmother, or Oma, is the event that launches the novel's investigation into the Reimer family's past, both Wendy and Sophie had already been wrestling with related questions. "This is something I've thought about for a while," Sophie insists (11). Reflecting that cis people have "timelines" and "benchmarks" associated with various ages, the women suggest the specificities and vulnerabilities of transgender lives—the physical changes of hormone-therapy or surgery, the new beginnings of coming out or transition, the foreshortening of life expectancy, and so on—mean that the ways that "mainstream society conceives of age doesn't apply to us" (12). It is worth noting, here, that the novel begins as a conversation strictly between trans women, as *Little Fish* will prove strategically uninterested in explaining itself to its larger audiences. When the conversation is interrupted when a waitress drops a tray of drinks, Plett positions the larger novel as its continuation by having Wendy retire to a bathroom stall to sip on a mickey of whiskey, "calmly thinking" about the question she had asked just moments before: "How do we think about our past?" (12)

The following chapters explore not only the novel's larger question about how the past is conceived but also the complex referents for those collective nouns—the "we" that is said to be thinking about "our past." In the first extended chapter, Wendy has returned to her grandparents' rural Mennonite town in Southern Manitoba for her Oma's funeral, when she learns, via an awkward phone conversation with an elderly Mennonite woman named Anna, that her beloved Opa may have been queer—or even trans. The possibility is staggering for Wendy, whose own experience of transitioning had left her to assume that the distance between the rural and conservative Mennonite community of her past and the urban transgender community of her present were all but unbridgeable. In the first tentative step toward what becomes months of effort to link her trans and Mennonite communities, Wendy decides to sneak several of her grandparent's photo albums back with her to the city. Back in Winnipeg, Wendy's decision to look into her family's past is gently encouraged by Sophie, who admits to having "thought a lot about old Mennonites being trans before" herself (37). When Wendy tries to dismiss the significance of her possible discovery, saying she would "bet a million fuckin' Mennonites were trans" and that they probably "killed themselves" or "added it to their triumphant burdens to bear for God" (36), Sophie urges her to consider how different her Opa's experience would have been in the closed Mennonite villages of his generation. "Their culture never built any of those skills," Sophie notes, adding, "It must be hard escaping that." Leaving "that world" for the city would have been difficult, Sophie continues, but "being in the world afterward" might have been "the hard part" (38–39). Sophie is, of course, describing the predicament that both she and Wendy now find themselves in, albeit a generation later. Might an investigation into her Opa's life provide the women with a new way to think about their past—and, in the process, build some skills to help them thrive in the world?

Although I will argue that one of the primary accomplishments of the novel is its demonstration of the fact that trans and Mennonite experiences are not mutually exclusive, Plett flatly refuses to underestimate their differences or the challenge of bringing them together. To the contrary, the episodic structure of *Little Fish* reflects the affective toll that comes with Wendy's attempt to negotiate what are presented as two profoundly different worlds, sharply juxtaposed so as to accentuate what Wendy calls the "infinite whiplash" that characterized Sophie's life as a trans Mennonite (280). The opening sentence of chapter 1 is indicative of what we might understand as a narrative strategy of maximum contrast: "The night Wendy's Oma died," it begins, "she had sex dreams." In case readers should miss the impact of this juxtaposition, Plett doubles down immediately. "When her grandmother died," it continues, "a girl was fucking her over an old television in an abandoned gym" (13). This type of strategic juxtaposition plays out over entire chapters: one chapter shows Wendy meeting up with Sophie and her mother to discuss the intricacies of faith and kinship among rural Mennonites and to reflect on the ways that religion "stays with you [. . .] in ways you don't expect" (142), and the next begins with a series of sex-work out-calls that Wendy undertakes across the city. At other times, it plays out from page to page: in one paragraph we see

Wendy vomiting while performing oral sex in a trucker's cab, for example, and in the next she is reflecting on "how light, sad, and peaceful" she feels while listening to "beautiful, haunting hymns" (153; 154). Readers might expect these types of sharp juxtapositions to ease with Wendy's efforts to delve into her Mennonite heritage, but Plett seems eager to emphasize that Wendy's whiplash continues. In one paragraph near the novel's close, for example, we see Wendy straining toward a tentative embrace of parts of her religious heritage—"*Maybe our God wasn't the lie*, Wendy suddenly thought about her people," Plett writes. "*Maybe our isolation was the lie*" (281)—only to shift immediately into a graphic description of the various sexual positions expected from a demanding John (281).

What is the function of these types of jarring narrative shifts? Surely they are meant to not only echo but to invoke in the reader something of the "whiplash" that Wendy experiences as she moves between these specific trans and Mennonite communities. In a 2015 essay entitled "Breaking the Binary: Queering Mennonite Identity," Alicia Dueck-Read reports on a series of interviews conducted with "transgender, genderqueer, and gender non-conforming" Mennonites in terms that strongly resonate with Plett's disorienting portrait of trans Mennonite life. Describing her interview subjects as people who have been "rendered unintelligible and unethical within the discourses of the Mennonite community" (115), Dueck-Read reports that it is not uncommon—though certainly not always the case—for nonconforming people to remain connected in some way to the community but warns that those "moving between Mennonite and secular gender contexts" describe it as "get[ing] whiplashed" (127).

If *Little Fish* is likely to invoke a certain "whiplash" in its audience, it is not simply because of its dramatic shifts between starkly different contexts but also because of Plett's strategic refusal to help her readers understand their specificities. Elsewhere, Plett has reflected on the importance of trans writing that has "dispensed with the worry of explaining ourselves to cis people" (Plett and Fitzpatrick), and several trans readers have appreciated *Little Fish* in just such a manner.[6] While the stakes are obviously quite different, something similar can be said regarding Plett's representation of Wendy's navigation of a Southern Manitoba Russia Mennonite world: what Kasdorf calls the "autoethnographic announcement" that seems all but obligatory in Mennonite literature in search of wider audiences is nowhere to be found here. Indeed, Plett details her novel with church acronyms such as EMC (14, 138) and MCC (85), and Low German phrases like "*Najo*" (15), "*Faspa* time" (170), and "*päpanät*" (248), all used without explanation or translation, just as references to trans women still in "egg mode" (24), books like *Whipping Girl* (78), and figures like Morgan Page and Andrea James (270) are left unexplained. The risk of such an approach, of course, is that the size of audience that could claim to be a fully informed readership—able to follow the nuances of the novel's portraits of these particular trans and Mennonite communities—is likely to be fleetingly small. "My book has to do with trans women, and Mennonites, and Winnipeg," Plett has noted elsewhere. "There's a very, very small Venn diagram of people who are intimately acquainted with all three of those communities" ("What"). The reward of such an approach, however, is substantial: *Little Fish* is a book that never seems to pander, is totally unafraid of contradiction, and is willing to risk being misunderstood in its drive toward a new kind of narrative.

As the novel proceeds, it becomes clear that Wendy's significant personal struggles are exacerbated by a lack of healthy models from the past that could help her navigate her own way forward. Plett underscores this absence in parallel scenes near the novel's conclusion. In the first scene, the elderly Anna rebukes Wendy for refusing to deny her earthly desires and sacrifice her life in service of a Mennonite faith she doesn't share. "God has *so much* strength to give," Anna says. "You may have thought you needed to be a woman or die," she continues, but you "choose the easy, selfish path" (263–64). Anna, who is closeted and has struggled to carve out a meaningful life within the community of her birth, believes herself to be offering a path forward through a hard truth, but in the context of the larger novel it appears to be a dead end. In the second scene, set almost immediately after this exchange, Plett turns to a similarly unhelpful effort from an earlier generation of trans women. Lila, a trans friend of the central protagonists, stumbles upon a paint-by-numbers online test called the COGIATI, which is meant to "tell you whether you're a transsexual or not" (268). The test is presented as simultaneously laughable, pathetic, and horrifying. When one woman says she thinks about "how desperate this woman probably felt when she was writing it, how much she must have thought she was doing the right thing, how she was helping the rest of us" (270) while she was, in fact, only causing harm, it is hard not to hear an echo of the advice that Wendy had just received from Anna about maintaining her position within a Mennonite community. Notably, Plett inserts a short chapter of a single paragraph between Wendy's difficult visit with Anna and her discussion of the COGIATI, and it is a brief description about how confusing the streets are in Winnipeg. "There aren't any freeways in the city of Winnipeg," it begins. "None of the streets have directionals, and nothing is numbered"; roads are assigned numbers "out of sequence," with "no meaning to a stranger"; the city's "map is a collection of stitched, makeshift grids" (265). Slipped between discussions of well-intentioned but hapless efforts from an earlier generation of Mennonite and trans women, the metaphor of Winnipeg's dizzying roadways seems clear enough: this is difficult, uncharted territory.

Without a meaningful and shared sense of trans Mennonite history, there is no simple path forward for Wendy. This is, of course, what makes Wendy's search for her Opa's past so difficult, but it is also what makes it necessary and full of promise. In a context where the possibility of her Opa's queer identity appears to have been unthinkable within the established norms and available history, Wendy must turn to alternative and often ephemeral expressions of the past in order to establish—quite literally—a genealogy of queer Mennonites. Notably, these unofficial, or alternative, lines of history are primarily oral: she first learns of her grandfather's "secret" through a chance phone conversation with Anna, and it is through her subsequent visits with Anna that she begins to piece together a portrait of her Opa as a closeted gay man whose lover in Winnipeg died of AIDS in the 1980s, after which he worked to suppress his sexuality as part of his earnest understanding of his Christian faith. Wendy's well-intentioned but often bumbling father, too, confirms "there were rumours" that Opa was gay (285). Other pieces of her grandfather's past arrive in a similarly haphazard manner, as in the family photo albums she scours for possible evidence (24, 36). And, in what might be considered the novel's (anti-) climatic scene, Anna provides Wendy with a letter from her Opa, purporting that it offers "black and white" evidence about his past (247).

Plett seems eager to underscore the archival nature of Wendy's efforts, including both a full-page image of Henry's letter, handwritten in wobbling Gothic script on a lined paper, as well as a typeset version for clarity. In yet another example of the ways in which the present shapes the community's engagement with the past, however, Anna selects only this one letter to share with Wendy, and it contains only vague reference to past "sins and misjudgements" that he is working to overcome (259). While oral narratives, letters, and photographs are standard primary sources for authoritative historical scholarship, Plett suggests the archive of queer Mennonite history as having remained, to this point, uncollected and uncollated.

The novel's archival project to uncover and insert queer identity into a narrative account of Russian Mennonite history is further complicated by a queer resistance to the linear modes of history, and the Mennonites' eschatological investment in the afterlife. As the prefatory chapter promised, the precarious, vulnerable nature of Wendy's life as a trans woman results in an episodic existence that moves swiftly between partners, jobs, parties, and, as such, resists the type of easy categorization available to cis conventions of marriage, long-term employment, and children. "Her life had kinda never really changed," we are told near the novel's end. "Her adult life at thirty looked a lot like it had at nineteen" (278). In this context, Wendy's efforts to explore her Opa's life throughout the novel are readable as an example of what Carolyn Dinshaw has called the "queer desire for history" (Dinshaw et al. 178)—that is, an archival desire to recover a queer past in an effort to counter the community's erasure and establish a historical legacy for the present. In her influential examination of queer temporalities, however, Elizabeth Freeman coins the term "chrononormativity" to caution against the "interlocking temporal schemes necessary for genealogies of descent" (*Time* xxii). For Freeman, who proposes that "we reimagine 'queer' as a set of possibilities produced out of temporal and historical difference" ("Introduction" 159), queer temporalities are—or can be—revolutionary in part because they disrupt the heteronormative time of the nation and the family that has forcibly excluded queer identities to date. From this perspective, Plett's archival efforts in *Little Fish* are double-edged: on the one hand, they work to productively write queerness into the deeply conservative history of Russian Mennonites in Manitoba; on the other they may risk containing trans history, rather than freeing Mennonite temporality. Or, put differently: to the extent the novel's archival process expands rather than reorients Mennonite identity, it risks affirming an exclusionary framework via its limited inclusivity—not unlike Jasbir Puar's critique of "trans(homo)nationalism," wherein nations interpolate trans subjects into the "national discourses and legal frames of recognition" (34). It is a risk Plett is clearly willing to take.

In a similar fashion, albeit in a very different register, *Little Fish* suggests the construction of queer Mennonite history is further complicated by the community's investment in a Christian eschatology that works to defer the affective elements of queer life into the afterlife. The temporal endurance of a sacrificial present life, in this model, is dwarfed by the immensity of eternal reward, with Christ's bodily sacrifice a model of physical martyrdom that gets reconfigured here as a queer denial of the self. Might it be possible, Sophie wonders, that Henry's complicated desires and identity would have been experienced as "just another earthly burden to bear," one that "God would be proud of him for resisting"? (39) Wendy is initially dismissive of the suggestion, but Plett returns to it in a key scene near the end of the novel. "There's so much that is hard in this life that God asks us to weather, for reasons we can't understand," Anna tells Wendy. "That's faith. Not judgment" (262–63). Like Henry, Anna uses scriptural references to support an argument for the need to sacrifice the present in the service of an eternal future.[7] How is one to think about reconstructing a past in the service of the present, Plett asks, in a context where all that matters is the eternal future?

Although Wendy is initially frustrated by the lack of "evidence" about her Opa's queer life and is hurt by Anna's judgmental language, the larger novel positions these as part of the larger challenges of attempting to build a framework in which queer Mennonite life is thinkable, and thus possible. Anna's decision to call Henry's family in the first place, her willingness to invite Wendy into her house, to share Henry's letter with her, to continue the conversation when it becomes clear that Wendy has been dishonest with her—all this can be understood as an example of Anna's flawed generosity, and evidence that Anna, too, is working toward this same project. Late in the novel Plett describes Anna and Wendy's relationship in terms that resonate for the book as a whole: "And if Anna had been a woman Wendy could talk to and be honest with, what would she have said? If Anna could have joined her wisdom to Wendy's truths, what would Anna have to tell her? And what if that trip hadn't hurt Wendy; what if Wendy had left the older woman's house full of warmth and unpoisoned insight?" (279). What if? Plett's effort to construct a genealogy of trans Mennonite identity in *Little Fish*, I want to suggest, is readable as an extended effort to answer precisely these types of questions. When the novel concludes just pages later, Plett shifts suddenly into the second person with reason for cautious optimism. "What kind of world does the core of your brain expect that you, you personally, get to live in?" Plett asks, addressing the reader directly. "Wendy wanted to be loved," she writes. "However easily she might have abandoned or ruined her prospects, Wendy did still believe she would have love" (292–93). With that, the narrative shifts back into the third person to show Wendy leaving an expensive hotel after a trick with an agreeable John, heading into a freshly snow-covered city that looks "pristine and quiet and footprint-less," almost like "outer space" (293). "She felt okay about where her life was headed," the novel concludes (293).

This is a final image that risks cliché in the larger literary world, but after several hundred pages of watching Wendy struggle mightily to uncover a past that could support a meaningful future, it arrives like a deep and hard-earned victory.

In reviewing *Little Fish* for the *Journal of Mennonite Studies*, Julia Michael notes that the novel's often explicit descriptions of violence and sex and are likely to dissuade some of the readers otherwise drawn to the novel's engagement with Mennonite characters and concerns. She is surely right on this point. I find *Little Fish* to be a hard novel, to be sure, difficult to read because of its graphic language and the violence endured by its vulnerable protagonists. Of course, claims of a book's difficulty tell us at least as much about the subject positions and sensitivities of readers as they do about the book itself, perhaps especially in a field like Mennonite literature. Beck's list of those books that have been considered "transgressive" in Mennonite writing—from *Peace Shall Destroy Many* to *questions i asked my mother* to *A Complicated Kindness* and on—suggests the aesthetic and social potential of uncomfortable writing, even if, as Beck suggests, these texts have offended mostly "through character defamation, negative stereotyping of Mennonites, or distortion of Mennonite history or theology" rather than "sadism and bodily function" (53). The frank and explicit descriptions of sex in Plett's debut novel suggests *Little Fish* is transgressive in a broader sense than that to which readers in the field have become accustomed, but here it seems important to recall Cruz's reminder about queer Mennonite writing more broadly: such work, Cruz notes, "often works to make readers uncomfortable in order to make its antioppressive messages clear" (*Queering* 4). Mennonite readers who pass on Plett's book because of its perceived transgressions not only risk affirming its critique of the community as refusing to engage its trans members. Ironically enough, they will also miss one of the more earnest attempts to re-engage and reanimate that community in contemporary fiction. This is a hard novel, too, then, because of the heartbreaking persistence with which Wendy pursues a relationship with a faith community that has hurt her repeatedly. When Plett has Wendy say she is "so, so tired of loving her people and them not loving her back" (150), is it a stretch to hear it echo into a description of the relationship between queer Mennonites and the broader Mennonite community?

"FALLOW": LOOKING TO THE FUTURE FOR A PAST

Few figures have risen so quickly in Mennonite studies over the past decade as the prolific American author and scholar Sofia Samatar. Winner of both the World Fantasy Award and the British Fantasy Award, Samatar's creative work includes the novels *A Stranger in Olondria* (2013) and its sequel *The Winged Histories* (2016), the short fiction collection *Tender* (2017), as well as *Monster Portraits* (2018), a collaborative illustrated project with her brother, Del Samatar. Daughter of the noted Somali-American scholar Said Sheikh Samatar, Samatar's faculty page at James Madison University suggests the broad range of her interests and expertise, including "Arabic Literature, African Literature, World Literature, Transnational Anglophone and Postcolonial Literature, Afrofuturism, and Speculative Fiction." Notable in its absence from this list is Mennonite studies, where her recent efforts have included influential postcolonial and feminist critiques of the field, and where her creative writing has found an eager audience.[8] Over the past several years, Samatar has begun to explore her Mennonite heritage in her speculative fiction as well, as in the remarkable novella I want to explore here, entitled "Fallow."[9]

First published in her 2017 collection *Tender*, "Fallow" is a lengthy story about a religious community that is recognizable (though never explicitly named) as Mennonite. Community members are presented as the descendants of a group of people who fled Earth in the aftermath of an environmental apocalypse to establish a colony on what proved to be a toxic planet named Fallow. Over the course of the novella, readers learn the colonists' plan is to abandon the Earth for some five hundred years in order to allow it to rejuvenate itself—to leave it fallow, in other words—at which point the colonists' distant descendants will attempt a return. The narrative is presented as the writings of a first-person narrator named Agar, who is recording her reflections of life on the colony with hopes that it will be accepted into the community's archives. The carefully crafted story is presented in three sections, each given the title of a major character. Section 1, "Miss Snowfall," is loosely focused on Agar's eccentric schoolteacher, who ultimately commits suicide. Section 2, "Brother Lookout," is focused on a quiet local man, who, as a leader of the "Young Evangelists," had once attempted a religious revival on the colony. Read carefully, this section establishes the colony's Mennonite heritage and includes a lengthy theological consideration of a community that has quite literally set itself apart from "the world." Section 3, "Temar," is focused on Agar's brilliant but deeply frustrated older sister and includes Temar's lengthy letter explaining why she fled the colony when the opportunity arose.

"Fallow" is typical of Samatar's speculative fiction in that it leaps into a highly detailed alternative world and slowly offers important contextualizing details intermittently throughout the work. Beginning *in medias res* is a common narrative strategy hardly limited to speculative fiction—we have seen a similar strategy put toward different ends in both *Silent Light* and *Little Fish*, after all—but it is particularly effective here. As the penultimate story in a larger collection of short speculative fiction, "Fallow" challenges readers to suspend nearly all their assumptions as they begin: when Samatar's narrator begins the story by saying she "once heard a beautiful story" (206), readers know the setting could truly be almost anywhere, at any time—even on a toxic planet in the distant future populated by intergalactic Mennonites. Reygadas decontextualizes a Mennonite colony to the point that it seemed *as if* it were cosmically isolated and works within that setting as fantasy, but Samatar begins by literalizing this fantasy and then slowly critiquing it by historicizing it. Over the next fifty-five pages, the larger context and setting is methodically drawn into focus with detail after enigmatic detail: first we learn early that Agar and her sister live near an important but inaccessible Castle; that their school and community are rigidly hierarchical; that there are dormitories for the colony's unmarried men and women. It takes several more pages before Samatar uses an extended classroom scene to provide the expository details necessary to understand the broader scope and setting of the story: that the small village is not on Earth; that the Castle is the headquarters where the colony's air, water, and food are produced; and so on. Significantly, withholding these details is fully in keeping with the conceit of the narrative being Agar's own writings, a strategic, fictional deployment of the intimacy of personal narratives written specifically for submission to the community archive, in which broad contextualizing details might be assumed. Indeed, the science fiction novella reads, as Chris Abani has suggested, as a type of "careful but casual realism." Importantly, it also works to disorient the reader, who rushes headlong into a detailed but clearly alternate world and must simply wait for the grounding details necessary to understand *where* and *when* the story unfolds, and what might be at stake in the narrative.

The Mennonite focus of the story is revealed slowly, as well. In introducing a section of the story published in *Electric Lit*, Abani suggests in passing that "the heart of *Fallow* is based on an actual historical event, the migration of Mennonites from Southern Russia to what is now Uzbekistan in the 1880's." This may well be true, but Abani offers no evidence or explanation for the claim, and it requires a careful reading to follow even the initial suggestions Samatar provides regarding the characters'

Anabaptist origins.[10] The opening epigraph, for example, reads "*Here is the Peaceable Kingdom*" (206), a phrase that returns to Agar pages later in secured facility that hosts the village's climate-controlled gardens (217). The italicized phrase is a reference to the well-known nineteenth century series of Pennsylvania landscape paintings of the same name by a Quaker minster, Edward Hicks, many of which feature a small child among placid lions and sheep with Indigenous people and Europeans together in the background. The first Mennonites in North America arrived as part of William Penn's Grand Experiment, and Samatar's invocation of the painting and its dubious theological interpretation of colonial contact—the large text on the border of several of the paintings in the series makes clear Hick's effort to equate the biblical account of a redeemed Earth (Isaiah 11:6–8) with Penn's founding of Pennsylvania—links the novella's community to Pennsylvanian history and signals its interrogation of religious discourses of utopian colonialism.

A firmer link to specifically Mennonite history comes in Agar's passing comment that she and her sister leave school each day under a gate that "bore the inscription ARBEITE UND HOFFE" (207). The use of German is a hint, of course, but it takes a reader alert to Mennonite history to connect the phrase to the opening pages of the *Martyrs Mirror*, the martyrology that has played a central role in Mennonite history and imagination since its first publication in the sixteenth century, where this inscription has traditionally been included alongside the image of a digging peasant.[11] In "Work and Hope," a fascinating essay that traces the long history of the phrase in transatlantic Mennonite history, for example, Kasdorf confesses that "each time I see that digging man"—even if it is in "another form" of some sort—she "feel[s] a flush of nostalgic recognition, connection, and hope" (*Body* 118). General readers, however, might feel a "flush" of a very different recognition, hearing echoes of another German phrase: the infamous lie, *Arbeit Macht Frei* ["Work will make you free"], that stood above the gate to Auschwitz. Did Samatar intend to invoke both Anabaptism and Auschwitz when she hung this phrase above the colony school? She would not be the first to make this connection, and placing the phrase on a gate suggests as much to me.[12] In one register, the phrase quietly connects the colony to specifically Anabaptist history and sets up the story's critique of the Mennonite community's historic practices of self-isolation; in another, it suggests that the strict rules, harsh punishments, and long labors demanded of its members in the name of survival are, in fact, lies.

As "Fallow" progresses, the community's heritage and history become increasingly clear for an informed reader, as does the novella's theologically informed critique. Early references to the community's pacifism, theology of yieldedness, its practice of shunning as church discipline, its conscientious objection to military drafts, and its longstanding efforts at isolationism—it was "so unfair, this senseless persecution, the pressing into evil of a people who only wished to be left alone," writes Agar (212)—transition into discussions of increasingly specific aspects of Mennonite history and theology. Many references are obscure, but they are nonetheless concrete: the sentence Brother Lookout reads at an early Young Evangelists meeting, for example, comes from an 1837 introduction to the Mennonite Confession of Faith by Joseph Funk (236);[13] what Agar describes as the "misguided prophets of old Earth: Jan van Leyden running naked through the streets of Munster, Claas Epp who heretically predicated the day of Christ's return" (235) are, in fact, references to well-known and controversial figures from Mennonite history. The critiques of Mennonite theology are clear, as well: on a toxic planet that cannot support life on its own, the practice of "shunning," or forcing members to leave the community, is quite literally a death penalty; we are told that the traditional Mennonite ideal of yieldedness (or *gelassenheit*) is prized highly, but Agar describes Miss Snowfall's suicide as its highest expression. "Miss Snowfall practiced, better than anyone else in our village, our highest value, what we call *yieldedness*," Agar writes. "She yielded and yielded until there was nothing left" (226). The Bishop's efforts to evangelize an Earthman who stumbled upon the colony are portrayed as similarly destructive. "Every day he was given sermons and injections," Temar reports. "If he accepted Christ he would be given a job in the Castle. If he remained stiff-necked he would be shunned" (254–55). "Shunned means killed," Temar explains, before ironically describing her own decision to turn away from the colony's faith as a conversion experience. "All I can tell you," she writes of her decision to turn away from the community, "is that I was born again" (255).

Nowhere is Samatar's theologically informed engagement with Mennonite history so clear as its caustic portrait of the community's longstanding effort to separate itself from "the world." The novella's larger critique is articulated with admirable passion by the Young Evangelist movement that is the focus of the teenage Agar's senior research project: "We belong to Earth, Brother Lookout explained, but we have abandoned it. We have cared only for our own salvation, our removal from the wars that blaze across its suffering continents, our preservation from its plagues and floods. Like the priest and the Levite, we have passed by the dying man on the road. Unlike true Christians, we have given no thought to our neighbors [. . .] we sit here like the carrion birds [. . .] waiting for others to die so that we might inherit the Earth" (236). While the larger story of "Fallow" affirms Brother Lookout's critique—in fleeing Earth to wait out the environmental collapse on another planet, these Mennonites *have* abandoned humanity—Samatar is far from the first to offer a stinging critique of Mennonite efforts to separate themselves from the world. Samatar raises the stakes of this critique by setting it on another planet, and by suggesting that the "separation debates" that had occurred on the colony, from which Brother Lookout's comments are taken, are now considered so dangerous that even the history of the debates themselves have become a taboo subject: Agar's efforts to research them for her senior project are sternly discouraged, even as she ostensibly undertakes her research in order to *affirm* the community's decision to remain separate.

Samatar's account differs from the field's long-established portraits of isolated Mennonite colonies in other ways as well, most notably in its incorporation of a racialized critique of the community's presumed homogeneity. Indeed, "Fallow" can be read not only as a work of Mennonite literature but also as a work of Afrofuturism, in which neglected Black histories and concerns are reanimated via time travel narratives. Coined by Mark Dery in a memorable interview essay entitled "Black to the Future," Afrofuturism offers, in Dery's original articulation, a means for "a community whose past has been deliberately rubbed out, and whose energies have subsequently been consumed by the search for legible traces of its history" to "imagine possible futures" (180). Subsequent work engaging Afrofuturism has refined this original critique while extending its politics. Kodwo Eshun, for example, suggests that the exclusion of Black subjects from the Enlightenment project resulted in a longstanding recuperative effort to "establish the historical character of black culture" by "assembl[ing] countermemories that contest the colonial archive" (288). It was in light of this "ethical commitment to history," he continues, that futurism was met with "suspicion, wariness, and hostility" (288). Eshun reads this suspicion as present through the work of early Black Atlantic studies but argues that today Afrofuturism is productively extending the tradition of countermemory, "reorienting the intercultural vectors of Black Atlantic temporality towards the proleptic as much as the retrospective" (289). "Afrofuturism," as Samatar herself puts it, "insists on lowercase histories as a means of unlocking other futures" ("Toward" 177).

The complex temporality of "Fallow" can be productively read as an Afrofuturist rendering, or re-visioning, of Mennonite history. Significantly, Samatar grounds this Afrofuturist portrait firmly in the present and past of the global Mennonite community. When Miss Snowfall instructs the colony children about how the community came to Fallow, for example, she invokes the Mennonite World Conference tradition that routinely brings together Mennonites from across the globe by describing a "Great World Conference" at which they first decided to depart. Miss Snowfall explains that the Mennonites who left Earth came from countries around the world (213), and she notes that the Mennonite engineers built their spaceship, or "Ark," in the "hills of Misraq Gojjam" (213). Samatar quietly underscores this Ethiopian connection throughout the story. A passing reference to the "eagle and the ossifrage" (236), for example, links the community's roots in North America (the eagle a common symbol for the United States) and Ethiopia (the ossifrage a vulture common in Ethiopia), while Agar's description of the community as "wandering farmers" notes that while their earlier "displacements" included Pennsylvania, Germany, Saskatchewan, and Russia, in Fallow they harvest "yellow-green fields of teff," an ancient grain common in Ethiopia (259–60). Descriptions of one friend's "soft brown body" (242) and a child's "halo of dense black hair" (259) further distance these intergalactic Mennonites from the presumptions of whiteness that routinely dominate the pages of Mennonite writing in North America. Near the novella's close, Samatar underscores these details once more, reiterating their significance for a community at risk of forgetting its past. Reflecting on the Mennonite's inaugural voyage to Fallow, Temar imagines the astronauts singing hymns as they hurtle through space. "*Unser Zug geht durch die Wüste. Hisboch hoy, des yebelachew, igziaheherin amesginu!*"[14] Temar writes, moving without comment between German, commonly spoken by the Russian Mennonites, and Amharic, commonly spoken by Ethiopian Mennonites (253). "It made me feel close to something," Temar writes. "We have a history, Agar, after all" (253).

Many of these details are likely to be overlooked by most readers, or to be considered inconsequential where they are noted. In a reading of the novella specifically as a work of Mennonite writing, however, they become central to the historicizing thrust of this futuristic project. In an essay published the same year as *Tender*, Samatar is blunt about the shortcomings of a field that has focused on Russian and Swiss Mennonite stories and histories while ignoring what she calls "postcolonial Mennonite writing," meaning to include "work by writers from Asia, Africa, and Latin America," as well as "the work of minority writers in North America" ("Scope"). "Fallow" may seem subtle in its assertion of a postcolonial Mennonite narrative, but there is power in that subtlety. After all, as Samatar writes elsewhere, postcolonial Mennonite writing is "the writing of the majority"—and indeed, a full half the world's baptized members of Anabaptist churches live in Africa, including more than 300,000 in Ethiopia alone.[15] The diversity of Fallow's community, in other words, is notable *only* from the perspective of a field still framed by its emergence as a form of white minority writing, bounded by its North American parameters. Outside this discursive frame, the story's blending of languages, its dovetailing of Ethiopian, Russian, and Swiss Mennonite geographies and histories, should be fully expected. Much as Cruz is right to recognize that Samatar's portrait of a Mennonite future in which queer relationships are so accepted as to be thoroughly unremarkable is itself a revolutionary act—two of the women in Fallow are in a longstanding and public relationship, but the story mentions this fact only in passing (*Queering* 136)—so too is the story's rendering of a postcolonial Mennonite community significant precisely because it is rendered normative.

Though "Fallow" is set in the future, then, it is very much a story about what constitutes the community's past. Having experienced the community's sanction for her efforts to revise its official account of its past—the cold response she received for her efforts to revisit the Separation Debates makes it clear such a project was unwelcome—Agar has turned to the community's archives. We learn that it was in these archives—in the documents, the personal interviews, and the snippets of closed fonds she has to access surreptitiously, and which she removes from the archive by copying the writing on her own skin—that she has been able to patch together some truth about the colony's past, and now she longs to add her own story to the collection. Agar knows that paper is in high demand and most writings submitted will be pulped and the paper recirculated for new stories, and she knows that the decision of which stories will be kept is determined by the sole discretion of a single man. The fact that this gatekeeper seems so well intentioned only adds to Agar's rising desire to attack him with her pencil. "Please accept these pages," Agar pleads in the novella's closing paragraph, referring to the document we have just finished reading as the story itself. "Accept, this time, my submission to the archives. Accept my absolute submission" (261). If she sounds desperate, it is not only because Samatar is positioning Agar's literary efforts within the Anabaptist language of yielding, or submission, but also because Agar truly *needs* her experiences—the "history" that Temar insists they have (253)—to be included in the official repository of the colony's past.

Elsewhere, Samatar has said she enjoys reading "literary criticism disguised as fiction, fiction disguised as literary criticism" (qtd. in Cruz "Fiction"), and it is in this vein that I would like to conclude my reading of her novella. In Samatar's portrait of a Mennonite community's archive that routinely pulps the stories deemed insignificant by its well-meaning gatekeepers, I see a compelling portrait of the stakes of Moretti's account regarding the mass of writings lost to the slaughterhouse of literature. Significantly, Agar explains she has "submitted a number of works, more than I care to remember," to the archives, but "all have been rejected." She continues, "I have submitted dramas, fantastical stories, novels of Old Earth, children's tales, even hymns. At this point, merely to pass by the archives gives me a queasy feeling. [. . .] It is a terrible feeling to have your work pulped" (217). It is no coincidence, in my reading, that most of the genres Agar describes as being rejected from the community's writing archives have been deeply underappreciated by conventional literary criticism—drama being the sole exception—including, of course, by the field of Mennonite literary studies itself. Might it be possible to hear also, in this passage, echoes of Samatar's critical argument, made explicit elsewhere, that hymns could be the logical place to begin a global study of Mennonite literature?[16] To hear in her portrait of a frustrated Mennonite writer with roots in Ethiopia echoes of Samatar's own exasperation with "anthologies of Mennonite writing, literary criticism and conference proceedings," which, as she points out, give little indication that "most Mennonites today live outside the United States and Canada"? Is it a stretch to hear in "Fallow" a response to her observation that in the discourse of Mennonite literary criticism, that "the time for postcolonial Mennonite literature is perpetually, it seems, not yet?" and to see in it something of her stated desire to "move toward that suspended time," to read her turn to a speculative work of Afrofuturism an effort "to trace, if possible, the contours of this project, which remains in the subjunctive, out of reach"?

ENDURE

Little Fish and "Fallow" are inescapably different works. One is a realist novel written by a Canadian, focused, in part, by its exploration of trans temporalities; the other a science fiction novella written by an American, focused, in part, by its exploration of Afrofuturism. One looks backward in search of a future; the other looks forward in search of a past. One foregrounds its engagement with Mennonite communities and concerns in its opening pages; the other actively avoids the title "Mennonite" altogether and weaves its engagement with Mennonite concerns into the deep background of a leisurely developing plot. It is difficult to imagine a context outside of North American Mennonite literary studies that is likely to bring these literary works into productive conversation. Together, however, they illustrate something of the startling range and vibrancy of writing by and about Mennonites at the present moment, and, at least in my reading, suggest something about how the field might continue to move into a most productive future.

I began this chapter with a return to the problematics of narrative history as explored in the early chapters of this study, noting a host of recent literary works published by or about Mennonites that explicitly invoke and reject the clarity and coherence of linear narratives. Whether poetry collections that rework traditional Mennonite hymns or novels that deploy "found manuscript" conceits to cast doubt on the order and content of its narrative, these works inscribe a narrative uncertainty that invite readers to acknowledge their own role in narrativizing the world presented by the work. Collectively, they inscribe versions of the same revisionary gesture that I have tried to trace in the contemporary critical field across this study: they recognize the past we inherit as being vital and important, but also as being in desperate need of reconsideration. Collectively, these books recognize the past is always shifting, always imagined in the service of a particular version of the present, and each work asserts—or confesses, as the case may be—that we are as readers and subjects complicit in its construction. Recognizing the fact that we are not simply the products but also the authors of our past means recognizing our complicity in the shape of the present, but it also means recognizing our opportunity to revisit and reconceive that past. Reading *Little Fish* and "Fallow" as works of Mennonite literature means following protagonists in search of the suppressed histories that are readable only in fragments—as oral accounts from unreliable sources, in rumors, in personal letters, in yellowed photographs, and archival papers, and so on—and whose efforts to uncover other pasts are motivated by a desire for more meaningful futures.

I began this study with Julia Spicher Kasdorf's parodic account of the "origin story" for Mennonite literary studies, in which she notes that it positions the author as a martyr-hero, whose act of truth-telling was "so transgressive that [he] became an exile" ("Sunday" 7). The originary hero in that originary myth, of course, is Rudy Wiebe himself, and that "first" novel, *Peace Shall Destroy Many*, tells a story that remains with us to this day: a closed, isolated community grapples unsuccessfully to control its members, who chafe under the prejudice and bigotry of its leaders. It is worth noting, in this context, that Wiebe himself has returned to this literary site in his 2014 novel, *Come Back*, to confirm what we might have expected: that Thom, the erstwhile hero of *Peace*, leaves Wapiti shortly after the first novel's conclusion. It is important to recognize this *leaving* is a central part of the legacy of Wiebe's novel as origin story, along with those works that Gundy calls the "kiss-it-goodbye" canon that has long stood at the heart of the field (*Walker* 25). Little wonder, then, that Cruz thinks to compare Fallow, the isolated colony of Samatar's short story, to Wapiti, the isolated village of Wiebe's novel, or that he points out how Temar "enact[s] the usual Mennonite literary trope of leaving the community because of its constrictions" (*Queering* 136). Indeed, when Temar discovered what she believes to be the colonists' plans to murder the Earthman via shunning, she feels she has little choice but to flee. As she writes to her sister in the letter she leaves behind, there may be "innocents" such as Agar who can thrive on the colony, but the only options for the "others" such as herself are to "Fade, fester, or run" (248). Fallow is a community full of colony members who have faded or festered. Temar's decision to flee the isolated colony of Fallow is fully in keeping with the tropes and scope of the fiction of Mennonite North America to date.

It seems important to conclude this chapter, then, by recognizing that several of these recent works offer portraits of characters who have remained. Just as Kasdorf's "Sunday morning confessions" includes a plea for Mennonite critics to stop celebrating only the Anabaptists who died as martyrs and be thankful, too, that there were those who managed to survive, it seems important to recognize and engage those literary figures who have been able and willing to stay. In *All That Belongs*, in *He'll*, and in *boneyard*, characters are all too aware of the community's limitations, but they continue to engage with it. At times, these authors even thematize these decisions as a shift for the field. In *Little Fish*, Plett has Wendy note that "the humble old desperate towns of Rudy Wiebe and Sandra Birdsell books were gone, or at least shrunk, or fast on their way to existing only in traces, photos, myth, and books" (22), for example, at once invoking and revising these canonical portraits of the community's past. Similarly, in Unger's *Once Removed*, a struggling ghostwriter named Timothy Heppner idolizes Elsie Dyck, the small town's literary "martyr" who dared to write the town in a poor light and who was promptly exiled to the city (30). Timothy, however, refuses to leave. "I figured it was about time all the 'rebel Mennonites' stayed in their small towns, drank their craft beer, played in their Springsteen cover bands, and wrote their trashy novels," he says (53).

Agar and Wendy, too, are characters who remain. In *Little Fish*, it is Wendy's difficult decision to engage Anna and her Mennonite heritage that opens the prospect of a broader history that might enable a more inclusive Mennonite community. And in "Fallow," Agar respects her sister's decision to leave but amends Temar's account of the options that face women in the colony. "For some of us there are only three choices—fade, fester, or run," she acknowledges, "but others have a fourth choice: to endure" (260). It is by staying and writing in the community, after all, that she discovers the Earthwoman they believed to have been murdered by shunning has been working in the castle all her life (246); it is by enduring that she has uncovered the histories that Temar insisted they have and has put them down in writing for the colony's archive. It is a point that Samatar reiterates in the novella's closing paragraph, where Agar acknowledges that her writings about the community may not always be easy but asks that they be received in the spirit in which they are intended. "If I have written of shame and sadness, I have done so out of reverence for the story we fight to preserve with every breath," she insists. "I have done so in the spirit of one who endures" (261).

Crucially, neither Plett nor Samatar appear to *prescribe* the hard work of enduring in these works. To the contrary, both authors take pains to show the high stakes being risked by those who stay, and to acknowledge the reality that others must leave. Wendy has suffered under the quiet violence of her narrow Mennonite heritage, and if she fights to make a place within it, Plett reminds us of the cost and stakes of such work. *Little Fish* has at least three other portraits of Mennonites who have endured, none of whom can be mistaken as models of full lives: the elderly Anna, a closeted lesbian who believes herself called to a life of strenuous self-denial; Henry, Wendy's grandfather, who was forced into living a doubled, guilt-ridden life; and Wendy's friend, Sophie, who has thought longer and more deeply about the trans Mennonite experience than Wendy herself, and who ultimately commits suicide. In "Fallow," Temar is the brilliant sister, the one of whom the most is expected, and the novella never criticizes her decision to run. Indeed, it is easy to read Temar as the novella's moral center, refusing the comfort of a community that has valued its own lives above others'. And yet Agar, like Wendy, chooses to endure and puts her hand to participating in the hard work of changing the way the community understands its past—and thus, perhaps, hopefully, its future.

CONCLUSION

Reading Toward the Future of Mennonite Writing

Mennonite literary studies in North America is a small field. According to Beck and Cruz's bibliography, roughly 150 scholars have weighed in with essays that comment substantially on Mennonite literature as a field over the past fifty years, and only twenty-five or so have returned to offer a second opinion.[1] Given the scale of the project, perhaps it is no surprise that scholars in Mennonite literary criticism sometimes speak of the field in familial terms. In *Making Believe*, for example, Redekop notes that she occasionally amuses herself by "thinking of the Mennonite literary scene as a family romance," with Rudy Wiebe as the "mostly benign literary father" and the critics falling into meaningful generations of relatives, including mothers, and siblings—and even a baby brother (xxiii). In *Queering Mennonite Literature*, Cruz anticipates Redekop's familial metaphor, but with a twist: "writing about Mennonite literature always feels like writing about family," Cruz writes, "and is therefore much scarier and more difficult" (17). In fact, these types of metaphors are as old as the field itself. In 1990, Robert Kroetsch began his reflections in the much-discussed "Closing Panel" of the very first Mennonite/s Writing conference with a caution about the particular type of squabbles and arguments that can arise in such families: "The first thing I noticed was the intensity of the family quarrel that's going on," he says. "There is the model of the family quarrel behind this incredible kindness, friendliness and generosity and

I am intrigued by that contradiction. A rather ferocious family quarrel going on behind the best of public manners, and I can't help but think of Greek tragedy as I sit here and listen" (223). Looking back on the Mennonite/s Writing discussion as a relative latecomer and from the distance of several decades, it would seem to be a field that has mostly avoided disaster—at least that on the scale of Greek tragedies. I have certainly appreciated the kindness, friendliness, and generosity of those working in the field, even as I recognize that kinship as a critical mode has both its strengths and challenges. It seems important to recognize that several prominent or promising voices have stepped away over the years, perhaps as causalities of the quarrels, and that it has sometimes been difficult to fully open the conversation to those who are not already sitting around the table. It also seems important, as I have argued in this larger study, to recognize that the scale of the field offers both challenges and opportunities.

I began this study by recognizing that Mennonite literary studies is in a period of productive uncertainty. Any questions being asked of the field's future, I have argued, cannot be about the availability of literature by and about Mennonites, and it certainly should not be about its broader relevance. Indeed, when the *New Yorker* paused its recent profile of Miriam Toews to earnestly define the practice of *schputting* for its highbrow audience—"There is a Plautdietsch term [. . .] for irreverence directed at serious or sacred things," readers are told, before being informed that "Toews is a *schputter*" (Schwartz)—I felt a frisson of recognition, but also as a certain sadness to find the oral slang from my Mennonite childhood in the pages of the magazine. It seemed as if the field had crossed a Rubicon of sorts, as if our little family quarrel had landed in the pages of . . . well, the *New Yorker*. From Cannes film festivals to reality TV, from bestselling novels to experimental chapbooks to popular websites and Mennonite Twitter, there seems to be little question of the ongoing relevance of Mennonite characters, settings, and concerns to audiences today. It will be important for such work to have an informed critical reception, one that is concentrated enough to be able to speak to the work in its specificity, robust enough to be able to offer a range of interpretative readings, and comprehensive enough to be able to position it in relation to a broader history of related work. Indeed, a central aim of this study has been to suggest that substantial work remains to be done not simply to engage with the ever-expanding body of contemporary Mennonite writing but also to more fully engage the broader histories of the field itself. The question, it seems clear to me, is not *whether* there is a future for the field or work to be done but rather *how* that work can be most productively undertaken, and what that future will be.

Part of the argument of this book, as I hope I have managed to make clear, is that this work is already underway. Even as established venues like *Rhubarb* magazine are shutting down, new venues and new avenues of critical thought are being opened by established and emerging scholars alike, including work in "world" and queer Mennonite writing, on theopoetics, form, and aesthetics, as well as on underexamined genres such as documentary writing, romance, and speculative fiction. It is in an effort to foster and sustain these expansive efforts that I have called attention to the critical drive for "new histories" that routinely accompanies such projects, cautioning that a reinvestment in the field's developmental literary history risks simultaneously reinvesting in the model of ethnic minority literatures and the patterns of critique so many of us are attempting to complicate. A strategic investment in the field as a case study in minor transnationalism, I have suggested, may be one way to help loosen its framing assumptions and continue moving the critical conversation forward. I am hopeful it might also encourage a deeper engagement with Mennonite transnational histories and lateral networks of intersecting identities in ways beyond those I have articulated here, even as others will rightly continue to historicize the field as it has emerged and functioned in its regional and national manifestations. What would happen, I wonder, if we were to continue thinking of Mennonite literature in functional rather than ontological terms, as a mode of reading, rather than of writing?

The chapters that followed this introductory argument, then, are offered not as a cumulative argument but rather as a series of methodological experiments exploring Mennonite literary studies in several of its specificities. They are, as a mentor of mine wrote in a different context, *essays* in the original sense of that word, as *essais*—as "a trial, a test"[2]—that attempt to join and further this critical conversation by identifying and testing the generic, geographic, and methodological boundaries of the field to date. For if it is true, as Moretti and others have insisted, that the sheer volume of works in most area studies makes the summative gestures of selective histories and canon formation an unavoidable matter of scale, I am hopeful that a field as small as Mennonite writing might be open to alternative forms of engagement, and, possibly, other forms of history. Accordingly, I undertook in chapter 1 a cross-sectional reading of all the literary books published I could find that were by or about Mennonites in North America in 1986, a year squarely in the midst of the field's emergence as a minority literature. The result was a dramatic expansion of the bibliographic accounting of this period that reminds us that Mennonite literature was already at this stage much wider and more varied than most conventional narratives of the field have been willing to allow. The various genres that have been overlooked by subsequent scholarship include life writing, children's and young adult's literature, as well as work by faith-based publishers and science fiction authors—all of which was set aside, presumably, under the now-dated logic that such work was somehow unworthy of scholarly critique. It also included a number of works that self-consciously engaged elements of non-European Mennonite identity that was being actively asserted in the broader North American Mennonite community in this period. What might happen, I wonder, if we attempted to broaden other years, or the entire history of the field, in a similar manner?

If the introduction and first chapter looked to test our understanding and expand the possibilities of Mennonite literary history, chapters 2 and 3 built on that work by reconsidering the field's strategic investment in identity. In chapter 2 I drew on work by Lejeune, Smith, and Watson, and others to position life writing as central to early Mennonite literary studies. What was it about Dietrich Neufeld's 1920 diary that made it an appropriate choice for the inaugural project of the Mennonite Literary Society, and why was it so thoroughly ignored by the Mennonite/s Writing critical conversation to follow? First written in French in what is now Ukraine, translated for first publication in Germany in 1921, retranslated for a second publication in California in 1930, and translated from German yet again for third publication as an unlikely bestseller in Winnipeg in 1977, *A Russian Dance of Death* serves as a compelling example of how life writing's complex negotiation of literature and history—its generic evocation of truthfulness—was key to the logic of the early field. In contrast to Neufeld's deeply earnest effort to strategically deploy an essentialized (but shifting) form of Mennonite literary identity, chapter 3 examined a range of contemporary writing that shows how a self-conscious and often ironic engagement with essentialized identity—reconfigured via Žižek as the "Mennonite Thing"—continues to structure much of the field imaginary today. Far from moving past or beyond identity concerns, I argued, much of what continues to circulate as Mennonite writing in Canada and the United States cleverly but clearly asserts an ongoing investment in identity, though it can no longer be read as a form of simple autoethnography.

In chapters 4 and 5, I looked to further test the implicit parameters of Mennonite literature in North America. In recognition of "North America" as a "relational designation" that marks it as part of the larger hemisphere, for example, chapter 4 tests the field's geographic, biographic, and generic assumptions to read the Canadian Mennonite author Miriam Toews's novel *Irma Voth* as writing back to the (decidedly non-Mennonite) Mexican director Carlos Reygadas's celebrated film *Silent Light*, set in a conservative Mennonite colony in northern Mexico. Reygadas's stunning presentation of Mennonite theology as fantasy vividly demonstrates the position of Mennonite cultural difference within a Mexican imaginary and reveals the need for an informed reading of such cultural representations—a reading offered, ironically enough, by the film's lead actress. The fifth and final chapter consists of close readings of two novels in genres that are fast becoming central to the field: in *Little Fish*, Casey Plett presents a vibrant but vulnerable community of trans women in Winnipeg, several of whom are looking to the Mennonite past in search of a future community; in "Fallow," Sofia Samatar weaves together theological and migration histories to present a colony of intergalactic Mennonites far in the future that continues to struggle with its community's utopian dreams of isolation. In the writing of Plett and Samatar we find not only two of the most acclaimed works of Mennonite writing in recent years but also two of its most thoughtful investments in possible Mennonite futures.

I am hopeful these individual efforts add up to a collective argument to suggest that reconsidering the parameters of Mennonite literature in North America through the logic of minor transnationalism can be helpful in estranging the generic, geographic, and biographical assumptions that have often structured Mennonite literary studies to date. My hope is that the book demonstrates how by loosening our investment in the specific set of paths and possibilities we've inherited by understanding it as a form of minority writing, we might better foster the work that has been underway to explore a more expansive version of the field. At the same time, rejecting the centripetal force of the field's desire to be readable within the conventional logic of minority literary studies—this the "cruel optimism" that Rak suggested was holding the field back—may enable Mennonite literary studies to further invest in the specific set of questions and possibilities that make it of value. As Lionnet and Shih suggest in arguing for the framework of minor transnationalism, the establishment of "strong and bounded terms" for transnationalism and minority studies have "rendered invisible subject positions that did not readily fall into such accepted categories" (4). Ironically enough, it is precisely these elements—the Mennonite literary studies' longstanding efforts to work across national and ethnocultural borders, its enduring concern with faith and theology, its migratory and institutional linkages across and beyond the continent, and so on—that could also make the field more relevant to those working in the larger world of contemporary literary studies.

NOTES

INTRODUCTION

1. Among the most prominent examples of the field's metacritical self-consciousness are the long-running explorations of the role played by the sixteenth-century martyrdoms and twentieth-century mass migrations within the contemporary literary/critical imagination. See Zacharias, "Garden of Spears" and *Rewriting the Break Event*. For related arguments, see chapter 1 of Jeff Gundy's *Walker in the Fog*, "Myths of Origin and Arrival" (25–43), and the introduction to Magdalene Redekop's *Making Believe*, "On Beginnings" (3–48).

2. See, for example, my introductions to *Rewriting the Break Event* and *After Identity*.

3. In her review of the collection, Jan Schroeder writes, "No one in the collection uses the word crisis" to describe the state of the field, but several "come close."

4. Redekop offers the "reluctant concession" that her critical book is also "an autoethnographic text" (xx) and can be read as "an exercise in life writing" (*Making Believe* 193). Cruz, too, suggests the "personal [. . .] leaks" into his own study (*Queering* 17).

5. This is the title of the fourth book of the *Report of the Royal Commission on Biculturalism and Bilingualism*, a founding document in Canada's movement toward formal multiculturalism.

6. The commonly used phrase is attributed to Andris Taskans, founding editor of *Prairie Fire* quarterly. See Taskans's "David Bergen."

7. See Ruland and Bradbury.

8. In her closing discussion of the differences between the American and Canadian contexts for Mennonite writing in *A Cappella*, for example, Hostetler notes "the popular use of the term 'ethnicity' in the United States as a euphemism for race differs from the Canadian use of the term to designate cultural features" (183).

9. See Roth and Beck, viii, and Hostetler, *A Cappella*, xix, for similar arguments. The American tradition of emphasizing Mennonite literature's religious elements manages to predate the writing itself, beginning with John Ruth's influential early call for writing that could share the community's "Salvation story" in his seminal study, *Mennonite Identity and Literary Art* (1978), and continues today in the growing field of theopoetics. See, for example, the special issues of *Crosscurrents* (64.4 [2014]) and *The Conrad Grebel Review* (31.2 [2013]) dedicated to theopoetics, the former of which includes essays by Gundy and Kasdorf as well as Anita Yoder and Scott Holland, and the latter by Holland and Gundy, again, as well as Jean Janzen and others.

10. This is not to say, of course, that the field is always imagined in transnational terms. Douglas Reimer's *Surplus at the Border* and my own *Rewriting the Break Event* focus solely on the Canadian context, for example, while Hostetler's "Coming into Voice" and Gundy's "U.S. Mennonite Poetry and Poets" focus on writing in the United States.

11. In the early 1970s, Felipe Hinojosa reports, just 6 percent of the Mennonite Church in the United States was nonwhite

("Goshen" 201), a number that did not change dramatically over the next decade (see Bechler 171 and Falcón 71).

12. See Taylor.

13. Notably, both of the collection's parallel projects—a collection of critical essays on Mennonite writing and an anthology of Mennonite poetry—move across the Canada–US border. *29 Mennonite Poets* has only a slightly larger purview, but at least offers a reflection on its frame. Though the "intention" was to "bring together a body of work that reflects the range and accomplishments of contemporary Mennonite poetry in North America," its editor takes some time to reflect on, and explain, the anthology's prevalence of Manitoba poets, and the relative lack of US authors included. See Foster.

14. Moreover, by presenting the field as a product of clash of cultures, he all but defines Mennonite literature as a temporary phenomenon. Again, the question here is not whether his account of the Manitoba Mennonite writing phenomenon as a reflection of a culture in transition has merit, as this is a well-supported argument: Froese Tiessen has argued that the "dominant" mode of those early Manitoba writers was to "project and evoke impressions of a fading ethos" with an "ambivalent lament" ("Introduction" 10); Royden Loewen has described it as a "Mennonite *Fin de Siècle*" in related terms; Di Brandt suggests its "main subject" was the "experience of transition" ("Paradigms" 154). The question, instead, is whether these tropes should be accepted as paradigmatic of, and as the parameters for, all Mennonite writing in North America.

15. Here I am gesturing to a recent essay by Brandt, in which her efforts to elaborate on the emergence of Mennonite/s Writing specifically within Canadian multiculturalism includes a remarkable suggestion. "It's tricky, of course, to make generalizations about a cultural group which includes various historical strands and diverse cultural organization in the present," she writes, before adding: "One must choose which specific instance might serve iconically for the whole. In this case, I am choosing the rural, peasant-based farming villages of Southern Manitoba and what happened when their children moved to the cities in the volatile decades of the 60s and 70s as the 'default' group for Mennonite cultural life in Canada, and beyond that, the U.S. and internationally" ("Paradigms" 154–55).

16. Froese Tiessen made this claim in the introduction to a journal issue dedicated to a conference entitled Mennonite/s Writing: Manitoba and Beyond—a frame that helps to explain her somewhat awkward explanation of how *Peace Shall Destroy Many* fits into such a frame: Wiebe is from Alberta and his novel was set in Saskatchewan, she acknowledges, but "he was living" in Winnipeg when it was published ("Foreword" 9).

17. Dunham's novel, along with a sketch of a Conestoga wagon, was included over the Kitchener-Waterloo area on the Macmillan Company of Canada's much-reproduced 1936 *Literary Map of Canada*.

18. The Mennonite/s Writing online bibliographies were created, updated, and maintained for several decades by Ervin Beck of Goshen College, and are currently maintained by Daniel Shank Cruz (see https://mennonitebibs.wordpress.com/general-discussions-of-mennonite-literature-bibliography). *The Trail of the Conestoga* has since been added to the bibliography.

19. For valuable critiques of my earlier study, see Brandt, "Paradigms" 162–63 and Brandt, "Postmodern Mennonite Identification(s)"; see also M. Redekop, *Making Believe* 30–32.

20. See his introduction to *Walker in the Fog*, "Myths of Origin and Arrival."

21. Also of note in this area is the promising dissertation work of Kyle Gerber at the University of Waterloo, who is

exploring the language of prayer in Mennonite literature through the lens of rhetoric studies.

22. See Daniel Shank Cruz's *Queering Mennonite Literature* (Penn State UP, 2019); Magdalene Redekop's *Making Believe* (U of Manitoba P, 2020); Hildi Froese Tiessen's edited collection *11 Encounters with Mennonite Fiction* (Mennonite Literary Society, 2017), and my own *After Identity* (Penn State UP, 2015; U of Manitoba P, 2016).

23. On this point, see Braz as well as Sadowski-Smith and Fox.

24. As Hostetler acknowledges, the "distinctive Canadian Mennonite literary community, which coalesced during the 1970s and 1980s, emerged before—and in many cases inspired—Mennonite poetry in the United States" (*A Cappella* xix).

25. I am aware, of course, of Deleuze and Guattari's influential account of minor literature as a deterritorializing force, used productively in Reimer's *Surplus at the Border*. With Lionnet and Shih, however, I worry that Deleuze and Guattari "end up falling back into a recentered model of 'minor literature,'" in which "the minor's literary and political significance rests on its critical function within and against the major in a binary and vertical relationship" ("Thinking" 2)—as it seems to function in Reimer's study.

26. More productive, in my view, is how their larger re-articulation of the "minor" insists that "minor literatures" have too long been understood only in relation to the major. It is only because "the minor *appears* always mediated by the major in both its social and its psychic means of identification" ("Thinking" 2), Lionnet and Shih suggest, that "we forget to look sideways to lateral networks" ("Thinking" 1).

27. Of course, it is one thing to "reflect on identity issues" and something else altogether to advocate for "a core or essence" of Mennonite identity. Epp's suggestion that the "idea of talking about 'a' Mennonite identity seems passé" and that looking for "a core or essence is elusive and perhaps useless" (12) would fit comfortably within contemporary Mennonite literary criticism, as would her accompanying proposal that "Mennonites are really a collection of very interesting stories—recipes perhaps—that reflect our multilayered beings as individuals or within families, as migratory or ethnic groups, as converts or colonizer" (13).

28. See Kamboureli (80–130).

29. See Dawson.

30. Writing in 1992, Douglas Reimer confesses himself baffled by the very idea of a queer Mennonite "ontology" (199), while the queer Mennonite protagonist of Jan Guenther Braun's novel *Somewhere Else* suggests her very identity seems to be "an oxymoron" (137).

31. This definition is taken from the "About" at the *Rhubarb* website, http://www.rhubarbmag.com/about-rhubarb, which is now discontinued.

32. In their landmark project in encyclopedic history, for example, King-Kok Cheung and Stan Yogi reflect briefly on a similar challenge and note that at times they simply included authors based on their last names alone.

33. On how form and identity might interact, see Jesse Nathan's effort to locate a North American Anabaptist sensibility in the call-and-response form in recent poetry in his "Question, Answer."

CHAPTER 1

1. There are two possible exceptions here. The first is Phyllis Pellman Good's *Three Mennonite Poets*, routinely acknowledged as a precursor to the contemporary field. It has not been the focus of a close analysis to date. (Ironically enough, Jeff Gundy's "Separation and Transformation: Tradition and Audience for Three Mennonite Poets," also from 1986, engages three

other poets.) Several early essays explored Janet Kauffman's *Collaborators*, though her work has fallen from critical attention in the field.

2. When revising this manuscript for publication, I was pleased to see Magdalene Redekop's effort to "bracket one decade"—she chooses the 1980s—and to offer a list of twenty-nine books (*Making Believe* 178). Although many of the conclusions we reach from our lists differ, I recognize her turn to bibliographic history as following a similar desire to rethink and expand our understanding of the field's past.

3. Of the seven books Beck lists as his canon, the chronology of the final six—Wiebe's *Peace Shall Destroy Many* (1962); Patrick Friesen's *The Shunning* (1980); Di Brandt's *questions i asked my mother* (1987); Julia Kasdorf's *Sleeping Preacher* (1992); Miriam Toews's *A Complicated Kindness* (2004); and Rhoda Janzen's *Mennonite in a Little Black Dress* (2009)—retraces the field's conventional literary history, beginning with Wiebe, moving on to the Manitoba Mennonite writing of the 1980s–90s, then moving on to the American context. Beck breaks from this most conventional account by including as his first "transgressive" Mennonite text Gordon Friesen's much earlier (and comparatively unknown) novel, *Flamethrowers* (1936).

4. Yes, that author is Rudy Wiebe. According to the bibliographies, the seven Mennonite authors whose work has been routinely engaged to date in critical essays are as follows: Rudy Wiebe (186); Miriam Toews (31); Sandra Birdsell (19); Julia Spicher Kasdorf (18); Janet Kauffman (15); David Bergen (10); Di Brandt (10); and Jeff Gundy (10). Notably, these figures refer only to essays that are explicitly focused on single authors, and do not include interviews, which provide another avenue for critical engagement.

5. The separate bibliographies for Canada and the United States reflect the nationalized contexts of their first creations: the Canadian bibliography is based upon a list first started for the "Mennonite/s Writing in Canada" conference; the American bibliography was begun for the subsequent "Mennonite/s Writing in the United States" conference. Cruz also includes links to (or provides citational details of) six other "specialized bibliographies" in the field, two of which are of relevant literary *criticism*, rather than literature, and the others of which—with the notable exception of a list of "Mennonite and Amish serial fiction," and a link to bibliographic material about a German Mennonite dramatist—are integrated into the relevant Canadian and American lists. The numbers included in this study were taken from the bibliographies as they stood at the end of 2019. The bibliographies are continually being updated and can now be found at https://mennonitebibs.wordpress.com.

6. In the following analysis, I have rounded the percentages to the nearest whole number, with the result that the sums may not add up to 100 percent.

7. The remaining percentages are made up of life writing, drama, and anthologies.

8. See https://mennonitebibs.wordpress.com.

9. *Odysseys Home* includes essays, selected reviews, and surveys, as well as a 110-page bibliography entitled "Africana Canadiana: A Select Bibliography by African-Canadian Authors, 1785–2001." Where Clarke looks to establish a Black writing in Canada in the broadest of terms, King-Kok Cheung and Stan Yogi's landmark project, *Asian American Literature: An Annotated Bibliography* (1988), divides its bibliographic entries by genre and, crucially, national/ethnic descent, and includes nearly 20 pages of "Literature by Non-Asians about Asians and Asian Americans," challenging the assumption that only literature *by* Asian authors is relevant

to the field of Asian American literature. Cheung and Yogi's project, however, is strictly bibliographic, offering simply an enormous list of Asian American publications. It is worth noting, perhaps, that neither Clarke nor Cheung and Yogi include the Mennonite North American authors of African or Asian decent that I engage later in this chapter.

10. See Loganbill.

11. Many self-published works are informal, with limited print runs, and it would seem simply impossible to include the category in anything other than an ad hoc nature. The gatekeeping function of publishing institutions, which has historically worked to exclude work by marginalized figures, should give us some pause before we ignore such works *en masse*, however, as should the fact that several of the best-selling works of both early and recent Mennonite-adjacent writing began as self-published ventures, including Joseph W. Yoder's *Rosanna of the Amish*, self-published in 1940, and Mary Ann Kirby's *I Am Hutterite: The Fascinating True Story of a Young Woman's Journey to Reclaim Her Heritage*, self-published in 2007. The year 1986 includes at least one other pair of works that might fit these parameters, but which I have left outside the expanded bibliographic count: two plays by Sandra Birdsell, each of which were produced by Winnipeg's Prairie Theatre Exchange. The first, *A Prairie Winter*, was a one-act play for children; the other, *The Revival: A Two Act Play*, was an attempt to bring the Mennonite-Métis Lafreniere family of her early short fiction to the stage. It is difficult to imagine a play written by Sandra Birdsell being "doomed by the script," as Robert Enright suggested of *The Revival* in *Maclean's*, or that it could have fully earned his dismissal as "five characters desperately in search of a short-story author" (66). Neither script was ever published, however, so it is a challenge to judge.

12. A note on the fractions in the lists: Sam Manickam's *Seed and Seasons* is half poetry and half fiction; Sharon and Thom Curtis co-wrote *Sunshine and Shadow*; and one work was published anonymously. Countries of origin reflect publisher location rather than authorial biography—except in the cases of Kindred Press and Herald Press, which have publishing ventures in both countries, where I have been able to list them by author. Edited collections are listed by editor alone.

13. Duerksen is well aware of how such sympathies might be read. When his reporting from the trial of Ilsle Koch seems to question her guilt, for example, he notes that if "someone might get the impression [. . .] that I attempted to minimize the crimes committed by some Germans during the Nazi period, even the days of the holocaust," he only means to suggest that there was insufficient evidence to convict Koch herself of such crimes (*Dear God* 334).

14. See Duerksen, "Wildcat Bus."

15. Occasionally, as in the chapter on Margarethe Willms Remple, the editor relies on a passage of direct quotation to allow a subject to recount the most personal and traumatic of accounts (248–49).

16. Cruz also notes the "rise of life writing" in "Mennonite literature specifically" as evidence of the "genre's ascendancy" ("Bibliography" 101).

17. Reimer's essay compares Smucker's two retellings of the Mennonite experience in Russia in her novels *Henry's Red Sea* (1955) and *Days of Terror* (1977) to argue that the latter is more "readable" and artistically successful "because it forces the Russian-Mennonite story to fit the conventional mold of the children's adventure story" (172).

18. The island is described as "hundreds of miles" away from the United States (71), long and narrow, Spanish-speaking, and with a notable valley region—likely in La

Plata Valley, where Mennonite missionary efforts in the country began. By 1986, the Puerto Rican Mennonite Conference had nearly nine hundred members across sixteen congregations (see Holsinger et al.).

19. Here I disagree with Cruz's use of this passage to suggest that Reimer "laments that queer-themed Mennonite literature is 'impossible to imagine'" (*Queering* 10). In my understanding, Reimer's claim comes as the conclusion to his argument that the "revolutionary efforts" in Lois Braun's writings throughout the 1980s and 1990s "take place in the sexual field'" (198), and his suggestion, phrased in the language of Deleuze and Guattari, is that her intimate portrayal of relationships between Mennonite women—writing that "women are much more interesting to women than men are"—"effectively deterritorializes Mennonite heterosexual metaphysics" (199). It is not queer-themed Mennonite fiction that is unimaginable for Reimer, in my reading, as he has just suggested that Braun offers precisely such work (rare as it may be). Rather, it is the *effect* that such fiction might have on a heteronormative, patriarchal Mennonite ontology that he cannot fathom. "What would a non-heterosexual Mennonite Canadian reterritory look like?" he asks. "It is impossible to imagine" (199).

20. Cruz counts six critical essays on Kauffman in venues unaffiliated with the Mennonite critical tradition, and two within it ("Bibliography" 97n18).

21. Ann Hostetler's paragraph-long discussion of the novel in her 2005 essay "Bringing Experience to Consciousness" is a notable but brief exception (145–46).

22. The quotation positioning *Rosanna of the Amish* as "the beginnings of Mennonite literature" comes from the back of the Herald Press's 2008 "restored" edition of the 1940 novel, edited by Joshua R. Brown and Julia Spicher Kasdorf, and categorized by Herald Press as "FICTION / Mennonite / Amish."

23. Weaver-Zercher traces the genre back to the 1905 novel *Sabina: A Story of the Amish*, by Helen R. Martin, naming it the "Ur-Bonnet book" (27).

24. My thanks to Daniel Shank Cruz for pointing out these connections.

25. While Togane's poetry implicitly engages with Du Bois's work on double consciousness, Bechler invokes it directly as part of his opening discussion of the Black experience in the United States, and in the rise of what he calls the "New black awareness" (22–23). Critical of the slowness with which "Anglo Mennonites" in the United States turned their attention to evangelizing their Black neighbors, Bechler notes the first Black members were baptized into the Mennonite church in North America in 1897 (37). In Bechler's account, those to whom he refers as "Anglo Mennonites" have been far too passive, rather than too aggressive, in their missionary efforts with the Black community, and Mennonite faith and cultural institutions have been paternalizing in fostering and maintaining the fruits of those efforts.

26. See, for example, Ashley 66.

27. The revival of the once-formative magazine would last just the one issue: Fall 1986.

28. Other contemporary science fiction written by Mennonites includes the work of Randy Nikkel Schroeder. See also the recent special issue of the *Journal of Mennonite Writing* (11.1 [2019]), edited by Gundy.

29. The issue includes interviews and/or excerpts from work by Sofia and Del Samatar, Tobias Buckell, André Swartley, Stephen Beachy, Jessica Penner, Chad Gusler, Keith Miller, Emily Derick, and William Squirrell. Importantly, Gundy acknowledges van Vogt as an early precedent to this "new" writing.

CHAPTER 2

1. Book 4 of the *Report of the Royal Commission on Bilingualism and Biculturalism*, entitled *The Cultural Contributions*

of the Other Ethnic Groups, makes dozens of extended references to the Mennonites, including one that positions them as the primary example of "ethnic endogamy" (92).

2. See the 21 Jan. 1977 letter from Department of the Secretary of State representative Ralph Friesen to Roy Vogt, president of the Mennonite Literary Society.

3. Reimer adds "A" to Neufeld's title, so it becomes *A Russian Dance of Death*, as well as a subtitle, *Revolution and Civil War in the Ukraine* (two articles too many, by my count). The other two sections of the book, titled in the 1977 edition as "The Ordeal of Zagradovka" (65–88), and "Escape from the Maze: By Horse Through the Ukraine" (89–126), continue Neufeld's account chronologically, but they drop the diary format, and shift into third-person narration. Although my interest in the diary itself and the limitations of space here have led me to set these sections aside for now, both are worthy of closer analysis.

4. See Zacharias, *Rewriting the Break Event*.

5. It is surely the sense of privacy and immediacy provided by the diary form that has made it a popular model in Mennonite fiction, including John Weier's experimental novel, *Steppe* (1995), structured as a collection of dated journal entries, and Patrick Friesen's *The Shunning* (1980), a long poem that begins as a diary, as well as in Rudy Wiebe's *Come Back* (2014) and Annie Jacobsen's *Watermelon Syrup* (2007), both of which include characters who discover important diaries, sections of which are presented directly to the reader.

6. See J. H. Janzen, "The Literature of the Russo-Canadian Mennonites," *Mennonite Life* 1.3 (1946–48): 22–25, 28, quoted by Froese Tiessen in *Liars and Rascals* (xii).

7. The series is clearly dedicated to exploring and expressing the history and culture of specifically Russian Mennonites. Of its fourteen titles, four are life writing, three are historical studies, four are historical fiction, and two are collections of historical and critical essays. The remaining book, *A Sackful of Plautdietsch: A Collection of Mennonite Low German Stories and Poems* (ed. Al Reimer, Anne Reimer, and Jack Thiessen, 1983), aims to establish a new orthography of Plautdietsch for future writers.

8. In Mennonite literary studies, Chang's insight has a correlative in Julia Spicher Kasdorf's description of what she calls the "autoethnographic announcements" common in Mennonite literary texts. See Kasdorf, "Autoethnographic."

9. See Letter to Mr. Frank Belle, 1977.

10. The pavilion was plagued by confusion about the community's "ethnic" status, with Russian Mennonite foodways and language exhibits standing next to religious materials. See Smucker.

11. These are among the diaries briefly discussed by Royden Loewen in "Diaries."

12. My thanks to Jon Isaak, archivist at the Canadian Conference of Mennonite Brethren Churches in Winnipeg, for giving me access to the Baerg diary.

13. See, for a notable recent example, the extensive and careful reliance on Mennonite memoirs in Jantzen and Thiesen.

14. In addition to the scholarly essays discussed in this paragraph, see B. Klassen's "Poet of Apanlee."

15. See Hostetler, "*Diary*."

16. The final form of the diary provides some clues as to what this might mean, including the editorial division of the diary into eight chapters that are given titles like "The Coming Storm."

17. Podnieks notes that recent scholarship on Samuel Pepys—often considered the "first 'real' diarist," whose diary is commonly held up as "a standard against which others are measured" (*Daily* 23)—has revealed that Pepys routinely wrote multiple entries at a time, rewrote at length, and even drew on newspaper articles for content. Similarly, Lejeune notes that Anne Frank "almost entirely rewrote" her diary expressly "with the intention of publishing it herself as soon as the war was over," with the result that multiple versions of her

"original" diary exist, both of which were unfinished at the time of her arrest and later shaped into a "coherent book" by her father (*Diary* 231). More recent work suggests there are at least four different versions of Frank's published diary. See Bunkers.

18. Hostetler's "Self in Mennonite Garb" is a notable exception, as is Jesse Hutchison's 2015 dissertation "Private People in Public Places: Contemporary Canadian Mennonite Life Writing" (University of Waterloo). Of particular note in the context of this chapter is Hutchison's valuable discussion of how Rudy Wiebe's memoir incorporates passages from his sister's diary as a comparison—and, at times, a counterpoint—to his own account. It can be accessed via the University of Waterloo's website at https://uwspace.uwaterloo.ca/handle/10012/9819.

19. On the provenance and appropriateness of the phrase, see Urry, "Mennonite Commonwealth."

20. I am quoting here from Reimer's biographical note on Neufeld in the 1977 edition of the diary (xiii). In addition to Reimer's note, my brief account of Neufeld's life draws on his entry in the Global Anabaptist Mennonite Encyclopedia Online, and Lotte Navall's "Dedrich Navall."

21. Early historical accounts emphasizing the Mennonite suffering during this period include John B. Toews's *Lost Fatherland: The Story of the Mennonite Emigration from Soviet Russia, 1921–1927* (1967). More recent historical studies have been more critical of the Mennonites' exclusionary ethos in the period leading up the revolutionary period, and have begun documenting Mennonite sympathies with German forces during the Second World War, as in Ben Goossen's *Chosen Nation* and Mark Jantzen and John D. Thiesen's edited collection *European Mennonites and the Holocaust.* My own *Rewriting the Break Event* examined the many fictional retellings of the 1920s collapse of the Mennonite colonies in Ukraine as a key story in Canadian Mennonite literary tradition.

22. See Zacharias, *Rewriting the Break Event*, 55–62.

23. Unless otherwise indicated, all citations of Neufeld's diary in English are from the 1977 edition.

24. The 1922 *Mennonitentum in der Ukraine; Schicksalsgeschichte Sagradowkas* opens with a page of endorsements of the significance of the 1921 diary, including a passage from a "Prof Ewart" from Kansas, who is quoted as suggesting it will prove a "lasting work of literature" (*Ich bin davon überzeugt, das Buch wird ein bleibendes Literaturwerk sein*).

25. Reimer cites from this document and attributes it to Neufeld in his introduction. A copy of the typed introduction, signed as "Dmitri Novopolye," can be found in the Al Reimer Papers, Fonds 054, Mennonite Heritage Centre Archives, Canadian Mennonite University, Winnipeg.

26. Notably, the introduction to the first German edition is signed as having been written in Huddinge (Sweden), though its cover page indicates it was published in Emden (Germany).

27. See MS103, 35: Correspondence re Russian Dance of Death. Dietrich Neufeld Papers, Mennonite Library and Archives, Bethel College, North Newton, KS. (available online; 29 May 2018).

28. Neufeld's archive includes several letters from Zona Gale expressing admiration for the diary and offering help in placing it with a publisher—as well as one (dated February 8, 1929) offering to "write the introduction" for a published version. See MS103, 26: "Willa Cather and Zona Gale re Russian Dance of Death," Dietrich Neufeld Papers, Mennonite Library and Archives, MS 103/ 26, Bethel College, North Newton, KS (available online; 29 May 2018).

29. Although the 1930 English edition does not declare itself to be self-published (as the 1921 edition does in naming itself a *Selbstverlag* on its title page), archival research strongly suggests that Key Books was incorporated by Neufeld himself, and that the diary was its only publication. The interior title page indicates that "Key Books" is in Claremont, California, where Neufeld lived at the time of its publication, yet the front matter also shows it to have been printed and bound by the "Antioch Press" in Yellow Springs, Ohio—near where Neufeld had worked earlier, at Bluffton College. The Bethel College archives also includes a fascinating German-language letter from a Mennonite correspondent in Barranquilla, Colombia, discussing a design for the Key Books logo that it seems Neufeld adopted (MS103, 20: Correspondence—Relatives and friends, 1914–36/. Dietrich Neufeld Papers. Mennonite Library and Archives, Bethel College, North Newton, KS. 29 May 2018). I can find no additional information about the publisher outside of Neufeld's work.

30. See Reimer's letter to Neufeld's widow, where he writes, "after translating close to half the book, I discovered, quite by accident, that Navall had himself translated his books in the early thirties," adding that "I have not been able to secure copies of the English editions" (2).

31. All three of these texts were first self-published in German by Neufeld, in Germany. *Ein Tagebuch aus dem Reiche des Totentanzes* was published first (1921). *Mennonitentum in der Ukraine: Schicksalsgeschichte Sagradowkas*, which is translated and retitled "The Ordeal of Zagradovka" in the 1977 edition, and *Zu Pferd 1000km durch die Ukraina*, translated and retitled "Escape from the Maze: By Horse Through the Ukraine" in the 1977 edition, were both published the following year.

32. The German term *Tagebuch* is conventionally translated as "diary," but it can be used to describe a wider range of writings, such as non-narrative daily records.

33. The original reads: "*Die Welt, sie muss es hören! / Denn unsrer Seelen Not ist schwer; / Es muss der Schrei die Lösung bringen!*"

34. "Machno" and "Chortitza" are alternate spellings for the names elsewhere in this chapter spelled "Makhno" and "Khortitza."

35. Here Neufeld appears to be referring to the review comments of a "Prof. Dr. G. Mentz-Jena," who praises the diary as being written "immediately and during the events" (*unmittelbar während der Ereignisse selbst*) as excerpted by Neufeld as a promotional blurb for the diary in his 1922 booklet, *Mennonitentum in der Ukraine.*

36. The essays are titled "The German Occupation and the Role of the Mennonite Self Defence" and "Makhno and the Makhnovschchina."

37. Cather's letter begins with the noted author expressing her frustration with "inexperienced writers" who have the "bad habit of sending their books to me and trying to extort some polite expression they can use in advertising" (1). There is some irony, then, to find that Neufeld quotes from Cather's letter his own promotional material for his book, and that her compliments are quoted at length on the back of later Hyperion editions.

38. A 1976 letter from his daughter claims that Dietrich changed his name because he "was such a liberal thinker and believer, as well as a protestor against the militaristic background of Germany," adding that his relatives were "not happy" about the decision. See Maya Navall McKenzie's letter to Mr. Hoeppner from 14 Oct. 1976.

39. Here Reimer is "correcting" the imprecision of the 1921 and 1930 editions, both of which suggest there are approximately twenty Mennonite villages in the area: "*herum 20 Hofdörfer begründeten*"

(1921, 5); "some twenty farm villages" (1930, 6).

40. The 1921 entry for October 19, for example, describes Makhno's men being outraged by false but inflammatory stories that were circulating (*sie erdachte Geschichten in Umlauf*) about the treacherous Germans (*die verräterischen Deutschen*) who had been pretending to be peaceful victims but shot at the Makhnovites from the windows, and so were killed in retaliation (44). These "Germans" become "colonists" (89) and "settlers" (90) in the 1930 edition, only to return into the Makhnovite stories, this time under the erasure of quotation marks, as "'treacherous Germans,'" and into the diary itself as simply "Germans" (38).

41. The 1988 edition of the diary is largely a reprint of the 1977 edition, with a couple of small paratextual changes meant to better attribute credit. One change made was to include a brief paragraph of correction to indicate the etchings that had been previously attributed to the diarist were, in fact, by his cousin of the same name. The other change was to update the photo of Reimer on the book's back cover.

CHAPTER 3

1. Examples of this joke recurring in Mennonite writing include André Swartley's *Leon Martin and the Fantasy Girl* (31), Darcie Friesen Hossack's *Mennonites Don't Dance*, and Di Brandt's *Dancing Naked* (36). See also M. Redekop, *Making Believe* 318–24.

2. In fact, the joke is not even specific to Mennonites at all: a quick Internet search turns up versions of the same joke poking fun at the moral conservatism of Baptists, Muslims, and others.

3. See, for example, Hildi Froese Tiessen's key essay, "Beyond the Binary."

4. Here I am thinking primarily of the critique of identity initiated in the 1990s in the context of postcolonial and poststructural theory, including influential work by Stuart Hall, Homi Bhabha, and Gayatri Chakravorty Spivak, extended more recently by critics such as Judith Butler, Rey Chow, and Slavoj Žižek. While their work obviously differs in important ways, each of these scholars has helped to advance a radical critique of identity as the transparent foundation of the liberal autonomous subject.

5. Here I am gesturing to Al Reimer's review of Miriam Toews's *A Complicated Kindness*, entitled "Look Homeward, Naomi."

6. The website for the Mennonite Artist Project, http://mennoniteartistproject.ning.com, is no longer active.

7. See Froese Tiessen, "Beyond the Binary," and Hostetler, "Unofficial Voice."

8. Notably, Patrick Friesen and David Waltner-Toews resist the title of "Mennonite poet" in their 1985 discussion with Margaret Loewen Reimer and Paul Gerard Tiessen (253).

9. See "Beyond Dr. Johnson's Dog: American Mennonite Poetry and Poets" (*Walker* 97–132).

10. Hostetler suggests that Gundy wrote "How to Write the New Mennonite Poem" in direct response to Kasdorf's "Mennonites" (*A Cappella* xviii).

11. Gundy, who points to this question as a sign of a certain frustration with Mennonite identity, is a notable exception (*Walker* 99).

12. Important note for the uninitiated: not all Mennonite poems have such stubbornly descriptive titles.

13. In *Tongue Screws and Testimonies*, Beachy disarms this gesture, adding an editorial note explaining that "606" refers to the hymnal pagination for the doxology, a favorite song among many Mennonite congregations (271).

14. See Zacharias, "'Learning Sauerkraut.'"

15. See Zacharias, *Rewriting the Break Event* 40–45.

16. I am gesturing here to the two meanings of "fixing tradition"—both in terms of restoring it and in terms of reducing it to a static entity—that are at play in the title of Kasdorf's *Fixing Tradition*.

17. As the names of the characters suggest, the joke of Season 6 turns on the sexual repression of the Mennonite community: Anita Dyck's daughters, Chastity and Charity Dyck, have not returned from their Rumspringa adventures, and the parents are worried. "Our Dycks belong in the hands of the Mennonites!" the mother declares. "Dyck's Slip Out" is the fourth episode in *Letterkenny*'s sixth season.

18. Although the film is otherwise clear about Suzie's Mennonite heritage, at one point she explains her Amish heritage to the school's director. It seems a simple plot error.

19. The motion and voting tally can be found online at https://www.ourcommons.ca/Parliamentarians/en/votes/42/1/1326.

20. See "Headlines from The Daily Bonnet" on MP Bergen's YouTube page at https://www.youtube.com/watch?v=-wo48FYAnCw.

21. See Goossen, *Chosen Nation*, and Jantzen and Thiesen. See also Goossen's "From Aryanism to Anabaptism" as well as a related attempt to grapple with Russian Mennonite antisemitism more generally in Schirch ("Anabaptist-Mennonite Relations") and Schirch and Gopin.

22. See Žižek, "Sexual Is Political," and Che Gossett's response, "Zizek's Trans/Gender Trouble."

CHAPTER 4

1. The two exceptions being the protagonist's wife and lover, each of whom Reygadas was (unsurprisingly) unable to cast from the colony itself.

2. See http://www.mwc-cmm.org/maps/world.

3. See, for example, the recently completed Global Mennonite History Series, an initiative of the Mennonite World Conference, which includes books on the history of Mennonites in Africa (*Anabaptist Songs in African Hearts*, 2006); Asia (*Churches Engage Asian Traditions*, 2011); Europe (*Testing Faith and Tradition*, 2006); Latin America (*Mission and Migration*, 2010); and North America (*Seeking Places of Peace*, 2012). See also Royden Loewen's forthcoming *Mennonite Farmers*.

4. When I watched the film with a group of Mennonite scholars gathered at Penn State, several Low German–speaking audience members laughed (and occasionally scoffed) as they contrasted the subtitles with the literal translations of the Low German.

5. See Urry, *Mennonites, Politics*.

6. See also Goossen, "Mennonites in Latin America."

7. See Beck, "Mennonite Transgressive Literature."

8. Also unsurprising: that *The Daily Bonnet* website would poke fun at this authorial hall-of-mirrors in a post titled "Mennonite Novelist Irma Voth Pens New Novel Called *Miriam Toews*," 1 Jan. 2019 (12 Aug. 2020).

9. See Kasdorf, "Autoethnographic."

10. See R. Loewen, *Horse-and-Buggy Genius*.

CHAPTER 5

1. For another example in this same vein, see Marlon Wiebe's "googly poetry" rendition of Thomas Ken's "Praise God from Whom All Blessings Flow," sometimes colloquially referred as "606" or the "Mennonite doxology." Wiebe runs the original English lyrics of the song through a series of Google translations—from English to Chinese, then to Urdu and Vietnamese before returning it to English. See http://ghjensen.com/googly-poetry/category/authors/thomas-ken.

2. See https://read.ridingsidesaddle.com/en.

3. See Zacharias, "Garden of Spears."

4. See Andrew Harnish's edited forum, "LGBT Mennonite Fiction."

5. For an account of the review literature's interest in the book's use of time, see Neilson.

6. "Plett's *Little Fish* shows what trans writers can do," Gwen Benaway writes, "when we are not expected to educate or entertain cisgender audiences."

7. Notably, Henry's letter—and a later voice mail from Anna—includes scriptural references that go unexplained but encourage the faithful to, in the words of Romans 12:1, "offer your bodies as a living sacrifice, holy and pleasing to God."

8. See, for example, Cruz, "Fiction, Theory, Memoir" and *Queering Mennonite Literature*, 131–36; Gundy, "Bad Mennonites"; and Gundy, "'There Is No Knife.'"

9. Other examples of her writings that engage her Mennonite heritage include her short story, "Hard Mary," first published in *Lightspeed* 100 (Sept. 2018) and anthologized in *The Best American Science Fiction and Fantasy 2019*, and an excerpt from her memoir-in-progress, *The White Mosque*, in the *Journal of Mennonite Writing* 10.4 (2018).

10. I can find only one direct reference to the Uzbekistan experience in the story: the invocation of the name Claas Epp as one of the "misguided prophets" (235), which comes in a section of the story not included in the *Electric Literature* selection. In the selection of *The White Mosque* published in the *Journal of Mennonite Writing*, which directly recounts Epp's journey to Uzbekistan, Samatar invokes the same hymn that she gives to the Mennonites in "Fallow." The migration is not, as far as I can tell, ever established as the primary reference within the pages of "Fallow" itself; instead, Samatar invokes a wider collage of Mennonite migration history.

11. On the impact of *Martyrs Mirror* on North American Mennonite writing, see Beachy.

12. Characters in Nathan Dueck's *He'll* explicitly call attention to the similarity in the two phrases (33).

13. While the Young Evangelists are working toward a reform of the church, the passage Samatar has Brother Lookout read at the young radicals' meeting is part of Funk's caution against church schisms: "How much good would result, if all the different denominations, who agree in the fundamental principles of christianity [*sic*], would lay aside their disputes about external things of minor importance—and uniting together to promote the redemption of Christ, by *the spread of his glorious gospel, and the extension of his kingdom from shore to shore*?" (461; italics quoted, unattributed, in "Fallow" 236).

14. It can be translated as "*Our train goes through the desert. O people, Rejoice and Praise God!*" My thanks to Ethiopia Language Services for help with this translation.

15. See Mennonite World Conference statistics on the global Mennonite community at https://mwc-cmm.org/sites/default/files/website_files/directory2018statistics.pdf.

16. See Samatar, "Scope of This Project."

CONCLUSION

1. These numbers reflect Cruz's "General Discussions of Mennonite Literature Bibliography" list, which is separate from work that discusses individual texts or authors. It can be found here: https://mennonitebibs.wordpress.com/general-discussions-of-mennonite-literature-bibliography.

2. "It is an essay as in *essai*: a trial, a test," writes Kamboureli (ix).

BIBLIOGRAPHY

Bibliographies of Mennonite Writing in Canada, the United States, and Critical Discussions of Mennonite Writing in North America, begun by Ervin Beck and currently maintained by Daniel Shank Cruz, are available at https://mennonitebibs.wordpress.com.

Abani, Chris. "A Dark Fairytale About Post-Earth Education: 'Miss Snowfall' by Sofia Samatar." *Electric Lit* 260 (10 May 2017). Web. 19 July 2019.

Alaszewski, Andy. *Using Diaries for Social Research*. London: SAGE Publications, 2006. Web. 3 Feb. 2021.

Alexander, Hartley Burr. Letter to Dr. Neufeld. 16 Apr. 1929. MS103, 35: Correspondence Re Russian Dance of Death. Dietrich Neufeld Papers. Mennonite Library and Archives, Bethel College, North Newton, KS. Web. N. pag. 29 May 2018.

Appiah, Kwame Anthony. *The Lies That Bind: Rethinking Identity*. New York: Liveright Publishing, 2018.

Arnason, David. "A History of Turnstone Press." Froese Tiessen and Hinchcliffe 212–22.

Ashley, Mike. "Science Fiction Magazines: The Crucibles of Change." *A Companion to Science Fiction*. Ed. David Seed. Malden, MA: Blackwell, 2005.

Baerg, Anna. *The Diary of Anna Baerg: 1916–24*. Trans. and ed. Gerald Peters. Winnipeg: CMBC Publication, 1985.

Barber, John. "Miriam Toews: It's a Mennonite Thing." *Globe and Mail*, 8 Apr. 2011. Web. 6 May 2013.

Barthes, Roland. "Deliberation." 1979. Trans. Richard Howard. *A Barthes Reader*. Ed. Susan Sontag. New York: Hill and Wang, 1983. 479–95.

Beachy, Kirsten Eve. *Tongue Screws and Testimonies: Poems, Stories, and Essays Inspired by the Martyrs Mirror*. Scottdale, PA: Herald Press, 2010.

Bechler, Le Roy. *The Black Mennonite Church in North America, 1886–1986*. Scottdale, PA: Herald Press, 1986.

Beck, Ervin. "Mennonite Transgressive Literature." Zacharias, *After Identity* 52–69.

Ben-Amos, Batsheva, and Dan Ben-Amos, eds. *The Diary: The Epic of Everyday Life*. Bloomington: Indiana UP, 2020. Ebook.

Benaway, Gwen. "Trans Writers Have More Than One Story to Tell." *The Walrus*, 3 Sept. 2019. Web. 5 Sept. 2019.

Berland, Jody. *North of Empire: Essays on the Cultural Technologies of Space*. Durham: Duke UP, 2009.

Berlant, Lauren. *Cruel Optimism*. Durham: Duke UP, 2011.

Boehr, Karren (Friesen). *Ants in the Sugar Bowl*. St. Louis, MO: Concordia, 1986.

Boll, Shirley. *At Every Gate a Pearl*. Harrisonburg, VA: Christian Light Publications, 1986.

Bottos, Lorenzo Cañás. "Transformations of Old Colony Mennonites: The Making of a Trans-Statal Community." *Global Networks: A Journal of Transnational Affairs* 8.2 (2008): 214–31.

Brandt, Di. *Dancing Naked: Narrative Strategies for Writing Across Centuries*. Stratford, ON: Mercury, 1996.

———. "In Praise of Hybridity: Reflections from Southwestern Manitoba." Zacharias, *After Identity* 125–42.

———. "Paradigms of Re:placement, Re:location, and Re:vision: The Creative Challenge of the New Mennonite Writing of Manitoba (and the World)." *Journal of Mennonite Studies* 36 (2018): 154–69.

———. "Postmodern Mennonite Identification(s): A Review of Robert Zacharias's *Rewriting the Break Event*." *Journal of Mennonite Studies* 32 (2014): 243–51.

Braun, Jan Guenther. "A Complicated Becoming." *Journal of Mennonite Studies* 34 (2016): 291–97.

———. *Somewhere Else*. Winnipeg: Arbeiter Ring, 2008.

Braun, Louis. *A Stone Watermelon*. Winnipeg: Turnstone, 1986.

Braz, Albert. "North of America: Racial Hybridity and Canada's (Non)place in Inter-American Discourse." *Comparative American Studies: An International Journal* 3.1 (2005): 79–88.

Brown, Hubert L. *Black and Mennonite*. Scottdale, PA: Herald Press, 1976.

Bunkers, Suzanne L. "The Complicated Publication History of the Diaries of Anne Frank." Ben-Amos and Ben-Amos. Ebook. N. pag.

Canada. "Vote 1326: Private Members' Business M-111 Vote." Web. N. pag. https://www.ourcommons.ca/Parliamentarians/en/votes/42/1/1326.

Carl-Klassen, Abigail. "Art, Migration and (Home)making: Mennonite Women, Mexico and 'the World.'" *Journal of Mennonite Writing* 10.1 (2018): n. pag. Web. 15 Jan. 2021.

Cather, Willa. Letter to Mr. Navall. 15 Jan. 1931. Mennonite Library and Archives. Bethel College, North Newton, KS. MS 103/ 26 jpegs 10–11. Web. 1 Nov. 2019.

Chang, Yoonmee. *Writing the Ghetto: Class, Authorship, and the Asian American Ethnic Enclave*. New Brunswick: Rutgers UP, 2010.

Cheung, King-Kok, and Stan Yogi, eds. *Asian American Literature: An Annotated Bibliography*. New York: Modern Language Association of America, 1988.

Chow, Rey. *The Protestant Ethnic and the Spirit of Capitalism*. New York: Columbia UP, 2002.

Clarke, George Elliott. *Odysseys Home: Mapping African-Canadian Literature*. Toronto: U of Toronto P, 2002.

Cramer, Michael. "Battle with History: Carlos Reygadas and the Cinema of Being." *The Global Auteur: The Politics of Authorship in 21st Century Cinema*. Ed. Seung-hoon Jeong and Jeremi Szaniawski. New York: Bloomsbury Academic, 2016. 235–52.

Cruz, Daniel Shank. "A Bibliography and Subject Index of Published Work from the Mennonite/s Writing Conferences." *Mennonite Quarterly Review* 91 (Jan. 2017): 93–130.

———. "Fiction, Theory, Memoir: Sofia Samatar's 'Request for an Extension on the *Clarity*.'" *Journal of Mennonite Writing* 11.1 (2019): n. pag. 20 Aug. 2019.

———. "Introduction: Queer Mennonite Literature." *Journal of Mennonite Writing* 10.3 (2018): n. pag. Web. 1 Nov. 2019.

———. *Queering Mennonite Literature: Archives, Activism, and the Search for Community*. University Park: Pennsylvania State UP, 2019.

———. "Reading My Life in the Text: Adventures of a Queer Mennonite Critic." *Journal of Mennonite Studies* 34 (2016): 280–86.

Curtis, Sharon, and Tom Curtis. *Sunshine and Shadow*. New York: Bantam, 1986.

Damrosch, David. *What Is World Literature?* Princeton: Princeton UP, 2003.

Dargis, Manohla. "Into the Mennonite World to Explore One Man's Test of Faith." *New York Times*, 23 Sept. 2008. Web. 19 Nov. 2018.

Dawson, Carrie. "The Importance of Being Ethnic and the Value of Faking It." *Postcolonial Text* 4.2 (2008): 1–10.

Deleuze, Gilles, and Félix Guattari (and Robert Brinkley). "What Is a Minor Literature?" *Mississippi Review* 11.3 (1983): 13–33.

de Luca, Tiago. "Carnal Spirituality: The Films of Carlos Reygadas." *Senses of Cinema* 55 (July 2010): n. pag. Web. 12 Nov. 2018.

———. *Realism of the Senses in World Cinema: The Experience of Physical Reality*. New York: I. B. Tauris, 2014.

de Man, Paul. "Autobiography as De-facement." *Comparative Literature* 94.5 (1979): 919–30.

Dery, Mark. "Black to the Future: Interviews with Samuel R. Delany, Greg Tate, and Tricia Rose." *Flame Wars: The Discourse of Cyberculture*. Ed. Mark Dery. Durham: Duke UP, 1994. 179–222.

Dinshaw, Carolyn, Lee Edelman, Roderick A. Ferguson, Carla Freccero, Elizabeth Freeman, Judith Halberstam, Annamarie Jagose, Christopher Nealon, and Nguyen Tan Hoang. "Theorizing Queer Temporalities: A Roundtable Discussion." *GLQ: A Journal of Lesbian and Gay Studies* 13:2–3 (Jan. 2007): 177–95.

Doerksen, Nan. *The First Family Car*. Winnipeg: Kindred Press, 1986.

Doerksen, Victor G. "From Jung-Stilling to Rudy Wiebe: 'Christian Fiction' and the Mennonite Imagination." *Mennonite Images*. 197–208.

Du Bois, W. E. B. *The Souls of Black Folk*. 1903. New York: Dover, 1994.

Dueck, Dora. "My Name Is Magdalene." *What You Get at Home*. Winnipeg: Turnstone, 2012. 43–53.

Dueck, Nathan. *He'll*. St. John's, NL: Pedlar Press, 2014.

Dueck-Read, Alicia. "Breaking the Binary: Queering Mennonite Identity." *Journal of Mennonite Studies* 33 (2015): 115–33.

Duerksen, Menno. *Dear God, I'm Only a Boy*. Memphis, TN: Castle Books, 1986.

———. "The Wildcat Bus." *Mennonite Life* 42.4 (1987): 16–21.

Dunham, Mabel. *The Trail of the Conestoga*. 1924. Toronto: McClelland and Stewart, 1945.

Dyck, E. F. "The Rhetoric of Plain Style in Mennonite Writing." *Mennonite/s Writing in Canada*, special issue of *The New Quarterly*, ed. Hildi Froese Tiessen, 10.1–2 (1990): 36–52.

Dyck, J. W. "The Image of the Mennonites in Josef Ponten's *Volk auf dem Wege*." *Mennonite Images*. 237–45.

Eagleton, Terry. *Literary Theory: An Introduction*. 2nd ed. Minneapolis: U of Minnesota P, 2003.

Edelstein, David. "Quiet Riot." *New York Magazine*, 11 Jan. 2009. Web. 9 Dec. 2018.

Ellis, Scott. "Surrational Dreams: A. E. van Vogt and Mennonite Science Fiction." *Prairie Fire* 15.2 (1994): 204–19.

Enright, Robert. Review of *The Revival*. By Sandra Birdsell. *MacLean's*, 24 Nov. 1986, 66.

Epp, G. K. Introduction to *Harvest: Anthology of Mennonite Writing in Canada, 1874–1974*. Ed. William De Fehr et al. Winnipeg: Centennial Committee of the Mennonite Historical Society of Manitoba, 1974. vi–viii.

Epp, Marlene. "Cookbook as Metaphor for a People of Diversity: Canadian

Mennonites after 1970." *Journal of Mennonite Studies* 37 (2019): 11–27.

Epp, Peter G. *Agatchen: A Russian Mennonite Mother's Story*. Ed. and trans. Peter Pauls. Winnipeg: Hyperion, 1986.

Erb, Peter C., "Critical Approaches to Mennonite Culture in Canada: Some Preliminary Observations." Loewen and Reimer 203–11.

Eshun, Kodwo. "Further Considerations on Afrofuturism." *New Centennial Review* 3.2 (Summer 2003): 287–302.

Falcón, Rafael. *The Hispanic Mennonite Church in North America, 1932–1982*. Trans. Ronald Collins. Scottdale, PA: Herald Press, 1986.

Ferguson, Roderick A. *The Reorder of Things: The University and Its Pedagogy of Minority Difference*. Minneapolis: U of Minnesota P, 2012.

Fish, Stanley. "One University Under God?" *Chronicle of Higher Education* 7 (Jan. 2005): n. pag. Web. 10 Feb. 2020.

Fitzpatrick, Cat, and Casey Plett, eds. *Meanwhile, Elsewhere: Science Fiction and Fantasy from Transgender Writers*. New York: Topside, 2017.

Foltz, Jonathan. "Betraying Oneself: *Silent Light* and the World of Emotion." *Screen* 52.2 (2011): 151–72.

Foster, Clarise. "Introduction." *29 Mennonite Poets*. Winnipeg: Mennonite Literary Society, 2016. 1–4.

Fothergill, Robert A. *Private Chronicles: A Study of English Diaries*. Toronto: Oxford UP, 1974.

Foucault, Michel. "What Is an Author?" (1969) *Modernity and Its Discontents*. Ed. J. Marsh, J. D. Caputo, and M. Westphal. New York: Fordham UP, 1992. 299–314.

Freeman, Elizabeth. "Introduction." *GLQ* 13.2–3 (2006): 159–76.

———. *Time Binds: Queer Temporalities, Queer Histories*. Durham: Duke UP, 2010.

Friesen, John V. *Never Never Give Up: An Autobiography*. Tsawwassen, BC: John V. Friesen, 1986.

Friesen, Ralph. Letter to Roy Vogt. 21 Jan. 1977. Mennonite Literary Society Papers. Vol. 1971–74, 4646. Mennonite Heritage Centre Archives, Canadian Mennonite University, Winnipeg. 3 May 2018.

Funk, Joseph, ed. and trans. *The Confession of Faith, the Christians Known by the Name of Mennonites, in 33 Articles*. Winchester: Robinson & Hollis, 1837. Accessed online via New York Public Library. 5 Aug. 2019.

Gingrich, Luann Good, and Kerry Fast. "Review of *Pure*, created by Michael Amo." *Journal of Mennonite Studies* 36 (2018): 279–82.

Gingrich, Luann Good, and Kerry Preibisch. "Migration as Preservation and Loss: The Paradox of Transnational Living for Low German Mennonite Women." *Journal of Ethnic and Migration Studies* 36.9 (Nov. 2010): 1499–1518.

Goertzen, Anna. *The Mbambi That Had No Ears and Other Congo Stories*. Lawrenceville, VA: Brunswick Publishing, 1986.

Good, Phyllis Pellman, ed. *Three Mennonite Poets*. Intercourse, PA: Good Books, 1986.

Goossen, Benjamin W. *Chosen Nation: Mennonites and Germany in a Global Era*. Princeton: Princeton UP, 2017.

———. "From Aryanism to Anabaptism." *MQR* 90 (Apr. 2016).

———. "Mennonites in Latin America: A Review of the Literature." *Conrad Grebel Review* 34.3 (2016): 236–65.

Gossett, Che. "Zizek's Trans/Gender Trouble." *Los Angeles Review of Books*, 13 Sept. 2016.

Greenblatt, Stephen. "Racial Memory and Literary History." *Rethinking Literary History: A Dialogue on Theory*. Ed.

Linda Hutcheon and Mario J. Valdés. New York: Oxford UP, 2002. 50–62.

Gundy, Jeff. "Bad Mennonites, Raspberry Migrations, and Usable Narratives: Grace Jantzen, Julia Kasdorf, and Sofia Samatar." *Mennonite Quarterly Review* 92.3 (2018): 423–38.

———. "Being Mennonite and Writing Mennonite." *Mennonite Life* 40.4 (Dec. 1986): 11.

———. "Doubt, Defiance, and Desire." *Conrad Grebel Review* 33.3 (2015): 336–58.

———. *Greatest Hits: 1986–2003*. Columbus, OH: Pudding House, 2003.

———. "How to Write the New Mennonite Poem." 1993. Hostetler, *A Cappella*. 86–87.

———. "Introduction: SF Special Issue." *Journal of Mennonite Writing* 11.1 (2019): n. pag. Web. 1 Nov. 2019.

———. "Mennonite/s Writing: Explorations and Exposition." *Mennonite Life* 70 (2016): n. pag. Web. 20 Aug. 2019.

———. "New Maps of the Territories: On Mennonite Writing." *Georgia Review* 57:4 (2003): 870–87.

———. "Separation and Transformation: Tradition and Audience for Three Mennonite Poets." *JMS* 4 (1986): 53–69.

———. *Surrendering to the Real Things: The Archetypal Experience of C. Wordsworth Crockett*. Normal, IL: Pikestaff, 1986.

———. "'There Is No Knife, but Only Flesh': Sofia Samatar and the Language of Other Worlds." Froese Tiessen, *11 Encounters* 69–85.

———. "U.S. Mennonite Poetry and Poets: Beyond Dr. Johnson's Dog." *Mennonite Quarterly Review* 71.1 (Jan. 1997): 5–41.

———. *Walker in the Fog: On Mennonite Writing*. Telford, PA: Cascadia, 2005.

Haas, Craig, and Steve Nolt. *The Mennonite Starter Kit: A Handy Guide for the New Mennonites (Everything They Forgot to Tell You in Church Membership Class!)*. Intercourse, PA: Good Books, 1993.

Habermas, Jürgen. "Faith and Knowledge." Trans. Hella Beister and William Rehy. *The Frankfurt School on Religion: Key Writings by the Major Thinkers*. Ed. Eduardo Mendieta. New York: Routledge, 2005. 327–37.

Hall, Stuart. "Who Needs Identity?" *Questions of Cultural Identity*. Ed. Stuart Hall and Paul du Gay. Thousand Oaks, CA: Sage, 1996. 1–17.

Harnish, Andrew. "LGBT Mennonite Fiction: A Panel from Mennonite/s Writing VII," *Journal of Mennonite Studies* 34 (2016): 279–302.

Hartman, Geoffrey. "Toward Literary History." *Daedalus* 99.2 (Spring 1970): 355–83.

Hellbeck, Jochen. "The Stalin-Era Diary." Ben-Amos and Ben-Amos. Ebook. N. pag.

Herbe, Sarah. "Life Writing Research Past and Present: Interview with Sidonie Smith and Julia Watson." *European Journal of Life Writing* 8 (2019): 8–20.

Hershfield, Joanne. "Nation and Post-Nationalism: The Contemporary Modernist Films of Carlos Reygadas." *Transnational Cinemas* 5.1 (2014): 28–40.

Hinojosa, Felipe. "From Goshen to Delano: Toward a Relational Approach to Mennonite Studies." *Mennonite Quarterly Review* 91 (Apr. 2017): 201–12.

———. *Latino Mennonites: Civil Rights, Faith and Evangelical Culture*. Baltimore: Johns Hopkins UP, 2014.

Holsinger, Justus G., David W. Powell, and James Adrian Prieto-Valladares. "Puerto Rico." *Global Anabaptist Mennonite Encyclopedia Online*. Apr. 2020. Web. 1 Mar. 2021.

Hooks, Angela R., ed. *Diary as Literature: Through the Lens of Multiculturalism*. Wilmington, DE: Vernon Press, 2020.

Hostetler, Ann, ed., with intro. and afterword. *A Cappella: Mennonite Voices in Poetry*. Iowa City: U of Iowa P, 2003.

———. "Bringing Experience to Consciousness: Reflections on Mennonite Literature, 2004." *Journal of Mennonite Studies* 23 (2005): 137–50.

———. "Coming into Voice: Three Mennonite Women Poets and the Beginning of Mennonite Poetry in the United States." *Mennonite Quarterly Review* 77.4 (Oct. 2003): 521–46.

———. "*The Diary of Anna Baerg* as a Source for Sandra Birdsell's *Katya*, or *The Russländer*." 1 Dec. 2013. Web. N. pag. 1 Nov. 2019. http://mennolitfall13.blogspot.com/2013/12/the-diary-of-anna-baerg-aa-source-for.html.

———. "In this Issue." *Journal of Mennonite Writing* 2.3 (May 2010): n. pag. Web. 19 Nov. 2019.

———. "Learning, Teaching and Creating Mennonite Literature." *Journal of Mennonite Writing* 8.1 (2016): n pag. Web. 13 Jan. 2021.

———. "The Self in Mennonite Garb: Where Does the Writing Come From?" *Mennonite Quarterly Review* 87.1 (Jan. 2013): 23–40.

———. "The Unofficial Voice: The Poetics of Cultural Identity and Contemporary U.S. Mennonite Poetry." Roth and Beck 31–48.

Hutcheon, Linda. "Rethinking the National Model." Hutcheon and Valdés 3–34.

Hutcheon, Linda, and Mario J. Valdés, eds. *Rethinking Literary History: A Dialogue on Theory*. New York: Oxford UP, 2002.

Hutchison, Jesse. *Private People in Public Places: Contemporary Canadian Mennonite Life Writing*. PhD dissertation. Waterloo: University of Waterloo, 2015. Web. 1 Nov. 2019.

Jantzen, Mark, and John D. Thiesen, eds. *European Mennonites and the Holocaust*. Toronto: U of Toronto P, 2021.

Janzen, Rebecca. *Liminal Sovereignty: Mennonites and Mormons in Mexican Culture*. New York: SUNY P, 2018.

Jay, Paul. *Global Matters: The Transnational Turn in Literary Studies*. Ithaca: Cornell UP, 2010.

Johnson, Theodore. Untitled review of "Russian Dance of Death" by Dirk Gora. *Progress Bulletin*, 9 Dec. 1930, n. pag. Accessed via Mennonite Library and Archives Online. 9 Sept. 2019.

Kamboureli, Smaro. *Scandalous Bodies: Diasporic Literature in English Canada*. Toronto: Oxford UP, 2000.

Kasdorf, Julia Spicher. "The Autoethnographic Announcement and the Story." Zacharias, *After Identity* 21–36.

———. *The Body and the Book: Writing from a Mennonite Life*. 2001. University Park: Pennsylvania State UP, 2009.

———. *Fixing Tradition: Joseph W. Yoder, Amish American*. Telford, PA: Cascadia, 2003.

———. "Introduction." *Rosanna of the Amish: The Restored Text*, by Joseph W. Yoder. Ed. Joshua R. Brown and Julia Spicher Kasdorf. Scottdale, PA: Herald Press, 2008. 11–23.

———. "Introduction: Documentary Writing and Mennonite/s Writing." *Journal of Mennonite Writing* 10.4 (2018): n. pag. Web. 1 Nov. 2019.

———. "Mennonites." Hostetler, *A Cappella* 129.

———. "Mightier Than the Sword: *Martyrs Mirror* in the New World." *Conrad Grebel Review* 31.1 (2013): 44–70.

———. "Sunday Morning Confession." *Mennonite Quarterly Review* 87.1 (2013): 7–10.

———. "'Work and Hope': Tradition and Translation of an Anabaptist Adam."

Mennonite Quarterly Review 69.2 (1995): 178–204.

Kauffman, Janet. *Collaborators*. New York: Knopf, 1986.

Kauffmann, Joel. *Wolfhunter*. Nashville, TN: Abingdon Press, 1986.

Kaufmann, Michael W. "The Religious, the Secular, and Literary Studies: Rethinking the Secularization Narrative in Histories of the Profession." *New Literary History* 38.4 (2007): 607–27.

Klassen, Betty Suderman. "The Poet of Apanlee: Anna Baerg (1897–1972)." *Women Among the Brethren: Stories of 15 Mennonite Brethren and Krimmer Mennonite Brethren Women*. Ed. Katie Funk Wiebe. Hillsboro, KS: Board of Christian Literature of the General Conference of Mennonite Brethren Churches, 1979.

Klassen, Pamela E. "Submerged in Love: An Interpretation of the Diary of Lydia Reimer, 1922–24." *Studies in Religion / Sciences Religieuses* 23/4 (1994): 429–39.

Klassen, Sarah L. "How to Prepare for Mennonite Heritage Week." *The Drunken Mennonite*. Web. 9 Oct. 2019.

Kroeker, Travis. "Scandalous Displacements: 'Word' and 'Silent Light' in *Irma Voth*." *Journal of Mennonite Writing* 36 (2018): 89–100.

Kroetsch, Robert, et al. "Closing Panel." Froese Tiessen and Hinchcliffe 223–42.

Lapp, Hannah B. *To Belize with Love*. Lawrenceville, VA: Brunswick Publishing, 1986.

Lapp, Jessica W. "Embodied Voices, Imprisoned Bodies: Women and Words in Janet Kauffman's *Collaborators*." *Mennonite Quarterly Review* 72.4 (1998): 615–24.

Lejeune, Philippe. "The Autobiographical Pact." *On Autobiography*. Ed. Paul John Eakin. Trans. Katherine Leary. Minneapolis: U of Minnesota P, 1989. 3–30.

———. *On Diary*. Ed. Jeremy D. Popkin and Julie Rak. Trans. Katherine Durnin. Manoa: U of Hawai'i P, 2009.

Lesher, Emerson L. *The Muppie Manual: The Mennonite Urban Professional's Handbook for Humility and Success*. Intercourse, PA: Good Books, 1985.

Lionnet, Françoise, and Shu-mei Shih, eds. *Minor Transnationalism*. Durham: Duke UP, 2005.

———. "Thinking Through the Minor, Transnationally." Lionnet and Shih 1–25.

Loewen, Harry. "Anabaptists in Gottfried Keller's Novellas." *Mennonite Images*. 209–19.

———. "Foreword." *Mennonite Images*. 1–3.

———. *Mennonite Images: Historical, Cultural, and Literary Essays Dealing with Mennonite Issues*. Ed. Harry Loewen. Winnipeg: Hyperion, 1980. 209–19.

Loewen, Harry, and Al Reimer, eds. *Visions and Realities: Essays, Poems, and Fiction Dealing with Mennonite Issues*. Winnipeg: Hyperion, 1985.

Loewen, Royden. "Diaries as a Source for Studying Mennonite History." *Mennogespräch* 9.2 (1991): 9–14.

———, ed. *From the Inside Out: The Rural Worlds of Mennonite Diarists, 1863 to 1929*. Winnipeg: U of Manitoba P, 1999.

———. *Horse-and-Buggy Genius: Listening to Mennonites Contest the Modern World*. Winnipeg: U of Manitoba P, 2016.

———. *Mennonite Farmers: A Global History of Place and Sustainability*. Baltimore: Johns Hopkins UP, 2021.

———. "A Mennonite *Fin de Siècle*: Exploring Identity at the Turn of the Twenty-First Century." Zacharias, *After Identity* 37–51.

———. “More Should Be Expected from the CBC.” *Canadian Mennonite* 21.4 (Feb. 2017). Web. 17 Oct. 2019.

Loganbill, Marilyn. “Radical Reformation and Mennonite Bibliography, 1986.” *Mennonite Life* 42.2 (1987): n. pag. Web. 1 Nov. 2018. https://mla.bethelks.edu/ml-archive/bibliographies/1986.html.

Longhurst, John. “Mennonite Heritage Week Creates Division.” *Winnipeg Free Press* (10 Sept. 2019). Web. 12 Sept. 2019.

MacDonald, Tanis. Review of *Gloryland*, by Carla Funk. *Journal of Mennonite Studies* 35 (2017): 388–90.

MacLaren, Eli. “Canadian Book History.” *The Oxford Handbook of Canadian Literature*. Ed. Cynthia Sugars. New York: Oxford UP, 2016. 799–812.

Manickam, Samuel. “The Other Mexico Through the Cinematic Eyes of Carlos Reygadas.” *Journal of Mennonite Writing* 5.1 (2013): n. pag. Web. 12 Nov. 2018.

———. *Seeds and Seasons*. Goshen, IN: Pinchpenny Press, 1986.

Martin, Guenn. *Forty Miles from Nowhere: A Winter Adventure in Alaska*. Scottdale, PA: Herald Press, 1986.

McKenzie, Maya Navall. Letter to Mr. Hoeppner. 14 Oct. 1976. Al Reimer Papers. Fonds 054. Mennonite Heritage Centre Archives, Canadian Mennonite University, Winnipeg. 3 May 2018.

Mickenberg, Julia, and Lynne Vallone. “Introduction.” *The Oxford Handbook of Children's Literature*. Ed. Mickenberg and Vallone. Oxford: Oxford UP, 2011.

Mierau, Maurice. “Introduction.” *9 Mennonite Stories*. Selected by David Bergen. Ed. Maurice Mierau. Winnipeg: Mennonite Literary Society, 2017. 1–6.

———. “The Voice Is Coming (Faintly) from the Grave, and It Says Mennonites Are Dead, and So Is Mennonite Writing.” *Rhubarb* 30 (2012): 27–29.

———. “Why Rudy Wiebe Is Not the Last Mennonite Writer.” *Conrad Grebel Review* 22.2 (2004): 69–82.

Michael, Julia. “Culturally Specific Forms of Life in Canadian Mennonite Writing.” *Emergent Forms of Life in Anglophone Literature: Conceptual Frameworks and Critical Analyses*. Ed. Michael Basseler, Daniel Hartley, Ansgar Nünning. Trier: Wissenschaftlicher Verlag, 2015. 273–84.

Millner, Michael. “Post Post-Identity.” *American Quarterly* 57.2 (2005): 541–54.

Mishra, Vijay. “Rev. of *Minor Transnationalism*.” *Intersections: Gender, History, and Culture in the Asian Context* 13 (Aug. 2006): n. pag. Web. 3 Nov. 2019.

Moore, Ruth Nulton. *Mystery at Camp Ichthus*. Scottdale, PA: Herald Press, 1986.

———. *Mystery of the Lost Heirloom*. Scottdale, PA: Herald Press, 1986.

Moretti, Franco. “Conjectures on World Lit.” *New Left Review* 1 (Jan./Feb. 2000): 54–68.

———. *Graphs, Maps, Trees: Abstract Models for Literary History*. New York: Verso, 2005.

———. “The Slaughterhouse of Literature.” *Modern Language Quarterly* 61.1 (2000): 207–27.

Nathan, Jesse. “Question, Answer.” Zacharias, *After Identity* 175–93.

Navall, Lotte. “Dedrich Navall—Writer and Teacher.” *Mennonite Life* 24.4 (1969): 161–63.

Neilson, Shane. “Zero Chronology—Notes on the Use of Time in Casey Plett's *Little Fish*.” *HA&L* 13.2 (2020–21). Web. 20 Feb. 2021.

Neufeld, Dietrich. (as Dmitri Novopolye). “Introduction.” Apr. 1927. Al Reimer Papers. Fonds 054. Mennonite

Heritage Centre Archives, Canadian Mennonite University, Winnipeg. 3 May 2018.

———. Letter to Albert Lugebuhl. 15 Feb. 1934. MS103, 20: Correspondence—Relatives and friends 1914–1936/. Dietrich Neufeld Papers. Mennonite Library and Archives, Bethel College, North Newton, KS. Web. 29 May 2018.

———. Letter to Dr. Rempel. 25 Sept. 1935. Al Reimer Papers. Fonds 054. Mennonite Heritage Centre Archives, Canadian Mennonite University, Winnipeg. 3 May 2018.

———. (as Dedrich Navall). "On the Banks of the Dnieper." *Mennonite Life* 24.4 (Oct. 1969): 157–61.

———. (as Dick Gora). *Russian Dance of Death*. Claremont, CA: Key Books Publishers, 1930.

———. *A Russian Dance of Death: Revolution and Civil War in the Ukraine*. Trans. and ed. Al Reimer. Winnipeg: Hyperion Press, 1977.

———. *Ein Tagebuch aus dem Reiche des Totentanzes*. Emden: Selbstverlag des Verfassers, 1921.

Niessen, Niels. "Miraculous Realism: Spinoza, Deleuze, and Carlos Reygadas' *Stellet Licht*." *Discourse* 33.1 (2011): 27–54.

Page, Carole Gift. *Rachel's Hope*. 1979. Scottdale, PA: Herald Press, 1986.

Patterson, Sean. *Makhno and Memory: Anarchist and Mennonite Narratives of Ukraine's Civil War, 1917–1921*. Winnipeg: U of Manitoba P, 2020.

Pauls, Peter. "Introduction." *Agatchen: A Russian Mennonite Mother's Story*, by Peter G. Epp. Ed. and trans. Peter Pauls. Winnipeg: Hyperion, 1986. 13–15.

———. "Rudy Wiebe's Frieda and Peter Epp's Agatha: Narrators and Narrative Technique in *The Blue Mountains of China* and *Eine Mutter*." *Journal of Mennonite Studies* 4 (1986): 70–76.

Penn, Sheldon. "The Time-Image in Carlos Reygadas' *Stellet Licht*: A Cinema of Immanence." *Bulletin of Spanish Studies* 90.7 (2013): 1159–81.

Perkins, David. *Is Literary History Possible?* Baltimore: Johns Hopkins UP, 1992.

Plett, Casey. *Little Fish*. Vancouver: Arsenal Pulp Press, 2018.

———. "Natural Links of Queer Mennonite Literature." *Journal of Mennonite Studies* 34 (2016): 286–90.

———. "On Creating Community in *Meanwhile, Elsewhere*, and *Little Fish*." Inv. by Arielle Spence. *Room*, 24 Sept. 2019. Web. 5 Oct. 2019.

Plett, Casey, in conversation with Madeleine Thien and Avi Cummings. "What Does It Mean to Belong?" *Literary Hub* 17 (Dec. 2020). Web. 13 Jan. 2021.

Podnieks, Elizabeth. *Daily Modernism: The Literary Diaries of Virginia Woolf, Antonia White, Elizabeth Smart, and Anaïs Nin*. Montreal: McGill-Queen's UP, 2000.

———. "The Literary Author as Diarist." Ben-Amos and Ben-Amos. Ebook. N. pag.

Poetker, Audrey. *i sing for my dead in german*. Winnipeg: Turnstone, 1986.

Prose, Francine. "Someone Else's Memories." *New York Review of Books*, 1 May 2013. Web. 8 Nov. 2018.

Puar, Jasbir K. *Terrorist Assemblages: Homonationalism in Queer Times*. Durham: Duke UP, 2007.

Rak, Julie. "Dialogue with the Future: Philippe Lejeune's Method and Theory of Diary." *On Diary*. Ed. Jeremy D. Popkin and Julie Rak. Trans. Katherine Durnin. Manoa: U of Hawai'i P, 2009. 16–26.

———. "The Hidden Genre: Diaries and Time." *European Journal of Life Writing* 7 (2018): 85–89.

———. "Mennonite/s Writing and Cruel Optimism: An Interview with Julie

Rak." Interview by Robert Zacharias. *Journal of Mennonite Studies* 36 (2018): 15–24.

Ratzlaff, Keith, Ardyth Bradley, and Brenda Hillman. *Three Winter Poems*. Omaha: Penumbra Press, 1986.

Redekop, Corey. "The Sexual Menno, Or, Wouldst Thou Accompany Me to the Barn Raising?" *Rhubarb* 32 (Spring 2013): 64.

Redekop, Fred. *Cornucopia: poems*. Goshen, IN: Pinchpenny, 1986.

Redekop, Magdalene. "'Is Menno in There?' The Case of 'The Man Who Invented Himself.'" Zacharias, *After Identity* 194–210.

———. *Making Believe: Questions About Mennonites and Art*. Winnipeg: U of Manitoba P, 2020.

———. "The Pickling of the Mennonite Madonna." Froese Tiessen and Hinchcliffe 100–28.

———. "Through the Mennonite Looking Glass." *Why I Am a Mennonite: Essays on Mennonite Identity*. Ed. Harry Loewen. Kitchener, ON: Herald Press, 1988. 226–53.

Redekopp, Elsa. *Dream and Wonder: A Child's View of Canadian Village Life*. Illustrated by Margaret Quiring. Winnipeg: Kindred, 1986.

Reder, Michael, and Josef Schmidt, SJ. "Habermas and Religion." *An Awareness of What Is Missing: Faith and Reason in a Post-Secular Age*. Ed. Jürgen Habermas. Trans. Caira Cronin. Malden, MA: Polity, 2010. 1–14.

Reimer, Al. "Introduction." Neufeld 1977. 1–5.

———. Letter to David Rempel. 28 June 1977. Al Reimer Papers. Fonds 054. Mennonite Heritage Centre Archives, Canadian Mennonite University, Winnipeg. 3 May 2018.

———. Letter to Lotte Neufeld. 20 Apr. 1977. Al Reimer Papers. Fonds 054. Mennonite Heritage Centre Archives, Canadian Mennonite U, Winnipeg. 3 May 2018.

———. "Look Homeward, Naomi: Misreading a Novel as Social History." *Mennonite Life* 60.2 (2005). Web. 8 Dec. 2020.

———. *Mennonite Literary Voices: Past and Present*. North Newton, KS: Bethel College, 1993.

Reimer, Kathy Meyer. "Passing on the Faith: Mennonite Writing for Children." *Journal of Mennonite Writing* 2.3 (2010): n. pag. Web. 1 Nov. 2019.

Reimer, L. Douglas. *Surplus at the Border: Mennonite Writing in Canada*. Winnipeg: Turnstone, 1992.

Reimer, Margaret Loewen, and Paul Gerard Tiessen. "The Poetry and Distemper of Patrick Friesen and David Waltner-Toews." Loewen and Reimer 243–53.

Reimer, Mavis. "'Literary and Artistic Voices' in T. D. Regehr's *Mennonites in Canada, 1939–70:* A Response, Two Observations, and Some Questions." *Journal of Mennonite Studies* 15 (1997): 115–23.

———. "A Question of Audience? Two Views of Home in the Russian-Mennonite Novels of Barbara Smucker." *Journal of Mennonite Studies* 6 (1988): 165–73.

Rempel, David G. Letter to Al Reimer. 8 June 1977. Al Reimer Papers. Fonds 054. Mennonite Heritage Centre Archives, Canadian Mennonite University, Winnipeg. 3 May 2018.

———. Letter to Al Reimer. Undated, titled "Response to questions raised in your letter of June 8, 1977." Al Reimer Papers. Fonds 054. Mennonite Heritage Centre Archives, Canadian Mennonite U, Winnipeg. 3 May 2018.

———. Letter to Al Reimer. 10 Jan. 1978. Al Reimer Papers. Fonds 054.

Mennonite Heritage Centre Archives, Canadian Mennonite U, Winnipeg. 3 May 2018.

Reygadas, Carlos. "Carlos Reygadas." Interview by José Castillo. *BOMB* 111 (Spring 2010): 70–77.

———. "The Impossible Becomes Reality." Interview by Robert Koehler. *Cineaste* 38.3 (Summer 2013): 10–15.

———. "The Sheltering Sky." Interview by Jonathan Romney. *Sight & Sound* 18.1 (2008): 42–43.

———, dir. *Silent Light* [*Stellet Licht*]. BAC Films, Nodream, and Mantarraya, 2007.

Romney, Jonathan. "Review of *Silent Light*, by Carlos Reygadas." *Sight & Sound* 17.7 (2007): 2, 17.

Roth, John. "In This Issue." *Mennonite Quarterly Review* 90.1 (2016): 9–10.

Roth, John D., and Ervin Beck. "Foreword." *Migrant Muses: Mennonite/s Writing in the U.S.* Ed. John D. Roth and Ervin Beck. Goshen, IN: Mennonite Historical Society, 1998. v–viii.

Roush, H. L. *Henry and the Great Society*. 1969. Scottsville, KY: Mennonite Church of Scottsville, 1986.

Royal Commission on Bilingualism and Biculturalism. *The Cultural Contributions of the Other Ethnic Groups*. Vol. 4 of the *Report of the Royal Commission on Bilingualism and Biculturalism*. Ottawa: Queen's Printer, 1970.

Rudd, David. "The Development of Children's Literature." *The Routledge Companion to Children's Literature*. Ed. David Rudd. New York: Routledge, 2010: 3–13.

Ruland, Richard, and Malcolm Bradbury. *From Puritanism to Postmodernism: A History of American Literature*. New York: Penguin, 1991.

Ruth, John L. *Mennonite Identity and Literary Art*. Scottdale, PA: Herald Press, 1978.

Sadowski-Smith, Claudia, and Claire F. Fox. "Theorizing the Hemisphere: Inter-Americas Work at the Intersection of American, Canadian, and Latin American Studies." *Comparative American Studies* 2.1 (2004): 5–38.

Said, Edward. *Beginnings: Intention and Method*. Baltimore: Johns Hopkins UP, 1975.

Samatar, Sofia. "Fallow." *Tender*. Easthampton, MA: Small Beer Press, 2017.

———. "The Scope of This Project." *Journal of Mennonite Writing* 9.2 (2017): n. pag. Web. 19 July 2019.

———. "Toward a Planetary History of Afrofuturism." *Research in African Literatures* 48.4 (Winter 2017): 175–91.

Schirch, Lisa. "Anabaptist-Mennonite Relations with Jews Across Five Centuries." *Mennonite Life* 74 (2020).

Schirch, Lisa, and Marc Gopin. "A Mennonite Agenda for Research and Action on Antisemitism." *Mennonite Life* 74 (2020).

"The Schleitheim Confession of Faith." 1527. Trans. and commentary by John Wenger. *Mennonite Quarterly Review* 19.4 (1945): 243–53.

Schroeder, Andreas. *Dustship Glory*. Toronto: Available Press (Random House), 1986.

Schroeder, Jan. "Who's a Mennonite?" *Journal of Mennonite Writing* 9.1 (2017): n. pag. Web. 1 Nov. 2019.

Schwartz, Alexandra. "A Beloved Canadian Novelist Reckons with Her Mennonite Voice." *New Yorker*, 18 Mar. 2019. Web. 23 Apr. 2019.

Sholl, Betsy. *Rooms Overhead*. Farmington, ME: Alice James Books, 1986.

Showalter, Shirley. "Mennonite in a Little Black Dress: An Old Mennonite Review." *Shirley Showalter*, 21 Nov. 2009. Web. 7 May 2013.

Siemerling, Winfried. *The New North American Studies: Culture, Writing, and the Politics of Re/Cognition*. New York: Routledge, 2005.

Smiley, Jane. "Mennonites, Marriage, Movies, Mexico." Review of *Irma Voth*, by Miriam Toews. *The Globe and Mail*, 8 Aug. 2011. Web. 19 Nov. 2018.

Smith, Leonard V. "Diary and Narrative: French Soldiers and World War One." Ben-Amos and Ben-Amos. Ebook. N. pag.

Smith, Sidonie, and Julia Watson. *A Guide for Interpreting Life Narratives: Reading Autobiography*, 2nd ed. Minneapolis: U of Minnesota P, 2010.

———. "Metalepsis in Autobiographical Narrative." *European Journal of Life Writing* 8 (2019): 1–27.

Smucker, David Rempel. "Faith Versus Culture? The Mennonite Pavilion at Folklorama in Winnipeg, Manitoba, 1980–1982." *Journal of Mennonite Studies* 33 (2015): 235–50.

Sollors, Werner. *Beyond Ethnicity: Consent and Descent in American Culture*. New York: Oxford UP, 1986.

Spivak, Gayatri Chakravorty. *In Other Worlds: Essays in Cultural Politics*. New York: Routledge, 2006.

Stahl, John Daniel. "Conflict, Conscience, and Community in Selected Mennonite Children's Stories." *Mennonite Quarterly Review* 55.1 (1981): 62–74.

Stanley, Liz, and Helen Dampier. "Simulacrum Diaries: Time, the 'Moment of Writing,' and the Diaries of Johanna Brandt-Van Warmelo." *Life Writing* 3.2 (2006): 25–52.

Stoll, Patricia Ann. *The Age of Fish*. PhD dissertation. Chicago: University of Illinois at Chicago, 1986. Web. 1 Nov. 2019.

Suderman, Elmer F. "Directions for Celebrating the Centennial of the Coming of the Low German Mennonites from the Steppes of Russia to the American Prairies." *What Can We Do Here?* St. Peter, MN: Daguerreotype Publishers, 1974. 2.

Suvin, Darko. "On the Poetics of the Science Fiction Genre." *College English* 34.3 (1972): 372–82.

Suzanne, Miriam. *Riding Sidesaddle**. Denver: Springgun Press, 2015.

Taskans, Andris. "David Bergen: In Country." *Quill & Quire* 6 (2005): n. pag. Web. 15 June 2020.

Taylor, Charles. "The Politics of Recognition." *Multiculturalism: Examining the Politics of Recognition*. Ed. Amy Gutmann. Princeton: Princeton UP, 1994. 25–73.

Teodoro, José. "On Earth as It Is in Heaven." *Film Comment* 45.1 (2009): 48–51.

Thiessen, J. "Canadian Mennonite Literature." *Canadian Literature* 51 (Winter 1972): 65–72.

Thiessen, Vic. Rev. "Show Not so Pure in Its Depiction of Mennonites." *Canadian Mennonite*, 23 Jan. 2017. Web. 19 Oct. 2019.

Tiessen, Hildi Froese. "After Identity: Liberating the Mennonite Literary Text." Zacharias, *After Identity* 210–25.

———. "Beyond the Binary: Reinscribing Cultural Identity in Mennonite Literature." *Mennonite Quarterly Review* 72 (Oct. 1998): 491–501.

———. "Beyond 'What We by Habit or Custom Already Know,' or What Do We Mean When We Talk About Mennonite/s Writing?" *Mennonite Quarterly Review* 90.1 (2016): 11–27.

———, ed. *11 Encounters with Mennonite Fiction*. Winnipeg: Mennonite Literary Society, 2017.

———. "Encounters: An Introduction." Froese Tiessen, *11 Encounters* 1–6.

———. "Foreword: Guest Editor." *Journal of Mennonite Studies* 28 (2010): 9–12.

———. "Homelands, Identity Politics, and the Trace: What Remains for the Mennonite Reader?" *Mennonite Quarterly Review* 87 (Jan. 2013): 11–22.

———. "'I Didn't Have Words for It': Reflections on Some of the Early Life-Writing of Di Brandt and Julia Kasdorf." *Journal of Mennonite Studies* 36 (2018): 25–41.

———. "Introduction." *New Mennonite Writing.* A special issue of *Prairie Fire*, ed. Hildi Froese Tiessen. 11.2 (Summer 1990): 8–11.

———, ed. and intro. *Liars and Rascals: Mennonite Short Stories.* Waterloo: U of Waterloo P, 1989. xi–xiii.

———. "Mennonite/s Writing in Canada: An Introduction." A special issue of *The New Quarterly*, ed. Hildi Froese Tiessen. 10.1–2 (Spring/Summer 1990): 13–16.

———. "Mother Tongue as Shibboleth in the Literature of Canadian Mennonites." *Studies in Canadian Literature* 13.2 (1988): n. pag. Web. 12 July 2019.

———. "'There Was Nothing to Be Read About Mennonites': Rudy Wiebe and the Impulse to Make Story." *Conrad Grebel Review* 22.1 (Spring 2004). Web. 1 Nov. 2019.

Tiessen, Hildi Froese, and Peter Hinchcliffe, eds. *Acts of Concealment: Mennonite/s Writing in Canada.* Waterloo: U of Waterloo P, 1992.

Tiessen, Paul. "The Confessions of Rudy Wiebe: Re-Positioning the *Peace Shall Destroy Many* Event of 192–63." *Journal of Mennonite Studies* 36 (2018): 137–51.

———. "Double Identity: Covering the *Peace Shall Destroy Many* Project." Zacharias, *After Identity* 70–85.

———. "'It Was Like Watching My Own Life': Moviegoers in John Rempel's *Arena* (1967–1970) and Miriam Toews's *Irma Voth* (2011)." *Mennonite Quarterly Review* 87.1 (Jan. 2013): 49–72.

Toews, Miriam. *A Complicated Kindness.* Toronto: Knopf, 2004.

———. *Irma Voth.* Toronto: Knopf, 2011.

Togane, Mohamud Siad. *The Bottle and the Bushman.* Ste Anne de Bellevue, QC: The Muses' Co., 1986.

Tompkins, Cynthia. *Experimental Latin American Cinema: History and Aesthetics.* Austin: U of Texas P, 2013.

Ty, Eleanor, and Christl Verduyn, eds. *Asian Canadian Writing Beyond Autoethnography.* Waterloo: Wilfrid Laurier UP, 2008.

Unger, Andrew. *Once Removed.* Winnipeg: Turnstone, 2020.

Unrau, Ruth. *Encircled: Stories of Mennonite Women.* Newton, KS: Faith and Life Press, 1986.

Urry, James. "The Mennonite Commonwealth in Imperial Russia Revisited." *Mennonite Quarterly Review* 84.2 (2010): 229–47.

———. *Mennonites, Politics, and Peoplehood: Europe—Russia—Canada 1525–1980.* Winnipeg: U of Manitoba P, 2006.

Vogt, A. E. van. "Prologue to Freedom." *Worlds of If* 23.1 (Sept.–Nov. 1986): 30–52.

Vogt, Esther Loewen. *Harvest Gold.* 1978. Hillsboro, KS: Kindred Press, 1986.

———. *Turkey Red.* 1975. Hillsboro, KS: Kindred Press, 1986.

Vogt, Roy. Letter to Mr. Ralph Friesen. 16 June 1976. Mennonite Literary Society Papers. Volume 1971–74, 4646. Mennonite Heritage Centre Archives, Canadian Mennonite University, Winnipeg. 3 May 2018.

———. Letter to Mr. Frank Belle. 21 June 1977. Mennonite Literary Society Papers. Volume 1971–74, 4646. Mennonite Heritage Centre Archives, Canadian Mennonite University, Winnipeg. 3 May 2018.

Vogt, Roy, and H. E. Duckworth. Untitled preface to *Dietrich Neufeld's A Russian Dance of Death: Revolution and Civil War in the Ukraine*, trans. and ed. Al Reimer. Winnipeg: Hyperion, 1977. N. pag.

Vogt, Roy, and Harry Loewen. Untitled preface to *Agatchen: A Russian Mennonite Mother's Story*, by Peter G. Epp, trans. and ed. Peter Pauls. Winnipeg: Hyperion, 1986. N. pag.

Waldrep, G. C. "Mennonite Poem." *Rhubarb* 24 (2009): 25.

Wall, Ann. "About Anna." *Mennopolitan*. N.d. Web. N. pag. 29 Nov. 2018.

Waltner-Toews, David. "Roots." *Good Housekeeping*. Winnipeg: Turnstone, 1983. 75–77.

Warner, Rick. "Filming a Miracle: *Ordet*, *Silent Light*, and the Spirit of Contemplative Cinema." *Critical Quarterly* 57.2 (2015): 46–71.

Weaver, Brenda. *Nuclear Pie: 14 Fables for Our Time*. Calgary, AB: B. Weaver, 1986.

Weaver-Zercher, Valerie. *Thrill of the Chaste: The Allure of Amish Romance Novels*. Baltimore: Johns Hopkins UP, 2013.

Weier, John. *After the Revolution*. Winnipeg: Turnstone, 1986.

Wiebe, Rudy. *Peace Shall Destroy Many*. Toronto: McClelland and Stewart, 1962.

Wright, David. "A New Mennonite Replies to Julia Kasdorf." *The Mennonite*, 25 May 1999, 5.

Wylie, Herb. "Hemispheric Studies or Scholarly NAFTA? The Case for Canadian Literary Studies." *Canada and Its Americas: Transnational Navigations*. Ed. Winfried Siemerling and Sarah Casteel. Montreal: McGill-Queen's UP, 2010. 48–61.

Yaguchi, Yorifumi. "Book Two: Poems by Yorifumi Yaguchi." Good 43–77.

Yoder, Joseph W. *Rosanna of the Amish*. 1940. Ed. Joshua R. Brown and Julia Spicher Kasdorf. Scottdale, PA: Herald Press, 2008.

Zacharias, Robert, ed. *After Identity: Mennonite Writing in North America*. University Park: Penn State UP, 2015.

———. "'A Garden of Spears': Reconsidering the Mennonite/s Writing Project." *Mennonite Quarterly Review* 90.1 (2016): 29–50.

———. "Introduction: After Identity: Mennonite/s Writing in North America." *After Identity* 1–18.

———. "'Learning Sauerkraut': Ethnic Food, Cultural Memory, and Traces of Mennonite Identity in Alayna Munce's *When I Was Young & In My Prime*." *Canadian Literature and Cultural Memory*. Ed. Cynthia Sugars and Eleanor Ty. Toronto: Oxford UP, 2014.

———. *Rewriting the Break Event: Mennonites and Migration in Canadian Literature*. Winnipeg: U of Manitoba P, 2013.

Žižek, Slavoj. *First as Tragedy, Then as Farce*. New York: Verso, 2009.

———. "The Inherent Transgression." *Cultural Values* 2.1 (1998): 1–17.

———. "The Sexual Is Political," *Philosophical Salon*. Web. N. pag. 1 Aug. 2016. https://thephilosophicalsalon.com/the-sexual-is-political.

———. *The Sublime Object of Ideology*. London: Verso, 1989.

———. *Tarrying with the Negative: Kant, Hegel, and the Critique of Ideology*. 1993. Durham: Duke UP, 2003.

Zook, Mollie. *From Wealth to Faith: A Tear-Stained Journey*. Harrisonburg, VA: Christian Light Publications, 1986.

INDEX

www.ingramcontent.com/pod-product-compliance
Ingram Content Group UK Ltd.
Pitfield, Milton Keynes, MK11 3LW, UK
UKHW042001260225
455621UK00004B/57